THE PILTDOWN MEN

by

RONALD MILLAR

ST. MARTIN'S PRESS

NEW YORK

ST. MARTIN'S PRESS NEW YORK

St. Martin's Press
175 Fifth Avenue
New York, N.Y. 10010

Affiliated Publishers:
Macmillan & Company, Limited, London
—also at Bombay, Calcutta, Madras and Melbourne.

Contents

List of Illustrations

PLATES

All photographs are reproduced by courtesy of the British
Museum (Natural History).

DIAGRAMS

Introduction

Piltdown man was unveiled to a densely-packed and excited audience at Burlington House, London, on 18 December, 1912. Piltdown man—or to give him his correct scientific title, *Eoanthropus dawsoni*—was the fulfilment of the half-century-old prophecy of the famous biologist Charles Darwin. He was the ideal 'missing link'. His noble brow postulated high intelligence but his most astonishing feature, an ape-like jaw, was a direct link with man's ancestors. Here was an ape halfway across the evolutionary bridge towards man.

Piltdown man was greeted in Britain with great enthusiasm. His arrival was long overdue. For many years now British archaeologists had cast envious glances across the Channel. It seemed that the French had but to dig anywhere in their native land to find a Neanderthal man. But Piltdown man not only gained redress. Crude flint tools and the bones of long extinct animals found with him in the Sussex gravel pit proved that he had lived many thousands of years before Neanderthal man. But compared with Neanderthal man, Piltdown man was an intellectual. Only Piltdown man could be the true ancestor of modern man. The brutish-looking Neanderthal man was a biological freak, it was thought, which had evolved in some remote backwater during the terrible Ice Age and had died out without issue.

Piltdown man was highly acceptable. And he was British. He transfused life into a British palaeontology feeble from the proliferation of discoveries of Neanderthal men and other prehistoric artefacts across the Channel. It was due directly to the fossil man from Sussex that London was now preferred to Paris as the seat of the study of fossil man. It was to London that the world looked for acceptance of Peking man. It was to London that Raymond Dart came to seek acceptance for his South African ape-man. It was London that rejected him.

Small wonder then that Piltdown man's discoverer, Charles Dawson, a Sussex solicitor, was congratulated and fêted. Only his death in 1916 robbed him of a knighthood and a civil list pension. But many years later the famous Piltdown site in Sussex was scheduled as a National Monument. A suitably inscribed stone was erected to the memory of the famous amateur. In the forty years of Piltdown man's credibility it is estimated that some five hundred essays were written about him. This does not take into account the myriad allusions to the Sussex relics in books of the 'highways and byways of rural Sussex' genre. The Piltdown site attracted visitors as new-laid concrete does dogs.

Then came the shock. In 1953—some forty years later—it was announced that Piltdown man was a forgery. He was an amalgam of a modernish skull with the jaw of a modern orang-utan. Obviously the human fragments, ape's jaw, flint implements and bones of extinct animals had been 'planted' at Piltdown. It was obvious also that the forger was Charles Dawson. He had duped Science and got away with it for forty years. Outraged Science tore his reputation to shreds. At the same time there was a great rush to explain that no one had really believed in Piltdown man anyway. Science, even the British Museum which had helped expose Piltdown man, closed its ranks (an almost unprecedented event) and adopted a defensive posture. But the scientists need not have worried. Thanks to a long-established indifference to the study of prehistory among British educationists, few could see the real joke. But the spectacle of the learned hoodwinked by the layman appeals to the vulgar sense of humour. An otherwise disinterested public picked on this aspect alone. Like the Australian bushranger Ned Kelly, Charles Dawson became a folk hero for a very brief period. Then he was forgotten.

The name 'Charles Dawson' meant nothing to me. I became acquainted with the spectre of Piltdown through another of the trickster's nefarious activities—a two-volume work, *The History of Hastings Castle*. In fact a considerable amount of time elapsed before I was made aware of the fact that the historian Charles Dawson was none other than the solicitor Charles Dawson; that I was in the literary presence of the 'Wizard of Sussex', the archduper and perpetrator of history's greatest archaeological fraud. By this time the damage had been done.

It is irrational but not unusual for one's good opinion of a work to be transferred to its author. The good opinion I had formed of the author of *The History of Hastings Castle* outlasted the discovery of his true identity. But even a superficial examination of the facts which surround the mysterious Piltdown forgery reveals that the assumption that because Dawson got the fame he should receive the blame is by no means unassailable. One other person got at least an equal share of the glory. Of the three main participants in the dig which brought Piltdown man to light there were two who were placed beyond shadow of suspicion merely because of their respective standing in Science and the Church. Another, who I firmly believe was the hoaxer, is never mentioned at all.

With this realization other issues began to intrude themselves. Who else could have been concerned with Piltdown? Why had the forgery remained undetected for forty years? Piltdown man so neatly fitted into the accepted evolutionary pattern, but why? What was this accepted evolutionary pattern?

As another layman I realized that to place Piltdown man in his correct historical perspective I should have to go back in time—to before the first fossil man astounded the scientific world. In order to understand Piltdown man's implications it was necessary to trace the history of the discovery of fossil man back to before the middle of the nineteenth century; to when it was never even suspected that such a progenitor of man had existed.

This then is a lay appraisal of the great fossil man hunt. It covers a period which is wishfully called (by scientists and encyclopaedias) a hundred years of scientific achievement. In fact it was a turbulent era of controversy, precipitate opinion, extravagant claims, fear, confusion and dilemma.

The present author gratefully acknowledges the kindness and patience with which Sir Wilfrid Le Gros Clark and Dr Kenneth Page Oakley assisted his enquiries about the Piltdown episode, and in the case of the latter, supplied him with the latest information on the Piltdown specimens.

He would also like to thank Williams and Norgate, Collins, Pitman Publishing, British Museum, and the editor of *The Times* for their kind permission to use material, tables, diagrams, etc.

Westhampnett,
Sussex
1972

Chapter 1

I T I S A L M O S T impossible for us to gain an adequate conception of the incredulity with which the majority of early Victorians received the first insinuations about the vast age of mankind. Unfortunately for our purpose we are too inclined to think of the Victorians as people like ourselves without the benefits of electricity; thus we mistake the acceptances of the latter end of a lengthy reign for the rejections of a major part of it, and interpret the contributions of the Victorian scientists as part of the Great Era of revelation when at the time these were often considered to be contentious hypotheses, even outrageous speculation.

It is unjust to single out the Victorians as uniquely antagonistic to new ideas and resistant to change, for they were not. Superficially, man is adaptable but he becomes notoriously ungymnastic when the rejection of attitudes based on fundamental principles is involved. For example, we too readily doubt the possibility of life on other planets without pausing too long to consider that some organisms might rejoice in an atmosphere of boiling sulphuric acid. It is not too much of an exaggeration to claim that a similar intellectual barrier was being assaulted by the early Victorians who were proposing that the Biblical conception of man's place in Creation might be entirely false. Such an insinuation at any time in the previous centuries would have been outrageous, even dangerous. Not much more than a hundred years had elapsed since unorthodox interpretations of the Bible had been purged in the fires of Smithfield. No such fate threatened the scientific heretics of the early nineteenth century but it was the view of the leaders of the Church that the exponents of this heterodoxy would be accorded the same fate at the Last Judgement.

There is no doubt that Victorian Britain was experiencing a religious backlash. Five years before Wellington's victory at Waterloo, George III, after one more lapse into insanity (although his critics say it was the reverse), retired to Windsor leaving his realm at the mercy of the Prince of Wales. The Prince Regent was the least reputable of a family whose common stock of virtue was not superabundant. He was not devoid of ability, as his frequent clashes with Parliament bear witness, nor lacking in dignity, and he possessed considerable personal charm; nevertheless, he was a shameless voluptuary, reckless spendthrift, rakehell, hard drinker and compulsive gambler. The Regent's conduct was an embarrassment to his ministers and a terrible example to his subjects, who slavishly followed it with an acquiescence and zeal which must have relieved its instigator of any feeling of responsibility. The brief reign of William IV brought some relief but there was a marked calming of the turbulent *mores* when the young Victoria, schooled in order, punctuality, obedience and self-sacrifice, succeeded to the throne in 1837.

The degree of profundity with which Religion smote the early Victorians is open to suspicion. Certainly a considerable proportion of the lower-class town dwellers were flagrantly lawless with but a thin veneer of religious observance and much hidden superstition. The effect of religious belief was most marked in the influential middle classes. But this manifested itself more in the form of a high-minded bigotry than in humanitarian uplift. A great age of social reform was ushered in but at its beginning, at least, Charity was dispensed with an ostentatious piety which raises doubts whether it did its donors or beneficiaries the more good. The workhouses to which the itinerant paupers were sent seemed to have been devised to rid the rich of the depressing sight of them. Not a few recipients of the grudging largesse of the New Poor Law designed to fight 'the growing evil of pauperism' wished they were dead and free of it.

The profundity of the early Victorian religion however need not concern us but its manifestation does. Having overcome the adversity of the previous reigns, the richly endowed and privileged Church of England now wielded authoritative power. But it was weak on the intellectual side. Its leaders were too obsessed with the temperature of Hell and the furniture of Heaven. Too much of their zeal came from belief in the eternal punishment of uncorrected sinners. They held too narrowly to a literal interpretation of the Bible. From all this stemmed a conviction that the swollen foot of scientific revelation could be squeezed into the narrow shoe of Biblical convention. This had a stifling effect on the teaching at the universities, which historically were religious foundations. Entry into the universities of Oxford and Cambridge was by way of religious tests which were not abolished until 1871. Most of the chairs of learning were occupied by men who were churchmen first and scientists second. Small wonder, then, that when the attack came it was extramural, from ex-university men to some degree emancipated from the theologio-scientific strait-jackets of their mentors.

By definition the prehistorian's material is unwritten and inscrutable. He creates his history of man out of the dumb evidence of tools and weapons, tombs, monuments, and indeed from his rubbish. For this reason much of the early study of prehistory was highly vulnerable to individual interpretation, fancy and invention. The equivocal material lends itself to all kinds of speculation. Anyone who could raise an audience used the relics as hooks on which to hang the most fanciful, astonishing and fallacious theories as to their nature and origin. This interpretation could be denied by the next describer. The ensuing debate, controversy, nose-pulling and name-calling seems to have added to the fascination of the subject for a great deal of it was indulged in for its own sake.

The historical study of man's development was by no means new even at the beginning of Victoria's reign. The Renaissance scholars of Italy studied not only the classical literature of the Greek and Roman Empires but also their archaeology. At the same time such men as William Camden explored Britain's ancient monuments with a view to discovering the nature of their builders. But in the main the study was more acquisitive than philosophical. It was the age of collectors of 'antiquities'. Great collections of antiquities were common. Most of the great houses had them. But, alas, it seems that at least some of the proud owners were none too scrupulous as to the qualities which distinguished a genuine artefact of pre-history from that which was not. Almost anything placed in a glass case assumed a value far beyond its intrinsic worth.

The year 1707 saw the formation of a club of enthusiasts who had met regularly at the *Young Devil* and *Bear* taverns in the Strand, London. From this bibulous beginning was born the Society of Antiquaries. Horace Walpole, it seems one of the more aesthetic members, cast considerable doubt on many antiquities which were extolled in the Society's journal (published for the first time in 1770). He condemned the collectors for their lack of discrimination, writing to a friend: 'Mercy on us. What a cartload of bricks and rubbish and Roman ruins they have piled together.' He also described his fellow club members as 'the

midwives of superannuated miscarriages'. Any lampooner short of
a target invariably kept his hand in with a tilt at the Society. The
hilarious highlight of a play by Samuel Foote performed at the
Haymarket Theatre in 1772 was a visit paid to the Society of
Antiquaries by the Nabob, who was preceded by negro slaves
bearing 'the twelve lost books of Livy', a piece of lava from the
last Vesuvius eruption, a box of bones, beetles and butterflies,
and a large green chamberpot described as a Roman burial urn
dug up from the Temple of Concord.

The Rev. James Douglas was no doubt referring to this sorry
state of affairs when he wrote, in the foreword to his *Sepulchral
History of Great Britain*[1]:'If the study of antiquity be under-
taken in the cause of History it will rescue itself from an approach
indescriminately bestowed on works which have been deemed
frivolous.'

But how old was antiquity? The Christian religion provided
the answer to this question. Early in the seventeenth century
James Ussher, Archbishop of Amagh, occupied himself with
the numerology of the Old Testament from which he deduced
that mankind originated with Adam in the year 4004 B.C. The
capacity for survival of the immediate descendants of Adam,
which ranged from the 365 years of the comparatively short-lived
Enoch to the 969 years of Methuselah, would render incredulous
anyone not firmly committed to complete faith in Biblical chronology, but not so Ussher. He published his findings in 1650[2] and
Ussher's calculation was widely accepted and considered as inspired as the Holy Writ itself, the year 4004 B.C. being duly
marked in the margin of the relevant passages of the Authorized
Version of the Bible.

The archbishop had supplied the missing element in a problem which had vexed theologians for centuries. Bede in the
eighth century had considered that the Creation must have been
accomplished in the spring, for how else had God so easily succeeded with the agricultural part of it? Vincent of Beauvais,
writing in the thirteenth century, supported Bede. Later it was
successfully argued that on the contrary there had been much
water about at the time of the Creation, the passages in Genesis
which lead up to the Dawn of Mankind were full of it, so
surely this would indicate a wetter period of the year, say September at the Equinox.

[1] Published 1793.
[2] *Annals of the Ancient and New Testament.* 1650.

One of the subscribers to this last view was Dr John Lightfoot, Master of St Catherine's College and Vice-Chancellor of
the University of Cambridge. Further consideration prompted
Lightfoot to amend the month to October. He declared in 1642
that he entirely endorsed Archbishop Ussher and that 'Heaven
and Earth, centre and circumference, were created all together
in the same instant and clouds full of water . . . this took place
and man was created by the Trinity on October 23, 4004 B.C.
at nine o'clock in the morning.' This precision owed nothing to
the Biblical text. It says much for Lightfoot's view of his calling
that he attributed the Dawn of Mankind to the date and time
of the commencement of the academic year.

Within the confines of this arbitrary chronology—let it not be
doubted that the Ussher-Lightfoot view was generally accepted
throughout the eighteenth and into the nineteenth century—it
seemed that little if anything remained to be discovered about
mankind's past. It was generally agreed that the great Assyrian,
Persian, Greek and Roman Empires had flourished before
Christianity. These would take up most if not all of the available
four millennia. But surely Britain, it began to be argued, must
have had some prehistory? What had happened in these islands
during the times of these great Empires? And there was the
evidence of the antiquities, the barrows, earthworks and stone
monuments which still stood in remote rural areas. Who were
the 'ancients' encountered by Julius Caesar and Claudius when
they came to Britain?

Scholars pondered this uncomfortable void but, gaining no
help from the monuments themselves, they resorted to inspiration and invention. The only rule of this game was that whatever race was selected as suitable inhabitants of this country during prehistoric times it must have some relation to what was
known of the other prehistoric civilizations.

Nennius, writing in the ninth century A.D., settled the Trojan
Brutus, grandson of Aeneas, together with his followers, in Britain
at the height of the Greek Empire. Belief that the early Britons
were the descendants of Greeks or Romans was strong until well
into the seventeenth century. As late as 1674, the Oxford
Almanack headed the list of the kings of England with Brutus.
Then Brutus was swept from power by a preference for a more
Biblical origin and we became descendants of Noah. Japhet and
the sons of Japhet were said to have peopled Britain very soon
after the Flood. Then the Phoenicians, one of the Lost Tribes of

Israel, even the Egyptians, were in turn canvassed and took their place as ancestors.

The supposed identity of the builders of Stonehenge, that conundrum on Salisbury Plain, varied with the prevailing ancestral wind. Inigo Jones was commissioned by King James I to make a study of Stonehenge. He declared in 1620 that it was a Roman temple. Dr Carlton, a court physician, countered that Jones was mistaken and that it was in fact built by the Danes as a place in which to consecrate their Kings. John Twyne and Aylett Sammes, strong for Phoenician settlement of these islands, saw no difficulty in recognizing strong Phoenician affinities in the stone pillars. Bishop Nicholson did not doubt that it was Saxon. Dr Bolton knew it as the tomb of Boadicea. The Elizabethan diarist John Aubrey and many others thought it the work of those conveniently ubiquitous mystics called 'Druids'.

At the beginning of the nineteenth century, amongst the more sober students of prehistory, at least, a certain frustration is discernible. After a study of New Grange, the megalithic monument in Ireland, thought in turn to be Mithraic, Danish, Egyptian and Phoenician, Sir Richard Colt Hoare wrote :

> I shall not unnecessarily trespass upon the time and patience of my readers in endeavouring to ascertain what tribes first peopled this country [Ireland]; nor to what nation the construction of this singular monument may be reasonably attributed for, I fear, both its authors and its original destination will ever remain unknown. Conjecture may wander over its wild and spacious domains but will never bring home with it either truth or conviction. Alike will the histories of those stupendous temples at Avebury and Stonehenge which grace my native country, remain in obscurity and oblivion.[1]

Thus one of the foremost archaeologists of those times summed up the extent of real knowledge by confessing his despair. In the imaginations of his contemporaries the phantoms of long-dead civilizations still flitted among the ancient barrows and earthworks. Scholars still detected Egyptian hieroglyphs and Phoenician daggers carved in antiquity on the sarsens of Salisbury Plain. But Colt Hoare's statement marked some improvement. One archaeologist was admitting humbly that the study of antiquities was based on little more than guesswork, that he had

[1] *Tour in Ireland.* 1807.

been unable to wrest from these evidences of prehistory any positive information, that the happenings of four thousand years were obscured by darkness.

Perhaps this was too gloomy a view. By the beginning of the nineteenth century there had been one palpable achievement, although it was by no means widely accepted as such. For centuries mysterious stone objects had been turning up. The triangular wedges of chipped stone, usually of flint or chert, were at first dismissed as metaphysical phenomena such as thunderbolts or elfshot. Ullisses Androvandi, an eminent seventeenth century zoologist, thought they were due to 'an admixture of a certain exhalation of thunder and lightning with metallic matter, chiefly in dark clouds, which is distilled from the circumfused moisture and coagulated into a mass (like flour with water) and subsequently indurated by heat, like a brick'.

But others took a more practical view. Sir William Dugdale was convinced that the flints were 'weapons used by the Britons before the art of making arms of brass or iron was known'.[1]

At the end of the century a stone axe together with the remains of an elephant were found. Unfortunately, the association allowed an entirely false interpretation to be placed on it. The stone axe and a portion of a molar tooth were recovered from building excavations in Grays Inn Lane, London, by William Conyers, an apothecary and antique dealer. The finder did in fact cherish the belief that he had stumbled across evidence which suggested that elephants could once have inhabited Britain and that the weapon must have belonged to an Ancient British hunter. His view caused great hilarity. John Bagford, a friend who delivered an account of the find to the Society of Antiquaries, confined himself to the observation that the elephant must be attributable to the Roman occupation of this country, in fact a Claudian import. The flint was presented to the British Museum.

The first recorded hint from a scientist at the probable vast antiquity of man was made by John Frere, F.R.S., in a paper read to the Society on 22 June, 1797. Of several flint implements recovered from twelve feet of earth at Hoxne, near Diss, Suffolk, he said that they 'were fabricated and used by a people who had not the use of metals ... The situation [depth] at which these weapons were found may tempt us to refer them to a very remote period indeed, even beyond that of the present world'.[2]

[1] *History of Warwickshire.* 1650.   [2] *Archaeologia.* 1800.

One wonders what Frere's fellow members made of his attempt to attribute his stone axes to a hitherto unsuspected region of time. It is probable, however, that the inference was ignored completely for the paper lay dormant until the mid-nineteenth century when it was held up as evidence of British pre-eminence in archaeological discovery.

At the commencement of the Victorian era prehistoric archaeology can usefully be likened to a fly in a bottle, ever buzzing for release. The bottle was its elder sister science—geology. If geology insisted that there was no time for prehistory then it was useless for archaeology to propose events to put into it. But at this time geology itself was engaged in internecine strife. Towards the end of the eighteenth century began the rift between those geologists who uncompromisingly believed in the Creation as described in Genesis and a few who had come to doubt whether what they saw in the rocks could be accomplished in the mere six thousand years allowed by the Ussher-Lightfoot chronology. Instead of rejecting Biblical exegesis, the new school proposed that as the many strata of rocks could not have been produced by conditions which prevailed in modern times, then in the past terrestrial energy must have operated at a higher intensity. They argued that at some time there must have been general catastrophes, of which the Biblical Flood was but one example, an age of geological chaos which had exalted the mountain ranges and folded the valleys, natural phenomena which had annihilated, and made chalk of, countless millions of sea creatures. The rival factions split into Diluvialists, Catastrophists and Fluvialists, each battling for general acceptance of theories involving the multiplication or permutation of any number of floods and other kinds of natural catastrophes.

The greatest Catastrophist of them all was Georges Cuvier (1769–1826), geologist, naturalist and foremost member of the French *Académie des Sciences*. Cuvier held that the many strata of rocks could only be interpreted correctly in the light of several catastrophes, the Noachian Flood of Genesis being one of many. He was the constant adversary of prehistoric archaeologists who claimed that man could have existed at the same time as the extinct animals. The science of geology, and its kindred science palaeontology, was advanced and advancing. That monstrous and strange animals, now extinct, once inhabited Western Europe was no longer denied but it was the entrenched belief of men such as Cuvier that these had perished during the age of catastrophes. According to these authorities time could be divided into three main epochs: the Antediluvium—that of the monstrous, now extinct fauna, and of catastrophes culminating in the Flood of Genesis; the Diluvium—during which were deposited the strata of rock in which the remains of these extinct species might be met with; and the Modern Age—that of mankind and the modern species of animals. At the Dawn of Mankind, it was believed, Adam and Eve had been born into the physical and moral perfection of the terrestrial Paradise. Therefore suggestions that man had once lived at the same time as the extinct fauna in a state of primitive destitution, as postulated by the crude flint implements, was preposterous, and anathema to men such as Cuvier.

But cautious claims that this might have been so were being made with increasing frequency. Men excavating in the Midi of France had found the bones of bears, hyenas and reindeer; many they said, clearly bore the cutting marks of the flint tools found with them. Indeed, some advanced to the view that they had found the bones of the primitive men themselves. But against them all stood Georges Cuvier. Playing with skill one game with the rules of another, with gusto he threw himself into the task of demolishing these alleged human relics. His objective approach was exemplified by what almost certainly is an apocryphal story of a jape perpetrated on him by one of his young students. Clad in red costume, horns and hooves, the pranker burst into the bedroom of the father of palaeontology crying: 'Wake up, thou man of catastrophes. I am the devil. I have come to devour you.' Cuvier regarded the frightening apparition with cold and critical gaze. He said: 'I doubt whether you can. You have horns and hooves. You only eat plants.'

To Cuvier's Paris laboratory came the supplicants. Each bore his remains of 'antediluvian man'. The 'pope of bones' examined each case with care, then rejected it for what it was—the remains of an elephant from Belgium, fragments of cetacean from Cerigo, parts of a tortoise from Aix-en-Provence and so on. If the remains were undeniably human they were dismissed as 'modern', as bones which had by some freak of nature intruded into the deposit where the extinct-animal bones were found, or judged wanting in corroborative evidence in the form of witnesses. A significant *coup* in 1811 was the destruction of an exhibit that had been going the rounds of laboratories and scientific exhibitions for ninety years as *Homo diluvii testis*. Cuvier incorrectly identified this human witness of the Flood as a slab of Miocene rock[1] in which was embedded the fossilized vertebra of the extinct reptile *Ichthyosaurus* to which was added the human skull of a recently deceased sufferer of hypertosis—an overvigorous activity of the pituitary gland causing malformation of the cranial bones. Cuvier summed up his ethic in a final verdict the year of his death on a human skull recovered with the remains of extinct mammals in what was thought to be ancient mud at Lahr on the banks of the Rhine. He wrote : 'All the evidence leads us to believe that the Human Race did not exist at all in the countries where the fossil [animal] bones were found, at the period of the upheavals which buried them.'

Such was Cuvier's reputation for infallibility that a grateful nation offered him the post of Minister of the Interior, but death intervened. But his work did not die with him. His disciples within the *Académie* drew up a list of twenty-seven successive acts of creation with intervening catastrophes which were said to have obliterated certain animals and plants, by which geological time could be measured. Similar tables were compiled in England at about the same time. William Smith, known as 'Strata Smith' (1769–1839), drew up a table showing thirty-two such layers of strata. He found distinguishing animal and plant organisms in each.

The Catastrophists, Diluvialists and Fluvialists were in command but a faint voice now called for a more rational interpretation of the succeeding layers of strata. This doctrine, which came to be known as Uniformitarianism—the basis of modern geological thought—had as its apostle James Hutton. He held no brief for catastrophes, extraterrestrial energy or heavenly fireworks. Hutton's *Theory of the Earth,* published in 1785, instead saw the layers of sand, gravel, clay and limestone as the normal, undramatic successive deposits of water, both river and sea. He argued that nothing more was needed than ordinary sedimentary deposition over an immense length of time. 'No processes are to be employed,' he wrote, 'that are not natural to the globe; no action to be admitted except those of which we know the principle.'[2]

Uniformitarianism made nonsense of Biblical convention and, as might be expected, Hutton's contribution was received with

[1] For explanation of geological periods, see *Table I.*
[2] *Theory of the Earth.* 1785.

anger and abuse by the seemingly impregnable phalanx of theologio-scientific geologists. Hutton, however, was soon forgotten.
The Diluvialists returned to haggling with the Catastrophists and
both raged against the Fluvialists. Thus frustrated by the Biblical
politicking of the mighty Catastrophists, the prehistoric archaeologists and palaeontologists sought another way to plead that
man and the extinct animals had at one time been coeval. This
impossible task was attempted by tricks of terminology of a kind
best illustrated by the following example.

During the clearing of rocky hazards to navigation from the
bed of the Jumna river in Bengal, North India, a large quantity
of fossil animal bones were dredged up together with a few
which were strongly canvassed as being human. A lively discussion took place in the British-Indian scientific journals of 1833
before it was proved that the human relics were nothing of the
kind. Although this debate was a waste of time it did, by attracting the attention of correspondents with similar interests, grease
the wheels for one of importance. Two years later, while interest
in the Jumna dredgings was still alive, Hugh Falconer, super-
intendent of the Honourable East India Company's botanical
gardens and an enthusiastic archaeologist then excavating ancient
deposits in the Siwalik Hills, uncovered the remains of a
Colossochelys atlas—a gigantic extinct tortoise, some twelve feet
long, eight feet broad and six feet high.

The enthusiasts seemed only too aware that a giant tortoise
figured prominently in myth and folklore. In the Pythagorean
cosmogony the infant world is placed on the back of an elephant
which itself is sustained by a huge tortoise. In Hindu mythology
a mighty tortoise grapples with an elephant. The dimensions of
both animals were expressed in terms of extravagant magnitude.
The tortoises of modern India are small. It would have been as
legitimate to speak of an elephant contending with a mouse as
with any one of these. Could man then, ran the speculation,
remember the days of these giant reptiles?

On this debate the Proceedings of the Zoological Society of
London for 1844 commented:

> The result at which we have arrived is, that there are fair
> grounds for entertaining the belief as probable that the
> *Colossochelys atlas* may have lived down to an early epoch
> of the human period and become extinct since.

In this careful way archaeological papers of the early and mid-nineteenth century pushed at the firmly closed door of Biblical conception. Many years later Falconer commented that if it were true that the giant tortoise may have *lived down* to man, then it must follow that man was alive on the earth at the same time as the tortoise. This way of expressing the relation was simply a semantic device calculated to minimize the likelihood of academic ridicule. A similar subterfuge was the statement that the primitive flint tool user was 'lived down to' by the extinct fauna of 'the *later* diluvium'. By such equivocation early nineteenth-century man was able to preserve his beliefs from direct conflict with established orthodoxy.

But the theologio-scientific cadre was not to be hoodwinked by such methods. Departing from its usual tactics of indifference or the swatting of reactionary gnats it closed its ranks. In 1802 William Paley[1] had published his *Natural Theology; or Evidence of the Existence and Attributes of the Deity collected from the Appearances of Nature.* Paley has been described as one of the most original thinkers on natural phenomena but his *Natural Theology* was a cringing testimonial to the old dogma. Dedicating the work to the Bishop of Durham 'to repair in his study his deficiences in the Church', he had written that although the world teemed with countless animal and plant 'delights' it could not have done so for more than six thousand years. Everything was part of a splendid, precise, design by God, the arch-watchmaker.

This was like balm to the sensitive hides of the theologio-scientists. It was thought that more needed to be done in this vein. In 1833 the Trustees of the Earl of Bridgewater commissioned a number of 'tame' scientific authors, selected by the President of the Royal Society in consultation with the Archbishop of Canterbury and the Bishop of London, to write treatises on the departed Paley's theme. The brief was that the account of the Creation in Genesis was literally exact and that Noah's Ark and the Flood were facts of prehistory. The contributions reached expectations, particularly that of William Buckland,[2] Dean of Westminster, a former Reader in Minerology in the University of Oxford.

Buckland's academic performance was superb from the point

[1] 1743–1805.
[2] 1784–1856.

of view of the ecclesiastics. He had spent a lifetime equating his religious faith with the contrary evidence supplied by his geological excavations. The doyen of university lecturers, his eloquence packed the lecture halls to overfilling. He insisted on a Universal Deluge, holding that geology proved it beyond doubt. As in the case of Cuvier, the stories about Buckland were legion—how he disinterred the heart of a French king from Sutton Courtenay churchyard and ate it, how he kept a pet orang-utan in his rooms at Christ Church, and how he breakfasted Ruskin on toasted mice. It was claimed that his field geology was so profound that when lost one day on a horseback journey from Oxford to London, he dismounted, scooped up a handful of earth, and remarked : 'Ah, yes, as I guessed, Ealing'.

Buckland's immense authority was instrumental in disposing of the claim of Father J. MacEnery, a Roman Catholic priest. MacEnery recovered from Kent's Cavern, near Torquay, Devon, a rhinoceros tooth and a 'flint weapon'. He hopefully communicated the find to the Dean only to be told that he was mistaken in his interpretation. Buckland said that the Ancient Britons must have scooped ovens in the cave floor, thus allowing the weapon to intrude amongst the fossil animal bones below. MacEnery argued that the floor was of unbroken stalagmite and that there were no such ovens—but in vain. The priest then enlisted the support of a local schoolmaster named William Pengelly and through him that of the Torquay Natural History Society. But Buckland's strong opposition was enough to convince MacEnery that he had better not publish. Many years later the British Association for the Advancement of Science was attracted by the story and conducted a new series of excavations at the cavern. In 1867 a human jawbone was brought to light.

But the Bridgewater Treatises were becoming an anachronism. Already the tide of opinion was making strongly against the Catastrophists and the Uniformitarianists were growing in number. The year 1833 saw the publication of the third and final volume of Lyell's *Principles of Geology*. It has been rightly commented that no scientific work except Charles Darwin's *Origin of Species* has during the author's lifetime exerted such a powerful influence on its subject. It is one of those ironies of life that Sir Charles Lyell claimed to have been attracted towards geology by William Buckland's brilliant Oxford lectures.

Lyell was an example of that quite common nineteenth-century phenomenon—the amateur turned expert. Destined by

his father for the legal profession, Lyell took a Master of Arts
degree at Exeter College and was duly called to the Bar. But
the seed implanted by Buckland exerted a powerful influence.
Lyell was shortly off on a series of geological excursions to the
Continent, principally to France with Roderick (later Sir) Impey
Murchison. This was the turning point in his life. He wrote to
his father that after the fullest consideration he had decided to
give up law and devote his life to geology. He did so to such
effect that by 1824, three years after leaving Oxford, he was
secretary of the Royal Geological Society, and two years later he
was elected to the fellowship of the Royal Society. The first
volume of his *Principles* was published that year.

To geologists who had gained their view of the formation of
strata from Georges Cuvier's *Theory of the Earth* the work was a
revelation. Instead of early convulsions and a higher intensity of
terrestrial energy culminating in periodic catastrophes, Lyell
proposed that the natural forces now existing were strong enough
to produce stupendous changes in the earth's crust provided they
were given sufficient time. The earth, Lyell argued, was millions
of years old and not just a few thousand as suggested by the
Catastrophists. Lyell's offering was not original. Hutton had said
the same sort of thing at the end of the previous century, but it
is a sad truth that a prophet out of his time rarely prospers.
Only when the minds of men are conditioned to the reception
of a new and strident hypothesis does it stand a chance of acceptance. Hutton was swept out of sight by the tremendous opposition. Lyell was lionized: knighted in 1848, honoured with the
doctorate of Civil Laws by Oxford in 1855 and the Royal
Society's Copley Medal in 1858.

Many Catastrophists, Diluvialists and Fluvialists joined the
ranks of Lyell's supporters; later many more were brought
round to his point of view. A notable English convert was the
Rev. W. D. Conybeare,[1] Dean of Llandaff, a renowned geologist
who not so long before had been postulating three deluges before
that of Noah. He now claimed that Lyell's work was 'in itself
sufficiently important to mark almost a new era in the progress
of our science'. But Lyell by no means had it all his own way.
Powerful men, such as William Buckland and Adam Sedgewick,
Woodwardian Professor of Geology at Cambridge in 1818, came
out strongly against the *Principles*. John Kidd, Buckland's former
teacher, was possibly typical of the majority who merely allowed

[1] 1787–1857.

the salt of Lyell's work to flavour the old Biblical mess of pottage. In his Bridgewater Treatise, published in the same year but subsequent to Lyell's *Principles*, he wrote that in the previous century it had been generally considered that shells and other organic remains found in chalk and other strata were proof of the Deluge of Moses. But today, he continued, without prejudice to the credibility of the Scriptures these same men were admitting that the shells and remains may have been deposited after the Deluge. Who can say, he asked, that this later view will not be adopted in respect of the extinct mammals found in gravel and caverns?

So the theologio-scientists of Britain began to admit that there might be some truth in assertions that the extinct species of animals had bridged the Deluge. By this admission the road was opened for eventual acceptance that man himself might have done so, but by crossing the Deluge in the other direction, by reaching backwards in time instead of forward.

But this minimal concession was open-handed by comparison with the uncompromising attitude across the Channel. By its nature British Protestantism is far more liberal than French Roman Catholicism and this manifested itself in the staunch rearguard action fought on behalf of Biblical convention and chronology by the *Académie des Sciences*, particularly in the way that body spurned men such as Boucher de Perthes.

Jacques Boucher de Crèvecoeur de Perthes[1] is invariably described as a retired customs official, even a mere lock-keeper. In fact he was a frequently published author of travelogues which described visits not only to the British Isles but also to Italy, Scandinavia, Russia and North Africa. But at this range Boucher de Perthes is an enigmatic character. It is by no means certain that he himself made the visits he described. His activities described later in this book suggest also that he was either an innocent victim of enthusiasm or a downright charlatan.

Boucher de Perthes was absorbed in the archaeology of his native Abbeville, then a small out-of-the-way town in Northern France. In 1846 he published *Antiquités celtiques et antédiluviennes: De l'industrie primitive ou des artes à leur origine*, the results of many years of excavation. He made no attempt at compromise, writing that he had found at various depths in the gravel pits about Abbeville numerous stone tools and the bones of extinct animals. There was no doubt in the mind of Boucher

[1] 1788–1868.

de Perthes that in spite of their imperfections these rude stone tools proved the existence of man as a contemporary of the extinct fauna.

It is traditional that the *Académie des Sciences* was outraged by the publication and that he was the scientific laughing stock of Paris. The renowned palaeontologist and foremost French commentator on the history of this science, Marcellin Boule, has written that 'contradictions, sneers and scorn' were forthwith heaped on Boucher de Perthes' head. But there seems no evidence to support this dramatic view of the reception. It is more likely that the *Académie* accorded Boucher de Perthes the treatment usually reserved for radical amateurs. It completely ignored him. For many years he and his work remained undignified by official rebuttal.

But if Boucher de Perthes lacked worldly fame he was not entirely unrewarded. He had achieved a great deal of local importance. His future scientific papers continued to delight his fellow members of the *Société d'Emulation d'Abbeville* and were widely circulated in the historical societies of rural France. Abbeville became the centre of a vigorous and profitable trade in stone axes. Boucher de Perthes established a museum which attracted a large number of visitors. One of the many Englishmen who later made the pilgrimage to Abbeville described this 'impressive' collection. According to Hugh Falconer, the museum was housed in a hotel which 'was from ground floor to garret, a continued museum filled with pictures, mediaeval art, and Gaulish antiquities, including antediluvian flint knives, fossil bones, etc.' He also reported that there was a not inconsiderable admixture of natural freaks such as water-perforated stones, and strangely-shaped pieces of glass and brick.

But the *Académie* was forced to notice Boucher de Perthes in time. In 1854, Dr Rigollet of Amiens innocently likened some stone axes found by himself in the sandpits of nearby St. Acheul to those found by Boucher de Perthes at Abbeville. Rigollet was a member of the *Académie*, but instead of abusing the scientist it turned on Boucher de Perthes.

It was not unusual even up to modern times for a scientific body to castigate an outsider while at the same time overlooking similarly offensive views when expressed by a fellow scientist.

Why this peculiar form of injustice was practised so frequently is not obvious. The usual clannish intolerance of unwarranted intrusion by outsiders does not seem to be the whole answer. It is possible, however, that it was a kind of diplomacy. By this means an authoritative body could warn a member that he had transgressed without directly offending him. In this way the risk that a faction might be formed about him would be greatly reduced.

Whatever the reason, undoubtedly Boucher de Perthes received the sniggers which by right should have been directed at Rigollet. Like the Londoner's attitude to the Society of Antiquaries many years before, Boucher de Perthes became the target for Parisian humour. But Paris is a long way from Abbeville.

Speculation on both sides of the Channel about the probable antiquity of man was a step forward. But no one yet doubted that these distant ancestors of mankind, if indeed they had ever existed at all, could have been anything other than like us in appearance. The Bible said, and the Church and Science, laity and geologists and amateurs, devoutly believed it, that God created man in his own image. This much was sure. When a fossil man was found at last nobody recognized him.

Chapter 2

THE UNEARTHING OF Neanderthal man in 1856—renowned as the first discovery of a genuine fossil man although events show that in fact he is not entitled to this preeminence—and the uproar which followed the discovery span a decade. In this decade speculation on man's antiquity received several shots in the arm in the form of the Darwin-Wallace paper to the Linnean Society in 1858, the publishing of the former's sensational *The Origin of Species* the following year and Huxley's *Evidence of Man's Place in Nature* in 1863. The story of Neanderthal man shows how little the minds of men responded to these historically momentous works.

The Neander valley (*thal*) lies near the town of Wuppertal about seven miles east of Dusseldorf in what then was called Rhenish Prussia. The valley, through which flows the Dussel river, gained its name from the seventeenth-century hymn-writer and recluse Joseph Neander. By 1856 however the 'sweet flowery bower' of the hermit had been mostly destroyed by the relentless quarrying of limestone for building. Neanderthal man was dug out of a deposit of mud on the floor of a cave some sixty feet above the river. How the quarrymen found the bones is clear but why they attached any importance to the remains is not so evident for it appears that similar discoveries were common. But in this case Neanderthal man, a skull with the facial bones entirely missing, a clavicle, a scapula, two ulnae, five ribs and a pelvis, was handed to Herr von Beckensdorff, the quarry owner. He presented the remains to Dr J. C. Fuhlrott of neighbouring Elberfeld who in turn passed them to H. Schaafhausen, professor of anatomy in the University of Bonn.

The choice was propitious. Three years before, in 1853, Schaafhausen had rejected the Catastrophists, even propounding a crude theory of evolution, writing that :

> living plants are not separated from the extinct by new creations, but are to be regarded as their descendants through continued reproduction.

A year after the discovery Schaafhausen published a paper on the Neanderthal remains. He said that they were undoubtedly human but had peculiarities of conformation. The skull appeared to Schaafhausen to be of unusual thickness with exaggerated eyebrow ridges. The thighbones were strangely curved but none of this could be due to deformation by disease. The brain-size, suggested by the capacity of the cranium, could not have been much less than 1,033 cc. (cubic centimetres) and so not much lower than the average capacity of the average modern skull.

But how old did Schaafhausen think the bones were? He found that the skeleton was of the same colour as other fossil animals' bones. The remains stuck to the tongue and when a fragment had been partially dissolved in hydrochloric acid no gelatine remained. When examined under a magnifying glass the bones were found to be covered with minute black specks. All this, wrote Schaafhausen, proved that the bones were genuine fossils.[1]

All this, Schaafhausen found himself able to conclude, pointed to the fact that the remains were those of

> an individual of a savage and barbarous race derived from one of the wild races of north-western Europe, spoken of by the Latin writers and traced to a period when the latest animals of the diluvium still existed.

Considering the professor's advanced views on evolution this finding is disappointing. His reluctance to make an ambitious claim for Neanderthal man, his lack of audacity, robbed him of any notable niche in history. But he had said enough, too much for some.

A colleague at Bonn, Professor H. von Meyer, immediately wrote to Schaafhausen that his allusion to the diluvium was nonsense for it was evident that the remains were of recent origin. If Schaafhausen cared to look at the notepaper on which the letter was written he could see the black specks which he had mistakenly attributed to vast age. The writer said he had in his possession the skull of a dog which was as recent as the

---

[1] The antiquity of bones was long thought to be established by adherence to the tongue, lack of gelatine and black specks sometimes identified as iron pyrites. Later these criteria were discarded as useless but in modern times the hydrochloric test was resurrected in another form and found to be valid.

Roman occupation of northern Europe and certainly not as old as the diluvium of which Schaafhausen had written. This skull stuck to the tongue and it did not differ in colour from the animal bones discovered in French caves, also erroneously lauded as being of vast age.

Professor F. Mayer, also of Bonn, thought that Schaafhausen's enthusiasm had carried him away. A little quiet reasoning, he said, would show him that the so-called ancient man was nothing of the kind. Over the years Mayer had examined many human remains for which claims of antiquity had been made. None, said Mayer, had lived up to the expectations of the discoverers. Mayer had a theory which accounted for the peculiar shape of the ribs and limb bones. A protuberance on the left elbow, said by Schaafhausen to be the scar of an old injury, was none other than a symptom of advanced rickets. The protruding eyebrow ridges confirmed this diagnosis. The owner was in fact a Mongolian Cossack on his way through Prussia in 1814 in pursuit of Napoleon's fleeing army. The pain of the disease had furrowed the forehead of the horseman, for such he was as only a professional equestrian would have such bowed legs. The Cossack, said Mayer, had crawled into the Neanderthal cave and succumbed in agony. Mayer did not explain how the stricken man had managed to climb up sixty feet of vertical rock to the cave, nor did he even mention this fact.

Another colleague, J. A. Wagner, was convinced that the remains were modern but, unkindly, those of a Dutchman. Schaafhausen had to wait until 1872 to be told by Dr R. von Virchow that the Neanderthal skull was that of 'a pathological idiot'.

The French *Académie des Sciences* pointedly ignored Neanderthal man entirely. In England the discovery passed almost unnoticed except for a brief mention in two journals of a semi-scientific nature. One, the *Westminster Review,* however, described the fossil as

the ruin of a solitary arch in an enormous bridge, which time has destroyed and which may have connected the highest of animals with the lowest of men.

The anonymous writer of these courageous words was not known. He anticipated scientific publication in England by almost four years, and general scientific thought by many more.

It is more than likely, however, that the prophet was Thomas Henry Huxley, for he was a regular contributor to the *Review*.

Huxley has that indefinable quality of being able to travel well through time. This is despite the efforts of many of his biographers who, with the best intentions in the world, tend to play up his idiosyncrasies. In 1856 he was just into his thirties but already of considerable authority. Of Huxley it can be fairly said that he had more talent than two lifetimes could have developed.

Of lower-middle-class stock, after a grammar-school education Huxley won a free scholarship to Charing Cross Hospital where he took prizes in anatomy, chemistry and physiology, winning the Gold Medal of the first University of London medical examination.

But his scholarship did nothing to obtain him a medical post and having to support himself he was forced into the only opening that was offered. He became an assistant surgeon in the Royal Navy, a turn of events which saved him for ever from a medical career, for his first—and only—appointment was to a survey ship with the unprepossessing name H.M.S. *Rattlesnake*.

With young Huxley aboard, the ship left England in December 1846 for a prolonged cruise of Australia's Great Barrier Reef and then up through the Torres Strait. This voyage would have been a major setback to the scientific pretensions of a lesser man, divorced as he was from instruction or guidance and with few books. Instead Huxley turned it to advantage. With the aid of a net adapted from a wire-mesh meat cover Huxley engrossed himself in the study of the anatomy of marine creatures. His scientific papers on the subject were of such peculiar brilliance that on his return to England in 1850 many established marine biologists sought to make his acquaintance. Within a few months he was elected to the membership of the Royal Society, and embarked on the first of the innumerable controversies which he provoked throughout his life.

Huxley blandly informed his Admiralty employers that he considered the body was obliged to pay for the publishing of his scientific description of the voyage. The Admiralty refused, considering that it had been more than generous in allowing the biological questing at all, for he had not accompanied the survey as official naturalist but as a doctor. He was informed that furthermore it was his duty as a naval officer to rejoin the Fleet immediately.

The argument between Huxley and the Admiralty raged on and off for three years, culminating on 1 February, 1854 with a direct order to proceed aboard H.M.S. *Illustrious*. Huxley refused, applying first for a postponement, then a cancellation, of the instructions. The Admiralty told him to report for duty or be struck from the Navy List. He did not and he was.

Now deprived even of the half-pay of the reserve fleet Huxley was penniless. Meanwhile he had married and necessity forced him to consider going to Australia to become a brewer. Nothing had come of his application for posts at the universities of Aberdeen and Cork or at King's College, London. But just before the effects of his expulsion from the Navy became too catastrophic he was offered the post of professor of palaeontology and naturalist at the Royal School of Mines, Jermyn Street, London, at a salary of £200 per annum.

Huxley's scientific papers were in great demand, and so was his writing for popular readership. Never was there a more potent purveyor of science for the layman. Although by training a physician and by inclination a biologist, Huxley embraced every related scientific subject and many that bore no resemblance. But all his articles were masterpieces of lucidity. The writer G. K. Chesterton remarked that Huxley was more a literary than a scientific man.

Huxley, however, did have an abrupt way with triflers or those he thought to be such, which has led to the charge of arrogance. But it would have been hard for the possessor of his staggering intellect to have been otherwise. Already he was developing a reputation for absent-mindedness. But it was noticeable that the suffering caused by his non-attendance at a scientific gathering was small compared to that caused by one of his surprise appearances at another where he was unlooked for. It is more than likely, therefore, that this feature was nothing more than a sudden change of mind precipitated by the last-minute discovery that adversaries more equal to his metal were to be found elsewhere. For Huxley dearly loved controversy. He was never better than on his feet dealing with some famous transgressor. He described himself as 'a peace-loving, good-natured man' and declared that 'controversy is as abhorrent to me as gin to a reclaimed drunkard'. In justice to his own case he could have added 'and just as irresistible'.

As might be expected Huxley made many powerful enemies and friends. Amongst the latter were the geologist Sir Charles

Lyell and Sir Joseph Hooker,[1] the famous systematic biologist who with his father built up the magnificent botanical collection at Kew. Both men remained lifelong friends of Huxley. Amongst the enemies was Sir Richard Owen[2], professor of comparative anatomy and palaeontology at the University of Oxford. Owen was a staunch theologio-scientist, a man of immense prestige and influence and equal quantities of arrogance and vanity. He was sometimes called 'the British Cuvier'. Huxley said privately that this was like comparing British brandy with cognac.

Owen had at first earned Huxley's gratitude by interceding with the Admiralty to prevent his untimely recall. But when Huxley at last spurned the Navy it seemed to the professor to be neither a reasonable nor a proper act. The next encounter was even more disastrous to the relationship. Huxley solicited a written testimonial from the great man who obliged with a condescension which stung the young biologist into a fury. It seems to have been of the 'not a *bad* sort of fellow' colour. Huxley said his first impulse had been to seek out the professor and knock him down.[3] Relations deteriorated further in 1856, the year of the Neanderthal discovery, when Owen arrogated Huxley's title of professor of palaeontology, as a repayment for being allowed the use of laboratory facilities at the Royal School of Mines. Huxley got something of his own back in his Croonian lecture to the Royal Society that year by describing Owen's contention that skull bones were modified vertebrae — then a widely accepted belief — as absolute rubbish. Owen never forgave him.

So far as England was concerned Neanderthal man had to be content with two notices, both of a non-scientific and philosophical nature. He certainly was not noticed by the British Association, the Royal Society, the Geological Society, all directly concerned bodies, or in the Press.

In France however the situation was considerably worse. Not only was the Prussian fossil man ignored completely but the proponents of the view that man had existed in the times of the extinct species of animals had made no headway. It is one of those paradoxes that the main scientific body of the country where stone axes and tools were being found in the greatest abundance persisted in ignoring the fact.

[1] 1817–1911.
[2] 1804–92.
[3] *Letter from Huxley to E. Forbes.* 27 November, 1852.

Marcellin Boule blames Elie de Beaumont[1], disciple of Cuvier, geologist and permanent secretary of the *Académie des Sciences,* for this state of affairs. He was certainly the leading figure in the conspiracy to ignore Boucher de Perthes. But the men within the *Académie* who respected the Abbeville amateur's view, such as J. L. de Quatrefages, Edouard Lartet, André Prevost and Jean Gaudry, did not strive for his recognition. They certainly encouraged Boucher de Perthes but it was well behind the back of de Beaumont and the other spiritual leaders of the *Académie.*

Boule attributes the *Académie*'s eventual tolerance of Boucher de Perthes to the intervention of British scientists, writing :

> Before the intervention of British archaeologists and geologists had deprived this great question of its wholly French bearing, for so long the entire French Academy followed its Permanent Secretary like a flock of sheep.

This view is anachronistic and unfair to the French believers. British support for Boucher de Perthes did not begin until 1859 and by this time many French Academicians themselves were publicly supporting their countryman although, it must be admitted, with little success.

Would Boucher de Perthes have fared any better in England in 1846—the year of his apostasy? The answer is in the affirmative but with a qualification.

There was no exact equivalent in Britain of the French *Académie*, to which only the most distinguished men of science and letters were invited as members. The nearest equivalents, the British Association for the Advancement of Science and the Royal Society, were again solely the platforms of the professional expert and beyond the range of the amateur. But lower down the order the views of Boucher de Perthes would certainly have received an airing on a scale that far exceeded that of the *Société d'Emulation d'Abbeville.*

The long, hot summer of Victorian prosperity, born of the Industrial Revolution, was at its height. As a result, for the middle and upper classes, came much time in which to do little. This idleness and the Victorian love of getting outdoors for some semi-scientific pursuit and talking about it indoors afterwards brought about a unique era of vernacular discovery. Many new societies were formed as escape valves for this energy. The

[1] 1798–1874.

already established learned societies received inrushes of new members, each one, it seems, with a view crying for release.

One of this latter kind was the Geological Society, with rooms at Burlington House, Regent Street, London. The interchange within this society was much freer from the strictures of religion than that within the French *Académie*. As has been observed earlier it was not too unusual for a speaker in pressing for the extreme antiquity of a find, to claim that this or that flint implement had been found with the bones of extinct species of animals which had somehow survived the Deluge. It is also certain, however, that such assertions were made in innocence of their implications, for what was being said would, within the still current interpretation of Biblical convention, send their authors posthumously to Hell.

So Boucher de Perthes would have certainly got a hearing. But such was the demand that the relentless 'papering' of the society tended to militate against itself. A paper almost invariably brought several against it, the proposition it contained often vanishing without trace in a confused sea of persiflage.

Chapter 3

THE *Beagle* TOOK up her moorings at Falmouth, Cornwall on 2 October, 1836, and Charles Darwin[1] returned home to Shrewsbury after five years. His father remarked that the shape of his head had 'quite altered'.

Darwin's output was enormous. With the help of Professor Sir Richard Owen, within six months of his arrival he had sorted his collection of specimens and arranged for them to be described by experts under his editorship in the official *Zoology of the Voyage of the Beagle*, and had written his own account, *Journal of Researches*. Then came three more books, *The Structure and Distribution of Coral Reefs* (1842), *Volcanic Islands* (1844), and *Geological Observations on South America* (1846).

While secretary of the Geological Society from 1848 to 1851 he studied and offered a solution to the problem of the origin of the 'parallel roads'—mysterious rock formations at Glenroy in Scotland. He erroneously attributed them to ancient marine beaches later divorced from the sea by land subsidence. Beaches they were but formed in a land-locked lake by glaciers. Several eminent geologists told him so with varying degrees of sarcasm. But Darwin also made the acquaintance of Sir Charles Lyell and Sir Joseph Hooker. It was to the latter that he first confided his theory of evolution by natural selection.

In an autobiographical sketch published in 1887 by Francis Darwin as part of *The Life and Letters of Charles Darwin*, the great man wrote that his main problem was how the changes in plant and animal species were brought about. He could see that man successfully applied artificial selection to animal and agricultural husbandry in farming, but how could this selection take place in the wild, with plants and animals living under natural conditions? Then the answer occurred to him. He read 'for amusement' Thomas Robert Malthus[2] who had written that animal populations increased in geo-metrical ratio unless checked. Darwin pondered the reason.

[1] 1809–82.
[2] 1766–1834.

Offspring in their early stages are always far more numerous than their parents, but in spite of this tendency to progressive increase the numbers of a given species actually remain more or less constant. The missing key then was the powerful and restless struggle for survival. Since all organisms vary appreciably only those advantageously equipped for the struggle can survive. Of this deduction Darwin wrote in a notebook : 'One may say that there is a force like a hundred thousand wedges trying to force every kind of structure into the economy of nature.'

This force was exerting itself just as powerfully on Darwin for he proposed to and was accepted by Emma, a daughter of Josiah Wedgwood, the potter of Maer Hall. The Wedgwood family had long been friends of the Darwins. Charles had known Emma since childhood. But it is typical of Darwin that before he took the plunge into matrimony he carefully weighed on paper the advantages and disadvantages of such a step. It is not even known whether Emma had come to mind before or after the favourable conclusion was arrived at. On 24 January, 1839, the thirty-year-old lover was elected to the fellowship of the Royal Society. Five days later the couple were married but there was no honeymoon; the nuptials merely inspiring a wedding-day note on plant-breeding.

In 1842 Darwin wrote a thirty-two-page abstract of his theory of evolution, or 'transmutation' as he called it. Two years later he had enlarged this to an essay of 250 pages. At first only Sir Joseph Hooker was informed of these developments but in 1856 Lyell was allowed to join the conspiracy.

Lyell and Hooker repeatedly urged Darwin to publish, for to delay, they advised him, was to risk being beaten to the post by someone else. In the case of Lyell there might even have been an element of self-interest in the whip-cracking, for the same vast quantities of time were required for the working of the Darwinian theory of evolution as Lyell had claimed for his history of the earth. Darwinism was likewise a direct negation of the word of God as interpreted by the theologio-scientists.

But Darwin fussed and prevaricated. He began to draft an epic work to be called *Natural Selection* which, on his own estimation, would have been some 2,500 pages in length. Two years later the Lyell-Hooker prophecy was fulfilled. On 8 June, 1858, to Darwin's complete consternation, he received a letter from Alfred Russel Wallace[1] which in twelve pages gave a brief

[1] 1823–1913.

but entire summary of Darwin's own theory of evolution by natural selection. According to Darwin, Wallace asked for help to get the paper published. Wallace, then in the Moluccas engaged in a biological survey of the Malay Archipelago, had been confined to bed by a bout of fever, during which he had set down his conclusions.

Darwin wrote plaintively to Lyell:

> Your words have come true with a vengeance—that I should be forestalled. I never saw a more striking coincidence; if Wallace had my MSS sketch written out in 1842, he could not have made a better short abstract! Even his terms stand out as heads to my chapters . . . So all my originality, whatever it will amount to, will be smashed.

In truth Darwin—and Alfred Wallace—had been anticipated by over forty years. In 1813, while Lyell was still a young man collecting data for his *Principles of Geology* and Darwin was not much more than a baby, a most extraordinary paper had been delivered to the Royal Society by an expatriate American physician named Charles Wells.[1] The paper, misleadingly entitled *An Account of a White Female, Part of whose Skin Resembles that of a Negro,* contained an almost complete condensation of Darwin's main thesis—natural selection. Speaking of artificial as opposed to natural selection Wells had said: 'What is done here by art (in the case of domestic animals) seems to be done with equal efficacy, though more slowly, by nature, in the formation of varieties of mankind, fitted for the countries they inhabit.' Wells then proposed that some stocks might better resist disease and multiply at the expense of others in particular areas.

A correspondent of Darwin's drew his attention to the Wells paper in the 1860s. Darwin mentioned it in the historical preface to later editions of his *Origin of Species* but said that Wells had confined his study to natural selection in the human races while he had extended his to embrace all organisms. Darwin was mistaken. Wells applies his remarks generally. He actually uses the phrase 'amongst men, as well as among other animals, varieties of a greater or less magnitude are constantly occurring'.

There is little doubt, therefore, that although Wells expressed his view more timorously and did not accompany it with such

[1] 1757–1817.

a wealth of evidence as Darwin did, a strong claim can be made for the former's priority. Like the geologist Hutton he suffered from being before his time.

On receiving the news about Wallace, Lyell and Hooker counselled Darwin that in fairness the only course was a joint publication. Darwin agreed and the paper was delivered to the Linnean Society on 1 July, 1858. The reception seems to have been non-committal for there was no report of any explosion. Possibly the implication of the paper was not realized. Darwin, however, now threw himself into his task with energy. Within fifteen months he had completed his *Origin of Species by Means of Natural Selection*. It was a much shorter work than he had originally intended, being only 502 pages long; but still a magnificent achievement.

Alfred Wallace's own account differs somewhat from the above widely accepted version of the events which led to the joint paper. Some forty years later, writing of his cordial relations with Darwin he pointed out that in 1854 he had already published *On the Law which has Regulated the Introduction of New Species*, a paper which set forth a reasoned denial that new species of animals were the result of direct and separate works of Creation. Wallace said also that he had briefly met Darwin in the Insect Room of the British Museum at the beginning of that same year just before his departure for Borneo. So Darwin must have been aware of a similarity of view on transmutation of species. He had written Darwin 'a very long letter' with special reference to his article. Darwin had replied at similar length telling him that he agreed with 'everything in my article' and that it was evident that both had been thinking very much alike on the subject. Darwin had also informed Wallace that 'this summer will be my twentieth year since I opened my first notebook on the subject'. Wallace further commented :

But never in this nor in any other letters did he give me a hint of his having already arrived at the theory of Natural Selection; while in December 1857 he wrote : 'My work will not fix or settle anything; but I hope it will aid by giving a large collection of facts, with one definite end. Yet he [Darwin] had already written a sketch in 1842, and in 1844 enlarged this to 230 folio pages giving a complete presentation of his arguments set forth in the Origin.'

But although he was outshone by Darwin, Wallace was not complaining. Indeed he claimed that Darwin's work had secured for himself 'full recognition by the press and the public'. Wallace was merely thankful that his work had compelled Darwin to write and publish without further delay.[1]

From abstract to completion it had taken Charles Darwin seventeen years to write the *Origin of Species*. Even taking into account the complexity of the subject this is about four times the length of time normally required for such a project. It is usual to attribute this prevarication to Darwin's earlier error over the 'parallel roads' of Glenroy, which made him wish to collect such an overwhelming mass of evidence for his new hypothesis that a repetition would be impossible. Lately it has been suggested instead that Darwin may have suffered from Chagas' disease, a chronic infection which produces lassitude and later affects the heart.

Chagas' disease is endemic throughout South America and it is known now that it can be contracted through contact with the armadillo, which is infected by the *Benchuca*, a bug which infests its burrows. Darwin could not have known this and he had certainly handled the armadillo, even eating its flesh. He had also encountered a *Benchuca* during his visit to Chile in 1853, allowing it to inflate itself with blood drawn from a finger. There is little doubt about Darwin's chronic invalidism, for soon after his marriage he started a daily log of his ill-health.

But it must be more than just coincidence that at this time he also began to rough out his *Natural Selection*. It could be that he prevaricated because of a deeper affliction—one of conscience. That he feared to publish. After rejecting medicine as a career at Edinburgh, Darwin had read for Holy Orders at Cambridge. He admits in *Life and Letters* that :

I did not then in the least doubt the strict and literal truth of every word in the Bible, I soon persuaded myself that our Creed must be fully accepted.

Darwin obtained a good pass degree in Theology, Euclid and the Classics. As a student he spent a considerable amount of his spare time with his mentor in botany, the Rev. John Steven Henslow. It was Henslow who obtained the budding biologist a place aboard the *Beagle*. Darwin's father, a deeply

[1] *Black and White.* 17 January, 1903.

religious man, was not at all pleased at this advent. Only the personal intervention of 'Uncle Jos' Wedgwood had overcome Robert Darwin's determination that his son should make a career in the Church. Darwin's wife Emma had very strong religious beliefs.

It is therefore not beyond the bounds of reason that Darwin was none too happy about the philosophical escalator on which his perception had placed him, that he would have been only too pleased to get off but for Lyell and to a lesser degree Hooker. He may well have feared that publication of his hypothesis—his affront to the word of God—would lead to damnation.

Darwin even made a last-ditch attempt to prevent publication. He wrote to his publisher, John Murray, 'If you feel bound to say in the clearest terms that you do not think it [the Origin] likely to have a remunerative sale, I completely and explicitly free you of your offer.' But Murray thought that it would, and it was published on 24 November, 1859. The first edition of 1,250 copies was sold out on the first day.

It is usual to account for the astounding success of the Origin on a happy chance which made the regular scientific book reviewer of The Times ill, his substitute being T. H. Huxley. This view is erroneous. In fact Huxley arranged for his review to be printed in the newspaper to the neglect of the staff writer. He told Lyell that 'the educated mob who derive their ideas from The Times shall respect Darwin and be damned to them'.

Huxley respected Darwin's hypothesis but it is debatable just how much he believed in it. Controversy was meat and drink to Huxley, and Darwin had handed him an intellectual bombshell which would explode inside those sepulchres of the theologio-scientists—the universities of Oxford and Cambridge. He had met Darwin in the autumn previous to the publication of Origin and had been allowed to read the final draft. He was enthusiastic, had been flexing his muscles for the fray ever since, but he was by no means an uncritical evolutionist. 'I by no means suppose,' he informed Lyell, 'that the transmutation hypothesis is proved or anything like it, but I view it as a powerful instrument of research. Follow it out and it will lead us somewhere.'

To Huxley, then, Darwinism was a working hypothesis; the current theologio-scientific view seemed to him to be no explanation at all. Of Darwin's contribution he said: 'Either it would prove its capacity to elucidate the facts, or it would break down under the strain.'

There can be little doubt, however, that no small element of the appeal of the Darwinian hypothesis to Huxley was that he knew it would be abhorrent to his old enemy, Sir Richard Owen. Darwin enjoyed protection, Huxley enjoyed giving it. He called himself 'Darwin's bulldog'. A palpable truth, for the principal evolutionist did precious little barking or biting himself. After reading *Origin* Huxley told Darwin that the work would be greeted 'with considerable abuse and misrepresentation'. On the eve of publication he had written gleefully to the author : 'I am sharpening up my claws and beak in readiness.'[1] This bloodthirsty attitude must have alarmed Darwin more than it gave him pleasure. But Huxley had to wait until the next year before the bloodletting.

As early as 1858 Hugh Falconer had visited Abbeville. What he saw convinced him that Boucher de Perthes' claims were valid; that the chipped flints were indeed the tools of primitive man. On his return to England he urged the geologists Sir John Evans and Joseph Prestwich and a Mr Flower to make a similar visit.

On 26 May, 1859, Prestwich proudly told the Royal Society the results of the visit, on 2 June the Society of Antiquaries was informed, the following day it was the turn of the Geological Society. Prestwich had to tell that his own digging at Abbeville had produced nothing but he had been able to purchase thirty flint implements from the locals. They were so well known to the peasants, said Prestwich, that they were referred to, by men, women, and children alike, as *langues du chat* (cat's tongues).

All the flint implements, said Prestwich, were formed in the same rude way, a blunt hand-hold at one end from which extended two rude cutting edges which converged to a point. As the meeting could observe, the cutting edges and points of the tools were as sharp as if they had been made yesterday. The unworked portions however had a high yellow discoloration which suggested long exposure to weather and which was probably due to some chemical change. Prestwich concluded that some interesting points were raised by the tools. Who were the manufacturers of the primitive tools? Why had not the remains of their manufacturers been found with the imple-

[1] Letter from Huxley to Darwin. 23 November, 1859.

ments? But these problems, said Prestwich, were the province of the archaeologist and not that of the geologist.

Two points emerge from Prestwich's concluding remarks. There was not even the barest suspicion that the flint tools could have been the work of a man of the kind represented by Neanderthal Man. Over three years had elapsed since the discovery of the Prussian fossil, but no one at any of the meetings of three of the foremost scientific societies in England had the faintest inkling of the possibilities of the discovery. The other point of interest is that Prestwich relegated the problem of the identity of the manufacturers of the flint tools. By doing so he made the first contribution to a state of affairs which profoundly hindered the study of fossil man.

As the years passed, the flint tools in the company of human bones were encountered with increasing frequency, the four most directly interested sciences—archaeology, palaeontology, anthropology and anatomy—developed four entirely different sets of terminology and methods of classification. The result was a proliferation of individual theories, unheeding controversy and unique interpretations. Until comparatively recently any attempt to gain a coherent picture of the study as a whole was like attempting a crossword puzzle while the clues were continually being changed.

The archaeologist differentiated flint implements by what he saw as cultural divisions, an ascending degree of refinement in manufacture. These were Abbevillian, Chellean, Clactonian, Acheulian, Levalloisian, Mousterian, Chatelperronian, Aurignacian, Solutrean and Magdalenian. The group names were derived from the localities where that type of worked flint was found in abundance. But as with other human products the flints by no means neatly dropped into strictly definable cultural pockets. This provided great sport and internecine conflict between individual archaeologists who could see 'great' differences between the flints they had excavated and any others hitherto discovered.

The palaeontologist had a different method. He dated flints or human bones according to the suspected age of the geological deposit in which they were found. As the progress of the science advanced and views changed as to the age of these sections, then of course the age of the flints or bones changed. Once again there was by no means a general view on the age of a deposit and so the dating, usually given in hundreds of thousands of years, varied with the individual palaeontologist.

The anthropologist attributed finds to cultural patterns of races and suspected racial migrations. The anatomist dated human fossils according to his individual view on the fossil's place in evolution.

But at the time of the Prestwich meetings the stampede into disorder was just beginning. The year 1859, the *annus mirabilis* as it has been called by enthusiasts for its recognition of fossil man, was marked by a declaration before the British Association meeting at Aberdeen by Sir Charles Lyell. He said that he was 'fully prepared to corroborate the conclusions recently laid before the Royal Society by Mr Prestwich'. The year also saw some astonishing activities on the part of the *Académie des Sciences* to prevent the spread of the flint-tool cult.

The Geological Society was honoured by the presence of Edouard Lartet whom Marcellin Boule has named as the chief founder of the science of palaeontology. Lartet was another lawyer turned scientist, awakened to his true calling, Boule said, in 1834 when he saw the molar tooth of a mastodon found by a peasant of his native village of Gers, Armagnac, south-west France. He began to explore the local ancient deposits and discovered the remains of a fossil ancestor of the modern gibbon, which he named *Pliopithecus*.

In 1850 Lartet forsook Gers for Paris on being elected to the famous *Académie*. The next few years were spent writing up his many discoveries of extinct animal bones, and tactfully supporting Boucher de Perthes. But he went too far. In 1858, he upset the *Académie* by writing that it was an abuse of the technical language of science to use high-sounding expressions such as upheavals of the globe, cataclysms, universal disturbances, general catastrophes and so on, for they gave exaggerated significance to phenomena which were, geographically speaking, very limited. This sounded remarkably like Lyell, but in the eyes of the *Académie* repetition was as big a crime as original sin and Lartet was shunned.[1]

But already Lartet had been forced to look to London for an audience. During his visit to the Geological Society he showed pieces of bone of the long-extinct European wild ox,

[1] This attitude was demonstrated in 1860 when Lartet submitted a paper on the probable antiquity of man. The *Académie* printed the title in its *Comptes rendus* but it did not publish it. This was strictly against custom.

found in Paris during construction of the Canal de L'Ourq. The deep incisions in the bones, said Lartet, were made with crude, unfinished flint tools usually discovered in the sandpits of St Acheul near Amiens. Similarly marked bones found at Abbeville seemed to have been made with flint tools of greater refinement. The marks on the bones, declared Lartet, established beyond all doubt the use of flint tools like those discovered by Boucher de Perthes and 'your learned countrymen, Prestwich, Evans and Flower'. Lartet concluded that the primitive people of Amiens and Abbeville might even have crossed the then dry land between France and England.

In this way Lartet included his English listeners in the great happenings across the Channel. What had been found at Amiens and Abbeville might be found in Britain. Could Lartet have detected in his British audience the first awakening of what was to become a general feeling that something was not quite right? Deeply rooted in each member of his audience was the conviction that their homeland was the priscan fount of knowledge, the epicentre of humanity. Inherent in every one of Lartet's listeners was the belief, never expressed, that if indeed God was not British then he at least had the nation's interests at heart. Where then were the British stone-implement makers? Why did not England have an Abbeville or St Acheul? This was the commencement of a unique era in which two nations vied with each other as to which of them had the most primitive ancestors.

But Lartet's departure from Paris was not undetected by the *Académie*. At the conclusion of Lartet's lecture the president of the Geological Society, Leonard Horner, read a note of denial from the *Académie,* which was a masterly confection of both concession and rebuttal.

The note read to the meeting by Horner described the Canal de L'Ourcq excavations in greater detail than had Lartet, then launched into a lengthy exposition of how the tongue test and the hydrochloric test had been applied to the wild-ox bones which had failed to come up to snuff. But, conceded the *Académie*, this was an instance of the unreliability of these tests, for the bones as proved by the species type were of no small antiquity. The *Académie* was prepared to go even further. The saw marks, read Horner, were too crude to have been inflicted with a modern blade. Lartet was correct to suggest that the marks had been scratched with flint implements. From this, said the *Académie* pointedly, it might be possible for some to argue that man was contemporary with the extinct animal in question. But when had the scratches been made? asked the *Académie*. They could have been made yesterday. Surely it was more likely that someone had chanced across the bones in modern times and had scratched them. Lartet's conclusions, therefore, were nonsense.

Before Lartet had a chance to reply to this disconcerting conclusion there was a rustle at the back of the hall and the president announced that the author of the *Académie*'s note had just arrived from France and wished to make a statement. Whether the *Académie* distrusted the postal service or just wished to gain a first-hand report of the encounter is not known. but here in the flesh was the distinguished Academician, Professor Delasse.

Delasse told the awed meeting that the note read by Horner expressed the *Académie*'s views precisely. He wished to reiterate, however, that the presence of gelatine in bone proved neither its antiquity nor its modernity. After a long series of tests conducted by Delasse nothing had been proved either way. Depending on the nature of the deposit in which they were found, some bones of high antiquity possessed gelatine whereas some comparatively recent bones had none. Delasse explained that his presence in London was entirely due to the *Académie*'s profound wish that the fullest possible evidence should be placed before such an illustrious gathering. Delasse did not doubt that the correct interpretation of Lartet's evidence would be made in any case.

Edouard Lartet appears to have been somewhat shaken by the *Académie*'s surprise intervention. Rising to his feet, he said that he was forced to agree with Delasse that the presence or otherwise of organic matter such as gelatine in bone was an unreliable indication of antiquity. But Delasse, he said, must agree that in this case the geological evidence proved that the bones could not be anything other than of vast antiquity. The Abbeville bones and flint implements had actually been found in 'diluvial' gravel which itself had been covered by an ancient deposit of loess. The Canal de L'Ourcq bones were found at a depth of twenty-eight feet. Only ages of time could have placed the bones so deep in these deposits.

Lartet said he had deliberately chosen the instances described in his lecture from a host of many such discoveries. He could, he said, have cited many instances of marked bones from caves but he had been on his guard. Critics of the evidence of marked bones would have doubtless used the accessibility of cave bones to destroy the value of the argument. But this accessibility certainly did not apply in the case of deeply buried bones, for how could they have been got at?

The contemporary accounts of such conflicts neglect to supply colourful details and therefore there is no record of the precise effect on Lartet of this intervention from Paris other than his words. But the bare fact that the *Académie* was prepared to send a representative to London shows that it went to great lengths to prevent its distinction being used by radical members to promote scientific hypotheses abhorrent to its inflexible view of the Creation.

The direct result of this collision was that men such as Prestwich, Evans and Flower reserved their verdict on bones of extinct animals alleged to have been marked by flint tools. But the general enthusiasm for the tools themselves continued unabated. In Britain, however, it was in the main an unrequited passion. Later in 1859 another Frenchman, Dr Rigollet of Amiens, told an envious Geological Society audience how flint tools were being recovered in large numbers from the Somme, Seine and Oise valleys of his native country. The lecture merely served to make the members even more jealous. Prestwich must have thought it necessary to bolster flagging morale.

Early in 1860 he told a meeting how an antiquary named S. Hazzledene Warren of Ixworth, Suffolk, had been handed a 'peculiarly worked flint' by a workman who said he had found it at a depth of four feet. He also described how twenty-five years had passed since a Mr Whitburn discovered a flint tool in a bed of sand between Guildford and Godalming in Surrey. Whitburn had not known what the flint was until he heard of the recent finds at St Acheul and Abbeville. He had now presented the flint to Prestwich.

Prestwich urged his fellow geologists to seek out the St Acheuls and Abbevilles of England in the brickfields of Kent, Essex and Wiltshire, and the gravel and clay pits of Somerset, Oxfordshire, Cambridgeshire, Middlesex, Surrey, Sussex, Hampshire, Gloucestershire and Berkshire. All that was required, exhorted the speaker, was diligence. Even at St Acheul the search had been long before it had been rewarded with the find of a single specimen. Prestwich concluded that, judging from such a precedent, 'our motto should be *Nil desperandum*'.

Oddly enough, the next find reported to the Society had

taken place in one of the Essex brickpits actually named by Prestwich in his harangue. But it was no flint implement.

The Rev. O. Fisher produced from what he grandiosely des-cribed as 'a cemetery for pachyderms' a 'singular red stone which looked as if it had been baked by fire'. The churchman had propounded an astonishing theory to account for its appearance. He said that it was possible that the kind of clay pots used by primitive hunters would not stand the heat of fire, so to boil water he was forced to heat stones and drop them into the pot.

Fisher's romantic explanation for his stone was adopted for future finds of stones which appeared to be blackened or cracked by fire. It was the first of an almost countless number of similar discoveries which have been reported ever since. The genuine-ness of these 'pot-boilers', as these stones came to be called, is still debated when nothing more pressing commands attention. Many who have experimented with this method of water heating seriously doubt whether there is any truth in the theory. The resultant explosions and the scattering of stone fragments smack more of warfare than cuisine.

Chapter 4

T. H. HUXLEY'S REVIEW OF Charles Darwin's *Origin of Species* saw it as a work of genius. But Darwin had short-changed his readers. He confined the scope of the work to the non-human part of Creation. In but one passage did he mention man, saying that 'light will be thrown on the origin of man and his history'. From this it is clear that Darwin did not wish to be exemplified as the holder of the torch.

Nothing is more indicative of the repressive theological atmosphere of the time than Darwin's reluctance to include man in his observations. His old collaborator of the Linnean Society paper, Alfred Russel Wallace, seems to have been somewhat dismayed by his neglect. Prior to the publication of *Origin* Wallace had written to Darwin asking whether it was the author's intention to include the evolution of man in the work. Darwin had replied, 'I think I shall avoid the whole subject, as so surrounded by prejudices, though I fully admit that it is the highest and most interesting problem for the naturalist.'[1] He had confessed to his friend, the Rev. Leonard Jenyns, that, 'With respect to man, I am very far from wishing to obtrude my belief; but I thought it dishonest to quite conceal my opinion.'[2]

In fairness to Darwin it is necessary to point out that with but one discovered example of fossil man available for examination, the author of *Origin* was wise to delay, to administer the medicine in swallowable doses. Indeed, it is quite possible that Neanderthal man was unknown to Darwin. If Huxley was the author of the advanced view expressed in the *Westminster Review* in 1856 his later scientific writings seem retrogressive. In the light of these he would hardly have been likely to commend Neanderthal man to Darwin's attention as definite evidence of the pattern of evolution of humanity. There was little other evidence. In 1856 Lartet had found bones of *Dryopithecus,* a primitive ape, *Ramapithecus*, during his excavations in the

[1] *The Life and Letters of Charles Darwin*, Vol. 2, p. 109. London, 1888.
[2] *Ibid.*, p. 263.

primitive ape, at St. Gaudens, and there was his earlier recovery of *Pliopithecus*—but that was all.

Though the vast majority of early nineteenth-century scientists did not suspect an actual genetic link between man and the ape they were conscious of some sort of connection. Travellers were inclined to confuse primitive races with the apes and *vice versa*. Many accounts show that there was by no means any clear standard by which one could be divided from the other. For example, the place in nature of the Hottentots of the Cape of Good Hope, whose low state of technology and language—desscribed as 'a farrago of bestial sounds resembling the chatter of apes'—was the source of great speculation. The primitive was often considered to be a kind of ape and the ape a sort of man.

But Darwin did not have to state coldly the evolutionary connection. The implication of his work appeared clear to all. As all the other animals had evolved, so had man. He had affronted the theologio-scientists and cast grave doubt on their view that God created man in his own image.

It is overstating the case to suggest that the entire body of the Church was outraged. Many churchmen greeted *Origin* with sympathy and understanding. Darwin's father did not disinherit him. On the contrary, he seemed rather impressed by his son's impact on science. But Darwin made many enemies in the Church.

Philip Gosse, a Plymouth Brother and another reviewer, said that although the work was rated as an hypothesis by a misguided few, it had done nothing to alter his own implicit faith in the Biblical interpretation of Creation. Gosse published a refutation of Darwin entitled *Omphalos*, in which he maintained that the world and all its works were created perfect. Adam and Eve, he wrote, were the sole parents of humanity and as direct children of God would have been born complete with navels, as in terrestrial birth. According to Gosse, in a similar manner trees would have been created with the annular rings which marked the season's growth. They had appeared on the earth as adult trees and not as seeds. Rocks had been created complete with fossils.

Gosse had neither originality nor Darwin's scientific standing. The real opposition came from a coalition between the theologio-scientists and the Church. The geologist Adam Sedgwick, a devout churchman and one of Darwin's Cambridge acquaintances, bitterly attacked him for deserting the only scientific method—that of Baconian induction. The Presbyterian geologist Adam White said that *Origin* was 'a lapse into pernicious error'. The ecclesiastical botanist Henry Triman thought that Darwin was the most dangerous man in England.

Darwin's most malignant opponent, however, and it must have brought Huxley intense pleasure, was his old collaborator Sir Richard Owen, the foremost comparative anatomist in England. Owen believed, and said so, that Darwin's conclusions were outrageous, incondite, incompatible with the Christian teaching on Adam and Eve, the Fall from Grace, the established time scale of the heavens and the earth, and the date of Creation, which was 23 October, 4004 B.C.

Owen is often seen as the scientific shadow behind the orator and Bishop of Oxford, Samuel Wilberforce.[1] He certainly supplied him with scientific ammunition. But the whole-hearted way in which he countered Huxley proved that he was by no means a behind-the-scenes manipulator.

The warfare between the exponents of Darwinism, or the 'evolutionists' as they came to be called—a name which seems to have rapidly acquired the same connotation as 'abortionists' —and the theologio-scientists was so far confined to heavy literary cannonade, Darwin keeping well out of sight, Huxley in his natural element. He successfully drew the fire on himself, choosing the *Westminster Review*[2] for a long and insulting article thinly disguised as a review of *The Origin of Species*.

He wrote that the 'species question' had overflowed the narrow bounds of purely scientific circles and was 'dividing with Italy [Garibaldi] and the Volunteers' the attention of general society. Everyone, he said, whether they had read Darwin's book or not, had given their opinion on it and 'pietists, whether lay or ecclesiastic, decry it with the mild railing which sounds so charitable; bigots denounce it with ignorant invective; old ladies, of both sexes, consider it a decidedly dangerous book, and even savants who have no better mud to throw, quote antiquated writers to show that its author is no better than an ape himself'.

Huxley said that all competent naturalists, whatever their ultimate opinions of the doctrine put forth, acknowledged that the work was a solid contribution to knowledge and that it

[1] 1805–73.
[2] April 1860.

inaugurated a new epoch in natural history. But he attacked what he described as 'the mistaken zeal of the Bibliolaters', among whom he named Owen, and recommended that these should read and attempt to understand the book before they condemned it.

This kind of writing was hardly likely to commend itself to the 'old ladies of both sexes' or to the 'savants who quoted antiquated writers'. Huxley was a marked man. The protagonists met face to face at the British Association meeting at Oxford in June 1860, at the traditionally famous debate between the 'apes' and the 'angels'; between the exponents of two books, one of which was alleged to have profoundly stimulated scientific thought and the other to have stifled it.

There can be no doubt that Huxley seized the Darwinian hypothesis and used it as a club with which to belabour his scientific adversaries. His altruism was suspect. Already he doubted the existence of God. Huxley did in fact coin the word 'agnostic' to describe his lack of belief. Just before the Oxford debate Huxley's four-year-old son Noel, his first-born, died of scarlet fever. This tragedy introduced an element of bitterness into everything that Huxley said henceforth on the subject of religion.

The Sheldonian Theatre at Oxford on 27 June, 1860, was well filled except for the upper gallery which, according to a witness, could have accommodated twice the number. A third of those present were ladies.

The theatre had begun to fill soon after three o'clock in the afternoon; at ten minutes past four the great doors were thrown open and the grand procession entered. First came the university bedels, then Albert, Prince Consort, Lord Derby, Chancellor of the University, then Dr Jeaune, Vice-chancellor and Master of Pembroke College. Members of the royal suite brought up the rear.

His Royal Highness Prince Albert was greeted with prolonged applause which he repeatedly acknowledged. He said that as retiring president of the British Association he wished to express the hope that the interests of Science had not suffered in his hands. He then paid a compliment to his successor.

Lord Wrothesly, duly installed, delivered his address, the burden of which has not come down to us. The report in *The Times* from which this account is taken says little more, three-quarters at least of the paper being taken up with a verbatim account of the debate in Parliament on the European Forces (India) Bill, a direct result of the Indian Mutiny. Indeed there is a complete abstention from public reporting of the famous debate. The *Proceedings of the British Association* was pointedly mute although the scientific paper which was used as the excuse for the *fracas* was printed fully. There does exist, however, a small number of private eye-witnesses, and hearsay accounts from which a glimmer of what took place can be sifted.

On the morning following the grand opening the Association's Section D, that of the zoologists, met at a lecture room for the first of the week's meetings. In the chair was Sir Richard Owen. Among the hundred or so scientists present was T. H. Huxley. Darwin was absent.

The first item on the programme was a Dr Daubeny's paper *On the Final Causes of the Sexuality of Plants with particular reference to Mr Darwin's Work on the Origin of Species*. The reading of the paper by its author passed off quietly enough, but a Mr R. Bowden rose and began to relate a series of anecdotes concerning monkeys. One was a pet which was fond of playing with a hammer, but although the animal was partial to oysters it could never be taught to crack the shells itself. From this, it was quite clear to him that the monkey was intellectually inferior to other animals, particularly dogs and elephants which could be trained to win food for themselves. The monkey, therefore, was no relative of man.

A flutter of anticipation greeted Bowden's final observation. Owen drew attention to the absence of Mr Darwin and wondered if anyone cared to reply on the biologist's behalf. No one felt so disposed and the president was forced to call on the sacrificial goat directly.

Huxley rose at last but to everybody's disappointment he said he considered that a general audience where sentiment would interfere unduly with intellect was the wrong sort for such a discussion. He resumed his seat.

But Owen would not allow the matter to be dropped so easily. He said he 'wished to approach this subject in the spirit of a philosopher' and that 'there were facts by which the public could come to some conclusion as to the probabilities of the truth of Mr Darwin's theory'. Bowden's point, said Owen, was in fact that the brain of man differed vastly from that of the monkey. As an anatomist of no mean distinction Owen begged to be allowed to draw Mr Huxley's attention to a feature of the human brain, the third lobe of the posterior horn of the lateral ventrical, called the *hippocampus minor*. This feature was

unique to the brain of man, said Owen, for no gorilla possessed
it.

Huxley thanked Owen for the anatomical instruction. He had
nothing to add to his previous remarks except to draw Owen's
attention to a major difference between man and gorilla. This
was, he said, the power of speech.

Owen glowered but he seems to have considered that as
Huxley had refused to come out of his corner the 'angels' had
won a tactical victory. A Dr Wright, who seems to have entirely missed the drift of the discussion, and the atmosphere,
innocently said that a friend had a pet female gorilla which he
took to the sea-shore for the purpose of feeding on oysters,
which the animal broke open with ease. But Owen cut the
speaker short. He guessed that Huxley was not to be drawn on
the issue of seafood-loving gorillas and he called the meeting to
a close.

The zoological section's meeting the following day, a Friday,
passed off uneventfully but it was common knowledge that the
great confrontation would take place on the morrow. Huxley
made no secret of the fact that he would attend. Nor did
Samuel Wilberforce, Bishop of Oxford, Fellow of All Souls,
nicknamed 'Soapy Sam' from his habit of rubbing his hands
together when winning a point in debate, which he did very
frequently and brilliantly. Wilberforce was pure churchman
and orator extraordinary of Biblical convention as applied to
science. Like Hindenburg and Falkenhayn, Wilberforce and
Owen offered an unassailable front to theologians and scientists
who might wish to transgress.

According to Sir Charles Lyell, the Saturday battle opened
with 'redoubled fury' over a paper by an American, Dr Draper
of New York, on *Intellectual Development, considered with
Reference to the Views of Mr Darwin*. The excitement was
tremendous. The audience proved too large for the lecture room
and so the meeting adjourned to the library of the university
museum, which was crammed to suffocation long before the
champions entered the lists.

Professor Stephen Henslow, old comrade and now enemy
of Darwin, was in the chair and 'wisely' announced that no one
should be allowed to address the meeting who did not have
a valid argument for one side or the other. This was a necessary
precaution, Lyell's account continues, as the audience had now
been swollen to some seven hundred by an influx of cheering

and counter-cheering students. Four scientific combatants were already shouting vague declamations over the general din.

Then Bishop Wilberforce was on his feet and launched into a speech which was described later (by an 'ape') as 'full of emptiness and fairies'. It was evident to this witness that the bishop had been crammed to the throat by Owen and knew nothing at first hand. But 'he ridiculed Darwin savagely but in dulcet tones and with such persuasion and well-turned periods that I [Lyell] who had been inclined to blame the president for allowing a discussion which would serve no scientific purpose, forgave him from the bottom of my heart! Unfortunately for the bishop, hurried along by the current of his eloquence, he so forgot himself as to push his advantage to the verge of personality in a telling passage in which he turned round and addressed Huxley.'

The bishop, polishing his hands, asked Huxley whether he was related on his grandfather's or grandmother's side to the ape. Huxley rose and replied to his opponent's scientific argument with, said the witness, 'force and eloquence'. He then passed to the personal remark.

'With remarkable restraint he said, "A man has no reason to be ashamed of having an ape for a grandfather or grandmother. If I had a choice of an ancestor, whether it should be an ape, or one who having a scholastic education should use his logic to mislead an untutored public, and should treat not with argument but with ridicule the facts and reasoning adduced in support of a grave and serious philosophical question, I would not hestitate for a moment to prefer the ape." '

The impact of this remark was described as 'tremendous'. Huxley himself said that there was 'inextinguishable laughter'. A lady is reported to have fainted, the usual Victorian metaphor for high drama. According to Lyell many blamed Huxley for his irreverent freedom but many more whom he had heard talk of the affair, including Hugh Falconer, assured Lyell that Vice-chancellor Jeaune declared that the bishop 'had got no more than he deserved'. Falconer said that the bishop just sat down and said no more, that 'although he had been much applauded, before the meeting was over opinion had quite gone the other way'.

According to Lyell, when Huxley informed Darwin of the outcome of the debate he tittered nervously: 'How durst you attack a live bishop in that fashion? I am quite ashamed of

you. Have you no respect for fine lawn sleeves?' But Huxley
himself could not see what all the fuss was about. On the subject of the relationship of the gorilla with man, he said that
to call man a modified gorilla was no more harmful, surely,
than the Church's insistence that man was modified dirt.

But had the debate achieved much else? Huxley himself
limited his popularity in Oxford to just twenty-four hours.
No great philosophical sluice gates were swung open. There
had not been one reference to Neanderthal man during the
entire Oxford meeting. Huxley had not mentioned him and
he was currently working on a scientific description of the
Prussian fossil man. Darwin's hypothesis still had a lengthy
uphill grind and many were the backslidings, even amongst
his most devout followers.

Men were much more preoccupied with God in those days.
By the majority it was thought to be far better to wait and
see. Some were amazed at the longevity of Darwin, and Huxley
even. That God did not strike them down forthwith amazed
them. Not a few pulpits cried out for Heavenly retribution. As
the years passed and the cries remained unanswered, it came
to be considered that a profounder punishment awaited the
leading evolutionists in Hell.

Possibly the most palpable achievement of the debate was,
as in the case of the Jumna river fossils, that it threw open the
windows of discussion with the maximum publicity. The next
few years saw a heightening of the controversy between Huxley
and Owen which raged in the scientific journals of the time.
Bishop Wilberforce watched helplessly while Huxley relentlessly
undermined his scientific colleague's authority.

Owen's statement that the *hippocampus minor* only occurred
in the brain of man—it is in fact a feature common to all
mammals—left him wide open to attack. As Huxley put it in
a letter to the editor of *Natural History Review* :[1]

Owen had declared the structure known to anatomists as the
hippocampus minor as occurring only in the human brain.
The fact is he made a prodigious blunder in commencing the
attack, and now his only chance is to be silent and let people
forget the exposure . . .

But Owen would not keep quiet and the lengthy dispute
[1] 3 January, 1861.

resulted in the printing of a series of comic verses in *Punch*. One, contributed by a 'Gorilla from the Zoological Gardens' and entitled *MONKEYANA*, read :

> *Then HUXLEY and OWEN,*
> *With rivalry growing,*
> *With pen and ink rush to the scratch,*
> *'Tis brain versus brain,*
> *Till one of them's slain;*
> *By Jove! It will be a good match!*

The final two verses were :

> *Next HUXLEY replies,*
> *That OWEN he lies*
> *And garbles his Latin quotation;*
> *That his facts are not new,*
> *His mistakes not a few,*
> *Detrimental to his reputation.*

> *To twice slay the slain*
> *By dint of the Brain*
> *(Thus HUXLEY concluded his review)*
> *Is but labour in vain,*
> *Unproductive of gain,*
> *So I shall bid you 'Adieu'.*[1]

Many similar verses appeared over the next three years and to the public the controversy seems to have been of absorbing interest. In 1863 an eight-page burlesque pamphlet for the not so sophisticated was on sale which bore on the cover '*A Report of a Sade (sic) Case Recently Tried Before the Lord Mayor. Owen versus Huxley. In Which Will be Fully Given the Merits of the Great Recent Bone Case.*' An extract must suffice:

Policeman X——: 'Well, your Worship, Huxley called Owen a lying Orthognatheous Brachycephalic Bimanous Pithecus; and Owen told him he was nothing but a thorough Archencephalic Primate.'
Lord Mayor : 'Are you sure you heard this awful language?'

The most enduring relic of the Great Debate, however, was the churchman-novelist Charles Kingsley's delightful fantasy

[1] *Punch*, XLIII, p. 164. 18 October, 1861.

for children, *The Water Babies,* published three years afterwards, in which he described how :

> The Professor got up once at the B.A., and declared that apes had hippopotamus majors in their brains just as men have. Which was a shocking thing to say; for if it were so, what would become of the faith, hope and charity of immortal millions?

But as Huxley wrote to Joseph Hooker after Oxford: 'Take care of yourself, there's a good fellow . . . We have a devil of a lot to do in the way of smiting the Amalekites.'[1] Owen was but one of many. But eventually the relationship between man and ape was passed down from science through the music-halls to become an accepted part of modern lore. It is hard for the late twentieth century mind to grasp the extent of the resentment which greeted the first suggestions that there was such a relationship. Owen was considered to be, and in fact was, an advanced thinker compared with many of his contemporaries. At the time there were many who did not believe that there was any such animal as a gorilla. Following the publication of Paul Chaillu's *Explorations and Adventures in Equatorial Africa* in 1861, the traveller exhibited a stuffed gorilla at the Ethnological Society. There was an uproar. One of the audience, T. A. Malone, denounced the gorilla as a fiction of Chaillu's imagination and his *Explorations* as a pack of lies. The author knocked him down with a blow. Sir Richard Burton, the African explorer, defended Chaillu in a letter to *The Times.*[2] Burton commented lustily that the gorilla was fact and that Chaillu was justified in striking his detractor.

[1] Letter from Huxley to Hooker, *August, 1860.*
[2] 8 July, 1861.

Chapter 5

BRITISH SCIENCE DISCOVERED Neanderthal man
in 1861. George Busk, Hunterian Professor of Anatomy and
Physiology at the Royal College of Surgeons, was a tireless
translator of German scientific papers. One was the Schaafhausen
description.

On the centenary of the discovery of Neanderthal man in
1956 Bernard Cambell wrote[1] that Busk's 'versatile mind
immediately saw the importance of the discovery'. He saw Busk
as the English discoverer of the Prussian fossil. But the view
could also be taken that translation was all in a day's work
to Busk and the role of pioneer was neither intentional nor
within his control.

Busk was an insatiable tongue-tester of fossil bones; his hydrochloric acid had disenchanted many a finder of his find. His
perception can certainly be called into question. Almost definitely
a Neanderthal skull had lain undetected in his own collection
at the Royal College of Surgeons since about 1848.

This skull has a peculiar history. It is believed that the discoverer was a certain Lieutenant Flint, Royal Artillery, then
stationed in Gibraltar. The officer found the skull at Forbes'
Quarry, North Front, and he presented it to the Gibraltar
Scientific Society. There is a minute to this effect in the society's
proceedings for 3 March, 1848. The skull then disappears into
the shadows until the 1864 British Association meeting at Bath,
where Busk stated that the skull was part of the Hunterian
Museum collection. It is therefore probable not only that an
Englishman found the first Neanderthal skull, for the Gibraltar
find was such a fossil, but also that Busk failed to notice it in
his own collection until long after the Prussian find had attracted
notice.

The British Association was much impressed by the Gibraltar
skull and voted a grant of £165 so that Busk and Hugh Falconer
could sail to Gibraltar to encourage further excavation. The
governor of the military prison on the Rock, Captain Broome,

[1] *Man:* 56.

himself a keen archaeologist, was an immense help to the visitors. On his return to England Falconer wrote to the Governor of Gibraltar, General Hugh Coddrington, recording the two scientists' appreciation of the work of Broome. He praised Broome's eagerness, energy and vigour, which had immensely helped the scientific enquiry. Coddrington forwarded the letter to the Secretary of State for War in London, and as a direct result Broome was cashiered for allowing military prisoners to be employed in private excavations.

Shortly before he died in 1865 Falconer wrote sadly of 'that unfortunate soldier Broome'. Of the troublesome Gibraltar skull itself he said at the same time that its owner was representative of 'a very low type of humanity—very low and savage, and of extreme antiquity—but still a man and not halfway between a man and a monkey and certainly not the missing link'.

With this denial Falconer was the first to use an expression which became a tradition and fascination for archaeologists, palaeontologists, geologists, and anatomists. The Gibraltar skull, however, the rejected 'missing link', remained quietly in the Hunterian Museum until rediscovered by Arthur Keith in 1906.

The first Englishman to attack Neanderthal man was a geologist named C. Carter Blake. In an article in *The Geologist* the same year as the Busk translation, Blake wrote that the great Cuvier had doubted whether human remains of the same age as those of extinct species of animals had ever been found. This was precisely his own conclusion, Blake said, and, despite the anatomist Schaafhausen's claims, the united opinion of German geologists. The English anatomist Busk had also said that there was no doubt about the vast antiquity of the Neanderthal bones but this theory too remained uncorroborated by any British geologist.

The singular characteristic of the Neanderthal skull, suggested Blake, was the large prominent eyebrow ridges. But these were also present in the modern gorilla, giving the animal its 'penthouse-like scowl'. So, challenged Blake, wherein lay the antiquity?

Busk replied that Blake's reasoning was at fault for many modern savage and barbarous races had considerable foreheads but had no eyebrow ridges.

But Blake was not after Busk. In a subsequent article[1] he said that he had hoped the appeal to English geologists in his first article would have thrown light on the age of the Neanderthal

[1] *Ibid.* 5:1862.

remains, but as this had not been forthcoming he had decided to give his own view. This was :

> The apparent ape-like but really maldeveloped idiotic character of its conformation is so hideous and its alleged proximity to anthropoid *Simiae* of such importance that every effort should be made to determine its probable date in time. The fact had not been conclusively demonstrated to English geologists that the Neanderthal skull is of high antiquity.

Blake said that the deposit of mud in the Neanderthal cave might have been modern. Also, he argued, there were several suspicious factors connected with the skeleton, for example, the bump on the elbow. The curvature of the ribs reminded Blake of those of carnivorous animals and might not belong to the skull at all. Most probably, concluded Blake, the skull belonged to 'some poor idiot who died in the cave.'

The anatomical content of Blake's tirade could suggest that its target was T. H. Huxley, whose part in the Oxford debate had by now been inflated by hearsay to the proportions of swashbuckling. Certainly at the time he was writing his *Evidences of Man's Place in Nature*, which contained an appraisal of Neanderthal man. But he was calling for a geologist to answer him. It is likely, therefore, that Blake was trying to come to grips with Sir Charles Lyell.

Not content with having caused a revolution in geological thought Lyell had now turned his attention to the nature of man. At the time of the Blake articles Lyell had just returned from a visit to Neanderthal. He had met Dr J. C. Fuhlrott of Eberfield, into whose hands Neanderthal man had first come. He had been presented with a plaster cast of the skull and a brief description of the discovery. Lyell passed on both to Huxley for his anatomical opinion which he wished to include in his new work *The Antiquity of Man*.

Huxley's performance on this occasion was disappointing. Of the Neanderthal skull and a similar one from Engis in Belgium—which like the Gibraltar skull had been brought from some museum cabinet by the Prussian bugle-call—he maintained before the Royal Society, and Lyell faithfully reproduced his view in *Antiquity*, that neither seemed much different from the skull of the modern Australian aborigine, the scientist's low water in human intellect.

Blake may possibly have sensed from Huxley's performance before the Royal Society that the Evolutionists were finding themselves on insecure ground. If he could get Lyell to confess that the Neanderthal skull could not be proved to be antique, then this would be a strong blow on behalf of the Bible. Blake was a friend and staunch ally of Sir Richard Owen.

Huxley did however make some kind of redress in his own account of Neanderthal man in his *Evidences of Man's Place in Nature* (1863). He wrote that he had obtained a fuller description of the skull and therefore was able to reconsider his earlier remarks. The skull, he maintained, was unknown even amongst the most savage and barbarous races which existed on the earth in modern times and possibly was that of a representative of the race dimly remembered and described by the Celtic and Germanic inhabitants of Europe to the Latin historians as 'autochthones'.

Beyond all doubt, wrote Huxley, the race represented by the Neanderthal skull could be traced back to a period in the earth's history when the latest extinct animals of the diluvium still existed.

Then Huxley faltered. In no sense, he wrote, could the bones be the remains of a human being intermediate between man and ape. At most they demonstrated the existence of a man whose skull could be said to have reverted back to the ape type.

This passage lacks Huxley's usual courage. The modern interpretation is that Huxley was proposing that Neanderthal man was a reversion towards a previous simian ancestor, that he was a throwback.

Lyell let matters rest, relying entirely on Huxley. But Neanderthal man at last found a firm friend in Professor William King of Queen's College, Galway, Ireland. In a paper to the British Association in 1863, King said that the mud on the floor of the Neanderthal cave must have been deposited at the end of the glacial period of the earth because of its similarity to deposits of the Meuse valley described by Lyell.

Here, said King, was an early forerunner of man. But because of his small cranium he did not believe that the 'brute' could have been capable of any moral or theological conception or inductive reasoning. King therefore proposed to distinguish him from his modern descendant by giving him the name *Homo neanderthalis*.

King's step was a bold one. No one before him had thought

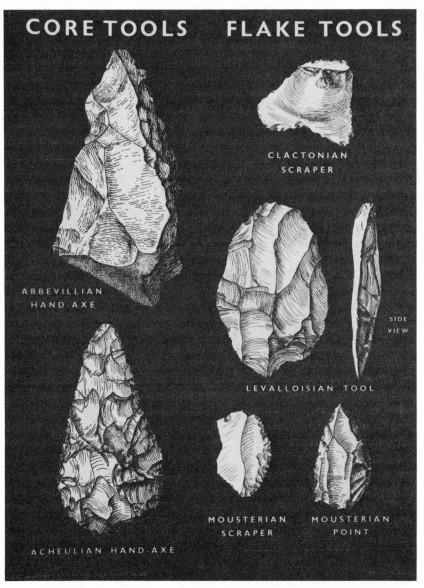

CORE TOOLS   FLAKE TOOLS

CLACTONIAN SCRAPER

ABBEVILLIAN HAND-AXE

LEVALLOISIAN TOOL

SIDE VIEW

ACHEULIAN HAND-AXE

MOUSTERIAN SCRAPER

MOUSTERIAN POINT

Palaeolithic flint implements ranging from the Clactonian scraper through the more sophisticated examples from St. Acheul (Acheulian), Le Moustier (Neanderthal) and La Vallois-Perret, Paris (Lavalloisian). Neanderthal Man's flint scrapers show a refined method of producing a sharp edge i.e. the 'pressure technique' where the flint is splintered away by bearing down on it with a pointed flint tool.

Forged flint implements from Moulin Quignon. Example on *left* bears label signed by the famous Abbeville amateur J. Boucher de Perthes.
Example on *right* clearly shows the sharp dividing ridges and shallow facets indicating modern production with a metal hammer.

of creating a distinct species for the fossil human. He also started a new name-game which has been the constant source of much anthropological preoccupation ever since.

At a meeting of the Anthropological Society in London on 16 February, 1864, came a collision between the friends of Neanderthal man and his enemies. Darwin's collaborator on the Linnean Society paper, Alfred Russel Wallace, was present but there were notable absentees. Darwin and Huxley were invited but Darwin always kept clear of such turmoil and Huxley forgot to attend. It was reported that Huxley set off for the meeting, but he never arrived.

C. Carter Blake opened fire with a paper *On the Alleged Peculiar Character and Assumed Antiquity of the Human Cranium from Neanderthal.* Blake said that some authorities were declaring that we had discovered the 'missing link' which binds together man and the apes. The speaker did not think so and he was, he said, strongly supported by the *Medical Times and Gazette.*[1] He begged leave of the meeting to read a portion of the article. It said:

'We strongly suspect that Mr Blake is right in his conjecture he throws out, that this skull belongs to some poor idiot. The description strongly reminds us of Sir Walter Scott's *The Black Dwarf.* A theory of rickets and idiocy, we suspect, goes some way towards unravelling the mystery.'

This, said Blake, was firm medical opinion. Nobody else, he said, seemed to agree about anything to do with Neanderthal man. King of Galway had said that a wider gap than a mere specific one separated the human species from the Neanderthal one. Schaafhausen disagreed with Busk on the issue of the enormous eyebrow ridges. Busk had said the cause was enlarged frontal sinuses. Schaafhausen said they were nothing of the kind. Huxley agreed with both that this peculiar conformation could not be pathological or artificial but that it suggested an ancient race. Then he said that the skull more resembles that of an ape than any race yet known. M. Pruner-Bey of Paris had recently said that the skull certainly belonged to a large Celt but he was unable to say for sure whether it was of an idiotic Celt or not. What, cried Blake in exasperation, was one to make of it all?

The next speaker was M. Broca of the *Société d'Anthropologie* of Paris. Broca said that he thought he could easily demonstrate that the Neanderthal skull was not that of an idiot, and launched

[1] 26 June, 1862.

into a long and intricate anecdote about a mental institution at Bicêtre where he had encountered an idiot with an enormous head. But at an autopsy, continued Broca, it was found that the brain was extremely small. So, said the Frenchman, skull size was no indication of idiocy.

Why Broca thought the case of the large-skulled but small-brained idiot of Bicêtre was relevant to that of the small-brained and small-skulled Neanderthal man, he did not explain. This contribution seems to have dumbfounded the meeting for there was no discussion on this point.

Blake returned to his feet next to attack King's statement that he doubted whether Neanderthal man was capable of moral or theological conceptions. This did not surprise Blake. Belief in God was not an inherent idea in the mind of all savages nor, if the claims that were being made for the so-called human fossil of Neanderthal were any guide, in some Englishmen. The skull was undoubtedly that of an idiot, said Blake. He did not belong to the diluvium at all.

A general discussion then followed. A Mr Redie said that whatever the opinion of the Neanderthal fossil's intellectual development and however low the state of man this might indicate, the skull was definitely that of a man not of an ape. The distinction between man and ape in intellectual capacity could not be mistaken. A gorilla had enough sense to warm itself by a fire made by negroes but did not possess enough sense to put more logs on the fire to keep it burning. It was a pity, said Redie, that a similar test could not be applied to the Neanderthal fossil.

Alfred Wallace was the next speaker. He told how he had compared the skulls of aborigines of New Zealand, Australia and New Guinea. Some, he said, were very similar to the Neanderthal skull, others not at all. He was satisfied, however, that the Neanderthal skull belonged to a member of a very savage race in a low state of development. It was certainly not that of an idiot.

Blake replied that George Busk had recently drawn attention to the Gibraltar skull in the Hunterian Museum in London, so it was beyond him why Wallace had to cite places as far away as Australia for skull forms which corresponded to that of the Neanderthal skull. It seemed to Blake that all sorts of evidence was being gathered together from the most unlikely places to lend weight to Charles Darwin's hypothesis.

The speaker said that nothing was further from his mind than to cast doubt on the transmutation theory. Indeed he considered it a very rational hypothesis. But what had the Neanderthal skull got to do with such an hypothesis? Blake was convinced that the misunderstandings, as he called them, had only arisen from original misrepresentations by Germans, who had possibly made the whole thing up. What was wanted, declared Blake, was real proof to confirm or deny the transmutation theory.

On this note the meeting ended. It cannot be doubted that Blake had no brief for the transmutation theory and merely made his spoken concession in deference to the presence of Wallace.

The debate on the antiquity of Neanderthal man was to continue for many years. The old arguments, indeed the old angers, were perpetuated until replaced by new ones, until the sheer weight of numbers of Neanderthal men made it impossible to reject them as isolated freaks. This meeting took place in 1864, eight years after the discovery of Neanderthal man, and four years after the famous Oxford debate which popular legend maintains changed men's minds and opened them to a new insight into man's place in nature.

Certainly Blake seems to have been outnumbered at this meeting but his stand did credit to his Biblical belief, which was at least unambiguous and single-minded.

Chapter 6

IN CONFINING OUR attention to events which bore directly on the belated discovery by British scientists of Neanderthal man, we have missed a *cause célèbre* which is now little publicized but which the Piltdown affair strongly echoed ninety years later.

While English enthusiasts were carrying out fruitlessly the Prestwich formula for archaeological success, the *Abbevillois* newspaper of 9 April, 1863, announced a momentous discovery. Into the possession of the local amateur Boucher de Perthes had come an ancient human jaw which contained a molar tooth. According to the newspaper, the human remains together with a number of flint implements had been recovered by workmen from a unique 'black bed' of earth discovered in the side of a gravel pit near Abbeville at a site known as Moulin Quignon. At last, Boucher de Perthes had told the newspaper, here was the primitive manufacturer of the flint tools for whom Science had searched for so long.

No flint tools had ever come from the Moulin Quignon gravel pit until the year of the discovery of the human jaw. Many times Sir John Evans and Joseph Prestwich had travelled to Abbeville, visiting this very pit on some seven or eight occasions, but they had neither been able to find a flint there nor been offered one for sale by local workmen.

But in 1863 things began to happen. Many finds of flint tools at Moulin Quignon were reported. Boucher de Perthes gave two specimens to Prestwich, and M. Marcotte, a local enthusiast, presented one to Evans.

But the flints from Moulin Quignon possessed some peculiar characteristics. Instead of the dark yellow or brown coloration displayed by the flints from the Abbeville district, the Moulin Quignon variety were bright yellow. This was explainable by the fact that the natural gravel of Moulin Quignon was much brighter in colour than was usual in the area, due to a local abundance of natural iron oxide in the soil. Another characteristic, however, was not so readily explained. No flints encountered anywhere else in France were so crudely manufactured as those from Moulin Quignon. This could only mean that the ancient humans of Moulin Quignon had occurred earlier in time than those living about the other Abbeville gravel pits. But this answer presented something of a conundrum to the British geologists. As Lartet had pointed out during his visit to London in 1859, Abbeville flint tools were more refined than those produced by the ancient toolmakers of St Acheul, near Amiens.

So it was with a sense of wonder that Evans and Prestwich, on hearing the news, hurried to France, arriving at Abbeville after a difficult journey, on 13 April to a cordial welcome from Boucher de Perthes. The Englishmen examined the ancient jawbone with care and were greatly impressed.

A pilgrimage was made to the Moulin Quignon gravel pit. The Englishmen gazed in awe at what must have been holy ground. But the famous black bed from which the human remains had been recovered was now obscured by a fall of gravel. As the pair were about to leave, a workman who had offered his services as guide took two highly coloured flint implements from his pocket and handed them to Prestwich. He said that he had found the flints while working in the Moulin Quignon pit. They were crude, badly-shaped and smeared over with a deeply iron-stained clay. With intense excitement the Englishmen realized that the dark soil must have come from the black bed. They eagerly gave the workman the two francs he demanded. It was while washing the dark earth from the flints at the first cottage they reached that Evans and Prestwich realized that they had been hoodwinked. Not only the earth came away but most of the colour as well.

The Englishmen hastened back to Boucher de Perthes. They asked him to wash some of his Moulin Quignon flints and watched in anguish as the high colour faded, then disappeared. Prestwich and Evans warned Boucher de Perthes of the serious doubt now cast on the jaw. The Frenchman does not seem to have replied or if he did neither Englishman bothered to report it.

With sad hearts Prestwich and Evans returned to England. The story of the bogus flints was conveyed to a meeting of the Royal Society on 16 April. On 19 April the *Académie des Sciences* rejoiced at the downfall of one of its minor enemies. An anonymous contributor to *The Times* of 25 April added that there was little doubt that the jaw was a forgery as well.

Neither Prestwich nor Evans seems to have entertained for a moment the possibility that Boucher de Perthes might have been behind the forgeries. But a batch of highly scurrilous stories began to be circulated about London and Paris concerning him. According to one of these, an unnamed Englishman staying at an Abbeville hotel was driven from his bed early by the sound of hammering. He came across a peasant chipping a flint, who replied to the obvious question : 'Why, making a *langue du chat* for M. Boucher de Perthes'. Another, on being reprimanded for selling a dishonest flint to a visiting Englishman, was supposed to have replied in exasperation : 'But what am I to do? The Englishman asks me for a flint. I say I have not got one. He insists. He does not believe me. So what am I to do? I make him one.'

Hugh Falconer told Prestwich that he had further evidence that not a few of the flints obtained from other sites at Abbeville were forged as well. Falconer had been experimenting with chipping flint and had made a surprising discovery. When pieces of flint are struck from a block by hammering with similar material, as would be the case with primitive man, the detached flakes leave behind facets that are broad and shallow, with rounded dividing ridges. If the flakes are detached from the parent block by striking with a metal hammer, however, the facets are deeper, narrower and more pronounced and the intervening ridges are more elevated and sharp.

The Geological Society unofficially communicated its views on the Abbeville flints to interested members of the *Académie des Sciences*. The result was a 'congress' which opened in Paris on 9 May and closed at Abbeville on the 13th, at which a large number of flints and the Moulin Quignon jaw could be tried. The French contingent comprised men who had devoted a major part of their lives to the excavation of their country's prehistoric sites—men such as De Quatrefages, Desnoyers and Lartet, all of whom had at one time or another incurred the wrath of the *Académie*. Also present was Lartet's old adversary Delasse, who appears to have undergone a change of heart since his surprise appearance in London. The Englishmen were Prestwich, Falconer, a Dr Carpenter, and George Busk, the translator of Schaafhausen's paper on Neanderthal man. Evans could not attend and sent his apologies. Boucher de Perthes was not invited. This must have been a time of extreme bitterness for most of the delegates. They were about to play devil's advocate for their bitter adversaries within the *Académie*. They were to try to prove that at least some of the flint tools—their objects of faith for many years—were modern forgeries, and at least partially to destroy what the *Académie* still insisted was an invention—antediluvian man.

Some forty flints were produced by the delegates. Some came from St Acheul, some from Abbeville, some from Moulin Quignon. In front of the assembly they were scrubbed in hot water. The St Acheul flints remained unchanged but many from Abbeville and all from Moulin Quignon soon lost their colour, changing from bright yellow to bronze and then to natural flint grey.

The facets of the suspect flints now presented the dull appearance of recent fracture, without 'glimmer'—the patina caused by ages of weathering. They were deep with sharp dividing ridges suggesting that a metal hammer had been employed to produce them. When a flake was struck from a flint the fresh facet differed in no way from the others. Another surprising feature was apparent. The suspect flints exhibited a striking similarity of pattern, as if all were produced by one person or at the most by two.

The English detachment was forced to conclude that although the St Acheul flints and most of those from Abbeville were genuine, a few Abbeville flints and all those from the black bed of Moulin Quignon were false. De Quatrefages, Desnoyers and Lartet were not convinced. They held that the appearance of newness exhibited by the flints was no proof of falsity.

Attention now passed to the Moulin Quignon jawbone with its single molar. To act as a 'control' two fossils of undoubted antiquity were produced; one was a molar tooth of some unknown species of animal, the other was a molar of the extinct cave-dwelling hyena (*Hyaena spelaea*). Delasse embarked on a series of tongue tests, considerably confusing the issue with a lengthy demonstration which proved that absolutely no reliance could be placed on it.

A debate ensued in which the Englishmen insisted that the human jaw could not have come from the black bed of Moulin Quignon because it showed little sign of staining by iron oxide —the great feature of the deposit in which it was found. To enforce this opinion Busk then demonstrated how irreverently fossils were handled in the mid-nineteenth century. The anatomist sawed the Moulin Quignon jaw in half. This produced,

according to Busk, the distinctive odour of limb amputa-
tions performed on live subjects, a feature he would hardly
expect of so-called ancient bones. The colouring, which was
found to be superficial, was easily scrubbed from one of the
portions of bone, revealing a surface which bore little of the
erosion common in old bones.

Busk produced a human lower jaw loaned by a Dr Robert
Collyer which he had found in a pit near Ipswich, Suffolk in
company with coprolites—roundish fossils resembling stones
supposed to be the petrified excrement of an animal. Busk said
that this jaw was presumed to have preceded the Roman con-
quest of Britain. He showed how the bone was infiltrated
throughout with iron from the soil from which it was recovered.
This infiltration, said Busk, was typical. He had seen bones
from Bolivian coppermines which had been filled with threads
of native copper. The Moulin Quignon jaw was virtually unstained, so the jaw could not have come from the black bed.
Busk doubted whether it was older than any other old bones
that could be obtained from cemeteries.

But the French would not give in. The implications of fraudul-
ence would allow the *Académie* to laugh them to extinction.
They considered that none of the evidence was conclusive and
that the jaw and the flints could be genuine relics of antediluvian
man. Desnoyers then proposed a simple method of proving
wheher the Moulin Quignon flints were genuine or not.
Whether colour came off the flints when washed, the evidence
of crude workmanship, the depth of the facets, said Desnoyers,
really proved nothing at all. The only real test was a search of
the Moulin Quignon pit conducted by themselves, secretly and
without giving prior warning to the locals. If only one flint was
discovered *in situ* which displayed similar characteristics, it
would prove beyond all doubt that the rest were genuine. This
logic was irrefutable and the motion was carried.

The congress, now joined by a large number of French
savants but, according to Prestwich, proceeding 'under utmost
secrecy', arrived at Abbeville and travelled undetected to the
Moulin Quignon pit. The archaeologists almost ran from their
coaches to the edge of the gravel but the famous black bed
was no longer to be seen. A workman explained that the bed
had been a very local deposit and had been quarried away.

This stage in the proceedings was chosen by an eminent
Académie geologist, Professor Hébert, to deliver an impromptu

address. He said that it was obvious to him that the Moulin Quignon deposit was comparatively modern. It certainly did not belong to the diluvium. Notwithstanding this oration, a large party of local workmen was set to work under the close supervision of members of the congress and the *savants*. To the surprise of the English and delight of the French 'believers' in the party the search was rewarded almost immediately. Five flint implements virtually sprang from the gravel. Falconer himself saw two revealed by a fall of gravel undermined by a pickaxe. All the newly-recovered specimens exhibited the usual strange Moulin Quignon features. The facets were deep and the ridges sharp and the colour could be removed by washing in hot water. But the conclusion was thought to be inescapable. All the Moulin Quignon flints were genuine. Prestwich hurried to Boucher de Perthes with the glad tidings.

The French 'believers' likewise wasted no time in transmitting the results to the *Académie*. But it availed them nothing. The permanent secretary, Elie de Beaumont, refused to accept that the Moulin Quignon was older than the 'modern age'. It was certainly not older, he said, than the Somme valley peat beds which had been found to cover the remains of a Roman road in the Département de Nord. De Beaumont added :

I do not believe that the human race was contemporary with *Elephas primigenius*. M. Cuvier's theory [to this effect] is born of genius. It is still undemolished !

Meanwhile Prestwich had communicated the favourable result of the Moulin Quignon 'dig' to the Royal Society and the Geological Society. Falconer followed suit in the August issue of *Natural History Review*.

Could this be the British support for Boucher de Perthes to which Marcellin Boule refers? If so, it must have escaped him that the British shortly had second thoughts. And with good reason.

Although convinced at first by the Moulin Quignon demonstration both Prestwich and Falconer soon began to wonder whether it had really proved anything. As a result, Prestwich again visited Moulin Quignon and conducted a test which had been omitted by the congress. He washed 135 fragments of flint which he personally recovered from the gravel. Unlike that of the flint implements, the high colour of the fragments could not be washed off no matter how hard they were scrubbed. It was now obvious to Prestwich that the Moulin Quignon flints were forgeries. Some unknown person or persons had manufactured the implements using modern tools and then dyed them to match the surrounding gravel.

To his enthusiastic paper in the Geological Society's quarterly journal which had already gone to the printer, Prestwich added a note rebutting it dated October 1863. He wrote that further and deliberate enquiry on his part had led him to revert to his opinion that the Moulin Quignon flint tools were forgeries. The entire congress, said Prestwich, had been mistaken in concluding that no fraud had been practised. He continued:

> Our verdict respecting the flint implements (leaving apart the question of the jaw) will, therefore, I fear, have to be reconsidered. The precaution against imposition by the workmen seemed to have made this impossible, but although it remained undetected, I cannot continue to accept the authenticity of the flints.

However, he concluded that the occurrence of genuine flint implements at Abbeville and Amiens continued to receive fresh confirmation with every fresh investigation and these placed Boucher de Perthes' original finds at Abbeville beyond all doubt.

So this then was the outcome. The Moulin Quignon flint implements were demolished, bringing down with them the jaw of antediluvian man. As far as the flints were concerned, Boucher de Perthes' failure to detect the imposition seems inexplicable unless, contrary to his many biographers' opinions, he was simple-natured. The weight of opinion at the time, however, seems in favour of the proposition that Boucher de Perthes was the innocent dupe of some unscrupulous workman who took advantage of the amateur's gullibility.

Certainly neither Prestwich nor Falconer attached any blame to Boucher de Perthes. No doubt it was at their instigation that Boucher de Perthes was, on 17 June of that year, honoured by the Geological Society by being elected 'foreign correspondent'. One wonders, however, whether the wheels had been put into motion before the deception had been detected.

But Boucher de Perthes was never elected to the *Académie des Sciences*. He was still laughed at in Paris. It was also rumoured that shortly before the jaw was brought to him by a workman, he had offered a reward of two hundred francs for any human remains found in the gravel.

Boucher de Perthes died five years later, in 1868, and because of strong opposition by the *Académie* his family withdrew all his scientific papers from sale. Even in 1875, A. V. Meunier's *Les Ancêtres d' Adam,* which contained an account of what he described as 'the martyrdom' of Boucher de Perthes, was withdrawn by the publishers after they had been informed that the work was offensive to the *Académie.* It was published at last, however, in 1906.

Chapter 7

THE MODERN GEOLOGIST employs aerogeophysical and seismic survey, and chemical and radiological assay. The Victorian geologist had only his eye and a geological hammer. We can gain some idea of the magnitude of the problem of the earth's crust for the Victorians by considering it in the light of what modern technology has revealed.

Unfortunately for the study of fossil man, particularly for the early attempts to date him, the Pliocene, the closing period of the Tertiary Age, and the Pleistocene, the first period of the Quaternary, which saw the emergence of man, man-ape and ape-man, are the most geologically turbulent.

During the early part of the Cenozoic Era, which culminated in the Pleistocene, much of Europe, North America and Asia was sub-tropical, with temperate forests of giant redwoods, elm and beech extending far north into Alaska, Greenland and Siberia. There were no mountains but instead monotonous rounded hills which offered little variation in either landscape or climate. Such humpbacks do not make for windward rain slopes or leeward deserts.

There had once been mountains, indeed the previous Meso-zoic Era, that of the giant reptiles, had been one of mountain building, but these had eroded away during the first forty million years of the Cenozoic.

During the second half of the Cenozoic however, to the accompaniment of volcanade and convulsions of the earth's crust, the Rockies, Andes and that great spine of Eurasia, the Alps and Himalayas, uplifted themselves.

This geological change was equalled climatically. The onset of the appalling Ice Ages of the two-million-year-long Pleistocene are attributed to the immense height of these new mountain ranges. Certainly a similar upthrust of mountains in the Permian, the final period of the Palaeozoic Era, some two hundred million years before, was accompanied by a similar but not so severe freeze-up. With the mountains came the glaciers.

Forming high in the Scandinavian mountains and fed by the increased precipitation of altitude, the glaciers pushed downwards. These glaciers met others formed in the foothills, uniting to bury entire mountain ranges, and pushed outwards. The build-up of ice produced its own impetus as it reflected back as much as eighty per cent of the sun's heat. The ice sheet now crept east, joining a similar one spreading from Siberia, and then west across the North Sea converting the water into ice as it went, to join the glaciers produced by the mountains of Britain. Thus one ice sheet covered two million square miles. In the region of the Gulf of Bothnia it was ten thousand feet thick. Similar sheets formed around the Pyrenees, Appenines and Carpathians to the south and in North America to the west. Thus a belt of ice girdled the earth down to about 50 degrees north of the Equator. At its greatest extent the ice locked up enough ocean to make the world sea level fall by four hundred feet. The northern ice-fields caused the belt of rain-bearing westerly winds to swing inwards towards the Equator by fifteen degrees of latitude, both north and south. Africa, the Mediterranean, Asia Minor, the south west of North America and South America experienced 'pluvial' periods: heavy and protracted rainfall with swollen rivers, rising lakes and floods.

At least three more times in the years of the Pleistocene the freeze was repeated. Three more times the ice-field pushed east, south and west. There was, it is believed, a similar encroachment by glaciers of the southern hemisphere but the effect on this area is difficult to plot, as it is mainly ocean.

Each of the four main Ice Ages, which occurred irregularly at intervals of roughly one hundred thousand years, was separated from the next by a warm period or 'interglacial'. During interglacials the ice contracted, but the retreat north was interrupted several times by checks and readvances.

With each climatic pulse there was a massive migration of animals, the less adaptable or less resistant species perishing. The considerable fall in sea level enabled the animals to move freely across desiccated sea beds. These land bridges connected Britain with Western Europe; Alaska with Siberia; Japan with Siberia; Tasmania with New Guinea; and the Asian mainland with the Celebes and the Philippines.

Each pulse of the ice, each advance, check, readvance, retreat, check, readvance, and retreat, left a legacy—massive ice-scarred ridges, banks and moraine, wide spreads of clay, gravel and wind-borne *loess*. Each change of climate left the bones of its own distinctive fauna.

Then some twelve thousand years ago the ice retreated for the last time. There was a wild see-sawing of land and sea levels. First came the floods as the melting ice released vast volumes of water. Then land surfaces, long crushed down by the weight of ice, popped upwards. This left a legacy of raised beaches, drowned forests and submerged land surfaces.

It is not surprising, therefore, that the nineteenth-century geologists, aided only by observation and percussion, could make little sense of it all. At first it was not realized that the Great Ice Age was not one but four Ice Ages. As knowledge advanced and more than one Ice Age was detected, there was much strife between factions that accepted and factions that rejected them. It was the glaciations which gave the Pleistocene its distinction, therefore estimates of its duration and the distance in time from the previous Pliocene period varied according to the number of Ice Ages postulated. For the geologist who subscribed to two Ice Ages the Pleistocene was twice as long as the Pleistocene of the geologists who could only see evidence of one.

Edouard Lartet was but one of a number of palaeontologists who proposed a chronological classification of fossil man by fossil animal remains found with his tools. He wrote:

'Thus in the period of Primitive man we shall have the Age of the Great Cave Bear, the Age of the Elephant and the Rhinoceros, and the Age of the Reindeer, and the Age of the Aurochs (wild ox); much after the names recently adopted by archaeologists in their divisions of Stone Age, Bronze Age and Iron Age.'

The Englishman Sir John Lubbock was the first to refine the Stone Age into two main cultural groups. In 1865 he wrote in his best-selling book *Prehistoric Times* that the polished flint tools now being encountered represented the work of a more culturally refined and therefore later kind of humanity. He proposed that this group should be called the Neolithic or New Stone Age. The crudely chipped flints belonged to the Palaeolithic or Old Stone Age.

But Lubbock's 'Palaeolithic' and 'Neolithic' were no more than broad labels for successive flint cultures. What was wanted by the archaeologist and palaeontologist was a more accurate chronology based on numbers of years. How long in years were the Palaeolithic and Neolithic Ages?

The geologists responded to the question with vigour. Not

fully aware of the geological contortions of the Pleistocene, at first they thought the answer straightforward. The chipped and polished flints seemed to align themselves with two distinct groups of fauna. The chipped flints were to be found in deposits which also contained the bones of mammoth, rhinoceros and hyena; the polished flints were usually accompanied by the bones of reindeer and wild ox. These Palaeolithic and Neolithic groups of animals were to be found in certain kinds of deposits. All that was necessary then was a calculation of just when in the Pleistocene, at what phase in the movement of the ice sheet, the deposit had occurred.

But at this point in the mental exercise, concordance ceased. The above principles had long held good for the science of geology. An animal or plant fossil could be reliably ascribed to the Cambrian, Ordovician, Silurian or Devonian periods because it was actually found in that kind of rock. The depth in the rock gave an indication of age. But it was not a critical classification. The Devonian, for example, had lasted for fifty million years. A million years or so error meant little. Faced with the short Pleistocene, it was a different matter. A suspected error of say ten thousand years would set one geologist howling for the blood of another. The main trouble was that opinion varied widely about how long it took a deposit to be deposited. Nor was it realized that the glaciers had bequeathed different legacies to different areas at the same time. For example, gravel in one geological section, hill wash in a second, loam in a third, lake sediment in a fourth were considered to be evidence of different geological periods, whereas they could have been placed by different glaciers at the same time.

So it was that one worker found from deposits around Geneva that the Neolithic began seven thousand years ago while another reported at the same time that he had calculated from Egyptian deposits that the Neolithic began thirteen thousand years ago. Sir Charles Lyell, working in the Somme, considered that the Palaeolithic began not less than one hundred thousand years ago, and the Pleistocene Ice Age endured for two hundred and twenty thousand years, while in England Joseph Prestwich considered that the Palaeolithic lasted but twenty thousand years.

But one man held the key to the problem. In his 1862 address to the Geological Society T. H. Huxley stressed that geological deposits occurring in the same order and bearing the same fossils were not necessarily contemporaneous. In doing so Huxley endorsed the principles of stratigraphy, a relatively workable method of dating deposits. Much subsequent confusion and name calling could have been avoided if more people had taken notice of what he said. But they did not.

Even today the prehistoric archaeologist is criticized for his folly in ascribing flints to time-divorced flint cultures, to the neglect of pure geological dating. This may be true of present times, but if he had done so before modern geological techniques had sorted something out of the great natural puzzle then commensurate chaos would have resulted. Frederick Zeuner, a leading authority on the turbulent Pleistocene, calculated that before the adoption of stratigraphic principles the chances of success by such methods would be of the order of one in a thousand.

There was yet another problem which vexed many geologists from the mid-nineteenth century onwards. The geological hammer had its limitations, it was thought, but it was an instrument of precision compared with the methods of the students of fossil man. Animal and plant fossils embedded in rock which could be reliably dated were one thing; flint implements found in association with the bones of extinct animals in caves were another matter entirely. In its enthusiasm, human palaeontology was far too prone to relate the age of the container to the age of what was found in it. Never or seldom was it asked, the geologists complained, whether the flint tool had arrived in the cave before or after the animal bones were deposited. No palae-ontologist seemed to consider that the cave was merely a dat-able box in which fossil bones and flints were placed by later eventuality.

But the evidence was slowly accumulating. In 1866 another representative of Neanderthal man—a jaw—had come to light in a cave called Trou de la Naulette, in a wooded hill at the conjunction of the Meuse and Lesse rivers near Dinant, Belgium. Found by a Belgian geologist named Dupont, the human remains were accompanied by the first tangible evidence of the antiquity of Neanderthal man, the bones of rhinoceros, mammoth and bear. This was a distinctly Quaternary collection. No bones were found with the Neanderthal man of Rhenish Prussia.

Rather strangely, the jaw was described by M. Pruner-Bey to the *Société d'Anthropologie*, Paris, as being extremely ape-like

with huge, projecting canine teeth. C. Carter Blake, to prove
Neanderthal man was an anthropoid ape, also spoke of enormous teeth. Even the methodical Darwin, quoting Blake,
mentioned them later in his *The Descent of Man,* published in
1871. In fact, when discovered the jaw contained no teeth at all.

A third Neanderthal man was discovered in Belgium the same
year in a limestone cave in a wooded hill above the Orneau
river, near Spy. Evidently the site had been well dug over a
number of times before and a number of implements of a type
which came to be called Mousterian, in deference to the French
(see page 97), had been found.

But Marcel de Puydt, a member of the Archaeological Institute of Liège, and M. Lohest, assistant geologist at the University of Liège, noticed a large neglected terrace in front of the
cave. A four-foot trench was dug at this point, revealing a
deep layer of bones and flints. The skeletons—there were two—
were accompanied by animal remains which also related the
find to the Quaternary.

Edouard Lartet was elected to the newly established chair of
palaeontology at the Paris National Museum of Natural History
in 1869, but he died some months later without having delivered a lecture. Lartet had however struck a last blow for the
credibility of fossil man.

Late in the year before his death Lartet had been called to
Cro-Magnon, near Les Eyzies in the Dordogne. Here railway
excavations of a limestone cliff had uncovered a rock-shelter
containing skeletons of five adult humans. But these remains
were neither modern nor those of the Neanderthal brutes. The
best preserved skull had a steep forehead with faint eyebrow
ridges. Indeed his cranial capacity of some 1,590 cc. was well
above the modern average of 1,350 cc. The other bones suggested a tall individual possibly in excess of six feet, exceedingly
muscular, definitely *Homo sapiens,* but with primitive features
which placed him slightly apart from modern man. It was supposed by some that because of his extreme muscularity 'Cro-
Magnon Man' could outpace a horse and bull-wrestle with ease
although he was not in fact a Stone Age superman.

With the human remains at Cro-Magnon were a large number of flint tools and sea shells, some pierced for use as neck-
laces. This suggested a ritual burial after death. The high degree of refinement of the tools, called Aurignacian, and bones
of bison, reindeer, mammoth and primitive horse found with

the human remains later led to the opinion that the Cro-Magnons had lived some time in the late Pleistocene, probably during the fourth and last glaciation known as *Würm*. Lartet found himself able to ascribe these fossil men to the Late Palaeolithic Age.

The impact of these discoveries on scientific thought would be hard to overestimate. The Belgian Neanderthal men swept aside the suggestions of idiot or imbecile hermit or rickety Cossack. One imbecile at Neanderthal was feasible but several similar imbeciles in Belgium not so. Even more important, coincidentally the men of Neanderthal and Cro-Magnon supplied two separate links in the chain of human evolution. For the first time Charles Darwin's *Origin of Species* began to bear fruit. Maybe, it began to be thought, man really did have primitive forerunners in the same way as the beasts of the field. It was at least a beginning.

But as it is true that all winds blow some good, sadly the reverse is the case also. The excitement induced by Abbeville and St. Acheul, and Cro-Magnon and Neanderthal, started Britain off on a great fossil man hunt. Flint implements were found in vast numbers but not the kind easily recognizable as such.

The Geological Society accords to a newly adopted president the right to devote his inaugural lecture to his particular interest. In 1857 Sir John Evans took this opportunity to cry out against the new craze. He said that formerly the antiquity of the human race could be proved by the class of fauna recovered with the remains and the geological changes which had taken place in the surface conformation since the human relics had been deposited. But today, complained Evans, increasingly it was becoming usual to consider as evidence of early man pebbles on which the finder could see the traces of human workmanship. He warned his listeners to be wary of the evidence of these alleged worked pebbles. No doubt Evans' disappointment over Moulin Quignon made him highly suspicious of those stones. He had reason.

The latest craze was due to Benjamin Harrison of Ightham, Kent. Inspired, it is said, by Lyell's *Principles* and not so evidently by Gilbert White's *The Natural History of Selborne*, Harrison, a general grocer, had begun to cast about for something to collect, to search the hills about Ightham for flint implements. The result was the 'eolith'—stone implements of such simplicity that human participation is barely detectable or, as Evans complained, extremely doubtful.

The authenticity or otherwise of the eoliths was enough to split British archaeologists into rival camps. The eoliths were considered by believers as something equivalent to the biological 'missing link'. The pebbles, it was claimed, bridged the gap between sticks, which possibly were the first tools of humans, and the easily recognizable chipped flints found at Abbeville and St. Acheul. The evidence of human workmanship, said the owners of vast collections of eolithics, was there for all to see if only it were looked for. Chipped, scratched, marked pebbles formed the focal point at many a historical society's winter evening gathering.

The disbelievers assigned the manufacture of the eoliths to Nature, to the dashing by waves of one pebble against another, to the grinding of pebbles by earthquakes, to the crushing of cart wheels. Indeed, cried the disbelievers, it was almost impossible for a pebble to remain whole when the number of debilitating forces at work down the centuries was taken into account. Oddly enough, one of the most telling arguments against eoliths was used as overwhelming evidence to support them—the large numbers discovered. Collections of several thousand eoliths were quite common.

Whether the stones are or are not the work of man is a debate which continues to this day. Evans did not believe in eoliths but a great many other influential men did. Alfred Russel Wallace regularly visited Ightham to examine the rapidly expanding collection. Harrison also received encouragement from Joseph Prestwich. Many years later, in 1899, the grocer was invited to show his collection of eoliths to the Royal Society. It was greatly admired. The same year he was awarded a Civil List pension. Then the Royal Society purchased an annuity for him. All this was to the delight of the believers and the chagrin of their opponents.

There is little doubt that Harrison's discovery of the eoliths was welcomed as a relief from the realization that the gravel and sand pits of Britain failed to live up to the standard set across the Channel. If it could be believed that the marked pebbles were crude tools, then this was evidence that a race of primitive humans had once lived in Britain, compared with which the Neanderthalers and the ancients of the Somme were but of yesterday.

The palpable achievement of these years was the publishing in 1871 of Charles Darwin's *The Descent of Man*, in which he more than made up for his sins of omission in the *Origin* by predicting with uncanny accuracy the kind of fossil hominids which had yet to be discovered.

When Darwin died after a heart attack at Downe, Kent, on 18 April, 1882, his achievement was magnificently recorded by J. W. Hulkes, president of the Geological Society. Hulkes saw Darwin as a man who had 'devoted his life to the development of those pregnant principles of evolution, the annunciation of which he had the happiness to see generally accepted'.

There was concrete evidence of this acceptance, for Darwin was laid to rest in Westminster Abbey. His pall-bearers included Huxley, Hooker and Wallace. Many of his old adversaries, or rather those of Huxley, such as Wilberforce and Buckland, had gone before him. One survivor was the seventy-eight-year-old Sir Richard Owen. Owen was buried at Oxford ten years later in 1892. It was a pity for Owen that he could not have held on another three years, for he undoubtedly would have derived great satisfaction from the fact that 'Darwin's bulldog', succumbing to influenza on 29 June, 1895, did not 'make the Abbey'. The agnostic-in-chief was buried without ceremony at Finchley Cemetery.

Chapter 8

THE NETHERLANDS EAST INDIES (now Indonesia) lie in the great volcanic belt which curves south and westward from the North Pacific to the Indian Ocean. Nowhere in the islands are the volcanoes far distant; lofty truncated cones which radiate ridges to the sea. Brown ridges of recent eruptions stand out bold and barren. Others covered with dense forests hem in mountain torrents. Towards the coast the ridges open out to embrace wide fertile plains through which wind sluggish rivers. There is either jungle or cultivation. Even on the old volcanoes the patchwork of plantations stretches to the summits.

Towards the end of the nineteenth century, however, there were disturbances other than seismic ones. The riches born of the fertility tended to stay in certain hands. Very little percolated down to the lower orders. The East Indies were to Holland what Australia was to the United Kingdom and, apart from the planters, they were populated by industrious adventurers, the destitute striving for riches, and the indolent seeking peace. They were also the repository for the scapegraces of good families.

These factions blamed their continued lack of prosperity on a Dutch government policy which eschewed free trade and imposed import tariffs which stifled enterprise. The administration, which represented the interests of the sugar and coffee plantation owners to the exclusion of all others, was unrepentant. It feared the intrusion of foreign interests. There was no guarantee that free trade would necessarily mean that the outside finance thus unleashed into the islands would remain in the right hands.

But by far the most serious threat to peace came from the native population. Remembering the philanthropy of British administration under Sir Stamford Raffles[1] the natives attributed the generosity of a personality to a nation. They were at best discontent, at worst in open rebellion.

[1] 1811–1816.

The ill-feeling had commenced when the British Crown sur-
rendered its Batavia protectorate in exchange for that of the
Gold Coast. By the end of the nineteenth century this had
deteriorated into the Achinese War, the expense of which was
threatening the whole economy of the Indies.

But the accompaniments of prosperity still survived. In Java
there were railways, steam-tramways and an efficient telephone
system. Important towns had splendid public buildings, pleas-
ances and botanical gardens. But outside the towns travellers
were warned not to pass beyond certain points or their safety
was not guaranteed. The capital Batavia (now Djakarta) had
become one vast military encampment, to the detriment of the
last survivors of the British settlement who complained that
their golf courses were being used by fat Dutch officers to exercise their ponies. This produced, they complained, an effect on
the greens similar to artillery bombardment. It is an irrelevant
but irresistible fact that one of these Dutch officers was Captain
Rudolph MacCleod, whose wife many years later aggravated
the French and the British military as the accomplished courte-
san and vastly incompetent spy Mata Hari.

Another arrival in the steamy atmosphere of the East Indies
summer of 1886 was a twenty-nine-year-old army lieutenant
named Eugene Dubois. Dubois seems to have been quite un-
qualified mentally to be medical officer at the military fever
hospital at Padang on the island of Sumatra, to which he was
sent from Batavia. His many scientific biographers say as much
but in a different way. They are more impressed by the fact that
even as a lecturer in anatomy at the University of Amsterdam,
Dubois had kept it no secret that he considered the 'missing
link' could be found in the East Indies, that he had come ex-
pressly to seek him out.

But everything written about Dubois has been so highly
charged with reverence that it gives rise to the suspicion that
romance has been preferred to fact. Even the real reason for
Dubois being in the East Indies—the Achinese War—is never
mentioned. Certainly many authors, Darwin, Lyell and Wallace
amongst them, had considered that a primitive forerunner of
man might be found somewhere in the East. But they all
specifically indicated Africa for the birth of humanity for the
cogent reason that anthropoid apes—the most plausible early
progenitors of man—were found in that continent to the almost
complete exclusion of all others. The only exceptions were the

islands of Borneo and Sumatra, the home of the orang-utan.

At first Dubois preferred Sumatra. He changed to Java only later when B. D. Van Rietschoten found a primitive Australoid skull in a marble quary there. Java has no anthropoid apes at all.

Within weeks of arriving at the fever hospital, Dubois published his first paper, entitled *On the Desirability of an Investigation into the Pleistocene Fauna of the Netherlands East Indies, particularly Sumatra.* Dubois wrote that he found it odd that such a large, peculiar and advanced animal as the orang-utan should be confined to the Islands of Sumatra and Borneo. He reasoned that this was significant. In other countries which had an animal stock confined to that territory, such as Australia with its kangaroos, the remains of primitive forerunners of these kinds of animals had been found. Surely a search of Sumatra would provide a similar early forerunner of the orang-utan. This might also be the forerunner of man himself.

Dubois then quoted R. von Virchow[1]:

All researches hitherto have only led to the presumption but not proof [of the existence of ape forerunners of man]. Is the question settled? Certainly not for the naturalist. Large regions of the world are still wholly unknown in respect of their fossil treasures. These belong precisely to the home region of the men-like apes; tropical Africa, Borneo, and the adjacent islands, are still entirely unexplored. One single new find can change the whole state of the problem.

Thus Dubois argued his case for a government-sponsored expedition to seek the forerunner of man. He was none too particular about his choice of authorities to support his argument. Von Virchow was still maintaining that the Neanderthal fossil was a microcephalic idiot. His 1870 paper was aimed at pushing the search out of Europe so as to exclude Neanderthal man from the running. When Dubois found his Java man, his glibbest opponent was von Virchow who said Java man was a form of chimpanzee.

Dubois negotiated a change from Padang to a small hospital for military convalescents at Pajokumbu in the interior. In the less demanding post of senior medical officer he had more time for exploration. He began his quest in the local limestone caves

[1] 1870.

which provided a wealth of animal fossils. But these were of the Quaternary and thus too recent to provide the 'missing link' of his ambitions. By now the sympathetic government had considerably augmented the search party with two military mining engineers and fifty military convicts. But Van Rietschoten, though not so fortunate in assistance as Dubois, was having more success in Java. The fossils he sent to Dubois were of much older fauna, more reminiscent of the Tertiary deposits of the Siwalik Hills of India.

In 1890, after five years of what Dubois considered to be disappointment, he transferred the search to Java. In a volcanic tufa, mostly soft sandstone, Dubois found a hippopotamus jaw-bone with strong Siwalik affinities. This deposit, a few kilometres in width, extended east-west across the island, to the north of the 10,000-foot Lawu and Willis volcanoes. Dubois recognized this as an old river formation, resting on Tertiary marine marls, limestone, and volcanic breccia of indeterminate age. The adjacent Bengawen (now Solo) river had cut down through the deposit exposing a natural geological section. The bones recovered from this deposit, chiefly mammals and reptiles, had a distinct local character but a high degree of affinity with the Pliocene fauna of the Siwaliks.

The first remains considered by Dubois to be those of early man were found in November 1890 at Kedung Brubus, forty kilometres east of the native village of Trinil. It was a fragment of a lower jaw which Dubois attributed to a human of hitherto unknown type, differing from any living or fossil man. In September 1891, at Trinil at the foot of the still-active Lawu volcano, on the left bank of the Bengawen, he found a right upper third molar tooth. He ascribed both finds to a very large and exceptionally man-like chimpanzee which he named accordingly *Anthropopithecus*. A month later, three metres from the tooth, a skull cap was excavated. The Bengawen site was flooded every 'wet' season, and Dubois had to wait until the next April before resuming his search. But in August 1892 he found another tooth, a left upper second molar, about a metre from the site of the first tooth, then a left femur ten metres from the skull cap.

Dubois published the results of his searches in 1894. He now attributed the remains to an extinct giant gibbon which he called *Pithecanthropus erectus*. Having discovered the first fossil man in the east, he became his own opponent. Dubois exhibited

what was described as 'a grotesque reconstruction' of *Pithecanthropus* in Batavia in September 1895 and then left the East
Indies for good. He now embarked with his fossil on a vigorous
series of lectures, appearing at the Third International Zoological
Conference at Leyden in Holland, Liège, Paris, London, Dublin,
Edinburgh, Berlin and Jena, and the Fourth International Conference at Cambridge in 1898.

But although the discovery was a sensation, it was greeted
with bared scientific teeth. Far from establishing any coherent
scientific view, the Neanderthal man controversy merely seems
to have served as a whetstone. Although the cranial capacity
of the *Pithecanthropus* skull was so low that it prompted its
discoverer to think it belonged to an ancient gibbon, the straight
shaft of the femur had a close resemblance to that of modern
man. This strongly suggested that *Pithecanthropus* was capable
of standing and walking erect. This paradox of ape skull and
human limb was seized on as clear evidence that the bones did
not belong to the same individual; that Dubois had mixed the
bones of an animal with those of a human being; that the
distance between the discovery sites precluded all possibility
that the bones belonged to the same creature.

By 1896, two years after the announcement of the find,
five authorities were convinced that *Pithecanthropus* was a
kind of anthropoid ape, seven asserted that he was human,
and seven thought that he was intermediate between the two.
Von Virchow was inclined towards the anthropoid ape theory
but then reverted to his usual one of microcephalic idiot. Yet
another authority disgusted his scientific colleagues by suggesting that the creature was the result of copulation between a
native and an orang-utan.

More famous arguments took place over the size of the
Pithecanthropus brain. Behind his heavy brow ridges, the frontal
region of the skull recedes sharply, far sharper in fact than in
Neanderthal man. Brain-room is further reduced by a sharp
inward 'nip' at the base of the forehead. The lower portion
of the skull was missing, so any estimate as to the cranial capacity
of the skull was equivalent to sounding a bottomless pit, and
therefore subject to the caprice of the measurer. Dubois estimated
this capacity at 850 cc. In 1939 this was enhanced by von
Koenigswald and Weidenreich to 914 cc., reduced to 850 cc.
again in 1957 by Boule and Vallois, but raised to 940 cc. by
Ashley Montagu in 1960.

It might be thought that it would have been wiser to arrive at a general concurrence of view on the brain capacity before the implications of brain size were debated. But it seems that the strong individualism of the many describing authorities made such concordance impossible. Brain size had more than an obvious importance. No pea-brained individual, it was argued, would ever have walked erect, so the small skull and straight limb bones belonged to two separate species of animal. Those that held that *Pithecanthropus* had a large brain considered that he had evolved to a point where erect walking was essential.

Dubois was deeply affected by the heated controversy· At length he withdrew from the debate entirely, retreating with *Pithecanthropus* to the privacy of a house at Haarlem. Only in 1920 was he at last persuaded to allow the fossil to be transferred to Leyden Museum. Over the years Dubois continued to debate with himself. He began to waver from his original view that *Pithecanthropus* was a gibbon, his writings describing the fossil as more human and less ape-like. He changed his mind again on at least three occasions, then finally reverted to his original opinion of fossil gibbon. In later years the old man kept his collection of bones in a cabinet protected from the view of his critics by sheets of newspaper pasted to the glass.

In 1907 the Berlin Academy of Science mounted a lavish expedition to Trinil under the leadership of Frau Selenka, the widow of a prominent German zoologist; but nothing further was found in the way of fossil man, in fact no remains other than those of a fossil antelope, which was named after Dubois. The expedition itself (at least according to von Koenigswald, a later and more successful searcher in another part of Java) left its own remains in the form of a litter of broken beer bottles.

Britain had to wait until 1898 for her first fossil man, although much later he was proved to be nothing of the kind. In fact the fossil had been discovered in 1888, or so the Geological Society was informed, the lack of immediate publicity being due to pressure of business on the part of the discoverer. For two years before the discovery, it had been the custom of Robert Elliot to visit at fortnightly intervals the gravel pits in the Northfleet area of Kent—Milton Street, Swanscombe, and Galley Hill. During a visit to Galley Hill, Jack Allsop, an employee at the pit, who on Elliot's behest had looked out for and saved flint implements and curious stones while the ballast was screened, informed Elliot that a human skull had turned up. Elliot could hardly credit the information at first but the pieces of bone were duly produced.

Allsop conducted him to the spot of the discovery where more bones still embedded in the shingle could be seen. As they were dug out the remains were found to be so soft that they were placed aside to harden in the wind and sun. Indeed, it was explained later, Allsop had left the remains in the gravel only for fear of damaging them by unskilful removal.

The fragments were then taken to Elliot's private 'museum' where, after being dipped in a hardening solution, they rested for a decade until a Frank Corner, of Poplar in East London, saw them and urged they be placed in the hands of someone qualified to describe them. The master of a local school, named Mathew Heys, appears to have been the first to see the skull after it was uncovered by the workmen excavating the gravel. He had hurried off, his intention being to obtain some indisputable evidence of the presence of the skull in the gravel either by photography or the testimony of two 'intelligent' witnesses. Heys did not consider that gravel pit workmen were qualified. Common workmen at the time were notorious for falsehood and drunkenness. But the schoolmaster's caution cost him the discovery. To his chagrin, when he returned the skull had been removed from the ground. It was retained by Allsop until handed to Elliot in exchange for a reward.

It fell to the lot of E. T. Newton, F.R.S., to present this exciting find to the Geological Society. The portions recovered were most of the skull but wanting the facial bones, the right half of the lower jaw with teeth, both femora, and parts of both tibiae and pelvis. When reassembled Galley Hill man resembled remarkably the Neanderthal man found at Spy. The skull possessed prominent superciliary ridges, and the femora were similarly curved, although the tibiae were less robust.

According to Newton, the flint implements found at Galley Hill in the past had been acknowledged as being of Palaeolithic type. Frank Corner possessed a hippopotamus tooth found at Milton Street. There also Elliot had found a deer antler. Lion bones had been found at Swanscombe. F. J. C. Spurrell had detected the remains of elephant, rhinoceros, horse and bison in a small patch of gravel near Northfleet railway station. Similar remains were found at Dartford Brent, west of the City Asylum.

No one was better acquainted with the North Kent Pleistocene gravel deposits than Spurrell, said Newton, who agreed that the Galley Hill deposit was part of one original stretch extending from Dartford Heath to Gravesend. Spurrell had further informed Newton that human bones had been met with before in these gravels but had been mislaid, and no record kept of the conditions under which they occurred.[1]

The possibility that the human remains were the remnants of a comparatively modern burial, said Newton, must have occurred to every one of his audience but the peculiar character of the remains and the depth of eight feet of gravel at which they were found, pointed to considerable antiquity. Elliot and Heys were reliable witnesses as to the undisturbed state of the gravel above the remains; therefore there could be little doubt as to the Palaeolithic age of the human remains from Galley Hill.

In the discussion which followed Sir John Evans said that it was unfortunate that such a long interval had elapsed between the discovery of the bones and the attention of geologists being called to them. The nearly perfect skeleton strongly suggested a recent burial. On the whole he was doubtful and preferred to wait for more evidence before accepting absolutely that the remains were contemporaneous with the gravel in which they were found, however ancient the bones might appear. Professor W. Boyd Dawkins of Owens College, Manchester, said he would go further than Evans, for he was convinced that the skeleton was a recent burial.

A Dr Gason, however, was sure that Galley Hill man was of the same race as the specimens from Neanderthal, Spy and La Naulette. W. J. Lewis Abbot took leave to point out to Evans that the completeness of a skeleton was no guarantee of a recent burial. On one occasion he had discovered at West Thurrock the bones of a mammoth which were laid out as if the animal had been recently interred. Abbot said that he too had excavated the Galley Hill pit and had found numerous Palaeolithic implements.

[1] This neglect may seem to be surprising, but at the time the misplacement of bones seems to have been so usual as not to give rise to comment. Footnotes in the Geological Society's quarterly journal frequently mention bones being mislaid on the way to lectures, even lost altogether. Often, it seems, parcels of elephant bones trundled across country by railway until they found rest at the Lost Property Office or were lost beyond recall.

J. Allan Brown thought the meeting was being over-cautious. In Brown's opinion, a more authenticated case of antiquity would be hard to find. He firmly believed in the continuity of mankind from the Palaeolithic through to the Neolithic. There had been no gap, said Brown, so why was it so surprising that a skeleton had been found which showed affinities with both periods?

Professor W. J. Sollas of Cambridge regretted that the evidence presented to the meeting was not more perfect. Hey, said Sollas, had seen the skull *in situ* but only for a few minutes; on the other hand, Elliot's evidence was less open to question. On the whole, said Sollas, the anatomical characters showed that the Galley Hill skull was of the same type as those found at Neanderthal and Spy, so he thought it highly probable that the British specimen was not a recent burial.

So Professor Sollas, a leading anatomist, was convinced that Neanderthal man had been found in Kent. Gason, Brown and Abbot supported him. Evans was not sure, and Boyd Dawkins, another leading palaeontologist, was strongly against the proposition.

In the event Galley Hill man passed to the British Museum as a rather late version of Neanderthal man. He was in fact a modern man, as suspected by Evans and Dawkins.

This debate provides an illustration of how enthusiasm can over-ride all other considerations, a not too infrequent occurrence in the case of fossil men. Animal remains and flint implements found over a wide area, and dubious pebbles claimed to be Palaeolithic, were all grist to the mill of the enthusiasts. We have also met W. J. Lewis Abbot, a curious, busy, dark-bearded little fellow, who was to play a minor role in the Piltdown controversy. In fact he claimed to have directed the attention of Charles Dawson to the antique gravel at Piltdown. As his kind was not untypical of the chronic enthusiast for 'antiquities' which throve about this time and into the 1930s, he deserves closer examination.

Abbot was a compulsive dabbler and in his own estimation an ignored scientific genius. At the time of the Galley Hill meeting he worked at Benson's, the London jewellers, but even as a young apprentice clockmaker he had been won over by T. H. Huxley's evolutionary biology as defined in *Evidences*. Self-educated, Abbot gave evening lectures on gem-stones at the Regent Street Polytechnic, London. He was one of a group

of amateur antiquaries which formed about Benjamin Harrison.
Like many others he had become infected with the cult of the
eolith.

But in the 1890s Lewis forsook Benson's—and Harrison—
and started a small shop on his own account at Hastings, Sussex.
Possibly the grocer overshadowed him and he looked for fresh
fields of undiminished authority. This move was rewarded.
In the eastern Sussex coastal town he became the local fount
of spurious geological information and general oracle on prehistoric archaeology. Indeed this esteem reached as far as the
Geological Society in London. Everything was 'new' to him.
He disinterred 'new' species of prehistoric mammals and reptiles,
'new' types of implements, which, if not immediately acceptable
as such to Science, would be acknowledged—or so thought
Abbot—in the fullness of time.

Abbot's great discovery was the 'Hastings Kitchen Midden
men', a 'Neolithic' culture now known to be non-existent. His
papers on scientific subjects multiplied, each one shamelessly
plugging his discoveries, each a masterpiece in the art of the
throw-away line which bolstered his scientific reputation. He
demonstrated his method at the Galley Hill meeting by his
carefree reference to the mammoth, while seeming to support
Elliot and Newton. Lacking academic training, he gave the
impression of such by peppering his writings with 'oids', 'isms'
and 'iths'.

Some of Abbot's finds were genuine, however. For his work
on Pleistocene fissures he was awarded 'the proceeds of the
Lyell fund' by the Geological Society. He opened a museum at
his Hastings shop, which unfavourably affected his trade as
clock and watch repairer without providing any pecuniary
return, and unprofitably sold lantern slides illustrating his views
on prehistoric anthropology. He got into financial difficulties,
and out of them, with a frequency which dismayed his more
staid contemporaries.

Chapter 9

WITH THE PASSING of such men as Darwin, Lyell, Falconer, Huxley, Prestwich and Evans, there was a perceptible dimming of the light of reasoned argument. In its place grew a predilection for the raspberry-flavoured wrangle. Alleged fossil human bones were found, described, disputed and ridiculed and rejected. Caves in Wales were discovered by one authority, only for it to be asserted that they had been explored years before by another. What a so-called 'discoverer' had mistakenly interpreted as the scratches of Ice-Age glaciers were in fact marks of the pickaxes of the real finder.

Popular Science Monthly (May 1903) was enlivened by a report of the find of a fossil man at Lansing, Kansas. The author said Lansing man was of very much the same stature as the Palaeolithic man of Europe, although he could be a woman. At roughly the same time Worthington G. Smith reported to the Geological Society the find of a human skeleton with Palaeolithic implements at Round Green, north of Luton, Bedfordshire. Unfortunately, said Smith, a temporary distraction had enabled the workmen to make off with the bones, causing them to fall to pieces during the rough usage. This news was received indifferently, as more likely to interest the police than a learned society.

Clearly British palaeontology was in the doldrums. The demand for news of discoveries, any kind of discovery, was insatiable. As a result all sorts of oddities were offered as evidence of Palaeolithic man in Britain. Pebbles alien to a district were claimed to have been brought there in antiquity by primitive hunters. Chalk bearing scratches, 'pot-boilers', stone 'loom-weights', played similar roles. Sticks with knotholes were revealed as 'arrow-straighteners', with knobs on one end as clubs, or with neither knob nor hole, as *'bâtons de commandement'*. The baton was supported by the intriguing reasoning that as primitive man wore no clothes he would need to carry some distinguishing stick as a badge of rank. A letter to *Nature*[1] said, however, that these

[1] 25 December, 1902.

sticks were in fact 'pomagans' or strikers. An example, said the writer, could be seen held in the hand of a North American Indian carved on 'Colonel' Townshend's tombstone on the south side of the nave of Westminster Abbey.

To the nudity of primitive man was also ascribed his evident frequent discarding of stone implements. In a paper advancing this view, he was referred to as a 'pocketless wanderer'.

But all this was very small beer compared with the happenings across the Channel. And the English knew and resented it, for in *Man*[1] appeared an article which was nothing more than a send-up of French enthusiasm. No reason other than pique could have prompted the editor of the magazine to consider that the tenor of the report on the first session of the *Congrès Préhistorique de France* held in September 1905 would be acceptable to his readers.

Although the report was anonymous, the touch is unmistakably that of Mark Twain. Certainly Samuel L. Clemens was in Europe at the time of the Congress on a lecture tour. The writer found it impossible to enumerate all the scientific papers that were read but found them all of peculiar and rare interest. He described a visit paid by the congress to the nearby prehistoric sites of La Madeleine and Laugerie Haut, where 'everyone fell upon the debris with any instrument which was ready to his hand: lance-heads were extracted with walking-sticks and [flint] scrapers with umbrellas'. Clemens told how he descended into a deep and dark cave and of the terror which prompted him to think that no cave man could have painted the animal murals for fun. The low roof, according to the famous author, 'bristled with stalactites, impartially distributing wounds and contusions with unpleasant frequency'. The congress was concluded 'with the need for literary expression which stirs any large gathering of Frenchmen', being satisfied with two poems which 'pictured in verse of excellent quality the heroic struggle of primitive races with nature and fierce beasts'.

But diluvian man was now highly acceptable to the officers of the *Académie des Sciences*. He had gained entry by the sheer exuberance of his proponents. This acceptance was also possibly given impetus by a wave of militant atheism and anti-clericalism which seriously rivalled that of the First Republic.

After its sluggish start French prehistoric archaeology and palaeontology had overtaken and well outstripped their British

[1] 6:1906.

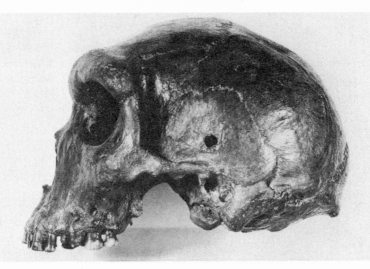

The skull of Rhodesian man: 'Cyphanthropus' or Stooping Man
according to the ornithologist W. P. Pycraft, head of the
British Museum (Natural History) Anthropology section.

Heidelberg man—a massive jaw discovered at Mauer, near
Heidelberg, in 1907 which later prompted Charles Dawson to at
first suspect an association with his thick-skulled
'Piltdown Man'. He entered Arthur Smith Woodward's office at
South Kensington crying: 'How's that for Heidelberg?'

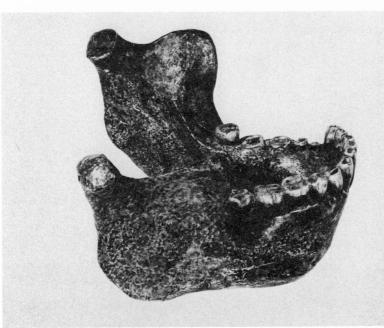

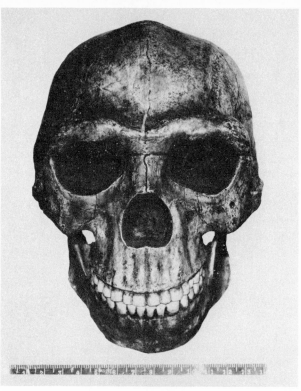

A reconstruction of Peking man (female)—one of the skulls that vanished sometime in 1941 when the Japanese occupied Peking, China. The entire Choukoutien assemblage said to have been aboard the s.s. *President Harrison* sunk by enemy action.

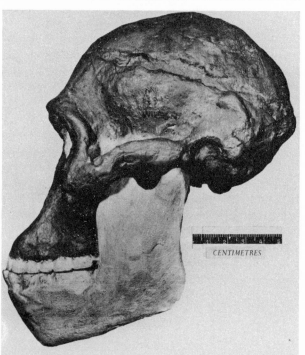

Australopithecus (africanus) The missing link which now occupies the place in evolution formerly occupied by Charles Dawson's 'Piltdown Man'.

counterparts. For example, at the second *Congrès Préhistorique* at Vannes, Brittany, in 1906, there were some thirty scientific communications producing a *Comptes rendus* of some seven hundred pages. At the third at Solutré in 1907, there were some forty papers producing a thousand pages; the fourth at Chambéry, Savoy, in 1908 produced one of nine hundred pages. This was after a strict attempt had been made to reduce the number of contributions, which now threatened to get out of hand.

These congresses, omitting the humour, were reported in envious tones in Britain's *Man* and *Nature*. Certainly the continentals had their controversies but these were conducted with an enthusiasm far removed from the parsimony of the English *chasseurs de cailloux* (pebble hunters), as the French disparagingly called them.

There was good reason for this sense of superiority. The French primitive man hunt had borne more fruit. Under the direction of the Prince of Monaco, excavations in the Principality in the caves of Baoussé-Roussé had produced two skeletons— adult and child—both of which presented very strong negroid features. But, as the describer Dr R. Verneau hastened to point out, the skeletons were not of true negroes but of a type somewhere between the Cro-Magnons and the Spy (Neanderthaloid) race, thus contributing a third ethnic element to the French fossil catalogue.

It might be noticed that the original Neanderthal man was now ignored in favour of the one found in Belgium. This did not intrude too much on Gallic priority.

Flint implements were being found in abundance, giving rise to the French names of the cultures which are still with us: Acheulean (St Acheul), Chellean (Chelles), Magdalenian (La Madelaine), Solutrean (Le Solutré), Aurignacian (Aurignac), Levalloisian (Levallois-Perret, Paris), Tayacian (Tayac, Les Eyzies), and Mousterian (Le Moustier). The last named flint culture was found in such abundance with the bones of Neanderthal men that until comparatively recently the human fossil was referred to as Mousterian man or *Homo Mousteriensis*, a fact of which France was particularly proud.

There were many such finds of Neanderthal men in France. A portion of skull was found in a brickfield at Brechamps, Eure-et-Loire (1892), a complete skeleton at La Chapelle-aux-Saints, Dordogne (1908), the remains of possibly six skeletons in a rock shelter at La Ferrassie, Dordogne (1911–13). All the discoveries follow the same general pattern, first finds of 'Mousterian' implements and then the Neanderthaloid bones.

From Chapelle-aux-Saints emerged a rare glimpse of what today is called 'humanity'. The Neanderthal skeleton, although considered to be that of an individual not more than 40 years of age, was toothless and deformed by osteo-arthritis to such a degree that he could not have hunted meat for many years before death. About the skeleton of 'The Old Man of Chapelle-aux-Saints' were many small mammal bones, Mousterian implements, and fragments of ochre suggesting a ritual interment. No great stretch of the imagination was required to deduce that despite the individual's economic uselessness he was important enough to warrant formal burial in the cave, that there was solicitude for the incapacitated. Such, anyway, is the interpretation, despite the discovery of the fragmented bones of some eighty Neanderthalers at Krapina, Yugoslavia—putative evidence that Neanderthal Man was a cannibal.

In 1904 trouble arose over some recently discovered Rivière cave paintings. The primitive painters—almost certainly the Cro-Magnons—had illustrated their human subjects with a fine disregard for propriety. Most of the early-twentieth century illustrators who were employed to copy the paintings omitted the huge genitalia for fear of giving offence. Some, however, were not so particular. Unfortunately, both versions—the virile and the castrated—came into the same hands and their owners were quick to conclude that someone was having an extremely vulgar joke at the expense of science, and that this someone was getting at the cave paintings. This threw doubt on the authenticity of the whole picture gallery, both human and animal. But the problem was quickly resolved. Albert Jean Gaudry was able to reassure his fellow members of the *Académie* that the offensive drawings were covered with the same smears of clay as the inoffensive ones. This was positive proof of antiquity. Oddly enough similar disbelief sprang from an identical cause some thirty years later when more cave paintings were discovered at Lascaux.

There was more trouble some four or five years later. It was a case of archaeological body-snatching which particularly incensed French palaeontologists and acquired an exaggerated significance because the site concerned was Le Moustier, French heartland of flint implement discovery. The culprits, said Marcellin Boule

darkly[1] 'came from beyond the Rhine'. The names in the indictment sound like a *mitrailleuse*—'Klaatsch, Virchow, von der
Steine, Hahne, Wüst and others'. According to Boule, one Hauser,
a Swiss dealer in antiquities 'who had only too long exploited
for German profit the deposits of the Dordogne, that is to say
the most valuable archives in France', had revealed how he was
paid the enormous sum of 125,000 francs. He admitted that with
his connivance a party of German scientists had exhumed a
human skeleton at Le Moustier.

Boule continued that the scientific value of the relic was
remarkably diminished by the 'poverty' of significant stratigraphical and palaeontological evidence and by the 'deplorable'
manner in which the skull was restored by the anatomist
Klaatsch. A second reconstruction in which Klaatsch was aided
by several distinguished colleagues was slightly more faithful,
the third was manifestly inadequate. Even the fourth reconstruction was still very imperfect, according to a countryman,
H. Taeger. Klaatsch, however, was unrepentant. In his scientific
description he said that the skeleton was that of a youth of
sixteen years who had been found lying on his right side with
legs slightly bent and head pillowed on a pile of flint flakes.
Mousterian implements were deposited about the skull and 'the
most beautifully worked of all the implements' lay within reach
of the left hand. The skeleton was presented to the *Museum
für Volkerkunde*, Berlin.

Germany made another contribution in 1907—a jawbone from
a sandpit at Mauer, near Heidelberg. This massive mandible
with modest teeth excited little comment, apart from an initial
quibble which likened it to the jaw of an orang-utan. From the
accompanying animal fossil remains, Heidelberg man is now
placed at the First Interglacial or Second Glaciation (Mindel).

Although the cult of the eolith was also detectable in France
by the end of the first decade of the twentieth century, for
Britain it seems to have acted as a kind of insulation against
thoughts of Gallic supremacy, certainly if the number of articles,
lectures and exhibitions on the subject is any guide. Of the
amateurs, and it must be admitted the cult was fostered mainly
by amateurs, S. Hazzledene Warren led the unbelievers. J. Reid
Moir and our old friend J. Lewis Abbot were strong for the faith.
But by far the most powerful supporter of eoliths was a professional, Sir Ray Lankester, a director of the British Museum.

[1] *Les Hommes Fossiles.* 2nd Edition. 1921.

Lankester, a former pupil of T. H. Huxley, was a large rum-bullion of a man with an immense literary output ranging from the life of the tsetse fly to prehistoric archaeology. In addition to his scientific works Lankester was a regular contributor of 'science for the layman' articles to the *Daily Telegraph* and semi-scientific and popular journals. With this large outlet for his opinions he was a powerful ally of any view he favoured and an almost insuperable adversary to any he did not.

At the age of seventy years Lankester embraced the cause of the eolith with a Johnsonian gusto. After an illustrated lecture before the Royal Society, as a prelude to the discussion that normally followed, Lankester hoped 'that no one would venture to waste the time of the society by suggesting that sub-crag flints (a kind of eolith promoted by J. Reid Moir) had been flaked by natural causes, as by so doing it would be plain that they had a very scanty knowledge of such matters'. The president, Sir Archibald Geikie, although himself a believer in eoliths, saw that the cause of free opinion was being subverted and called on the meeting to ignore the outburst, urging the members 'in spite of what Sir Ray Lankester had said, to express their opinions freely'. One did, only to be told by Lankester that he had been listening with 'amazement to the sort of thing I would expect to hear from a savage'.

On another occasion, following a talk given to the Society by Lankester, Worthington Smith said that nothing would induce him to believe in the pebbles. He said : 'We have here choppers that do not chop and borers that do not bore.' 'You, sir,' said Lankester, 'are a bore who does bore.'

The old man did not confine his homilies to the lecture room. A friend's wife hoped that he would not take any notice of the foolish womanly things she had said, and was informed 'gravely' that 'they were nothing to the foolish things your husband said'.

The collector of these anecdotes of the scientist's irascibility was J. Reid Moir[1] and as they advanced the cause of the eoliths by making Lankester's victims seem ineffectual and stupid they are not beyond suspicion. To the contrary, Lankester's writings suggest a calm, reasoned, perceptive approach. It is possible, however, that advancing age and ill-health lent him an intolerant attitude regarding what had been a life study of flint implements. As a young man he had visited Abbeville and one of the favour-ites of his large collection of flint implements was an artificially

[1] *Prehistoric Archaeology and Sir Ray Lankester*. Ipswich, 1935.

stained implement which he said had been given him by Boucher de Perthes.

Flint implements of one kind or another were the main diet of the British palaeontologist. Finds were reported from India, Mombasa and Somaliland, in Chinese Turkestan and German East Africa, near the south end of the Victoria Nyanza, and in Egypt. The most important find was some Neanderthal teeth in Jersey, Channel Islands, during excavations conducted by the *Société Jersaise*, but this did not bring much solace, being too near the French mainland, and apart from lengthy reports in *The Antiquarian* was little noticed.

Chapter 10

I N 1903 Professor Johnson Symmington, titular head of the Royal College of Surgeons, in his presidential address àpprised the British Association's anthropological section of the marked similarity between the skull of Neanderthal man and that of a chimpanzee. But, cautioned Symmington, as nothing would ever be known of the kind of brain the fossil skull had contained any conclusions arising from the similarity were a waste of time.

This sweeping observation went unchallenged by the meeting. No contradiction would ever be offered at the time as a matter of precedent, but no British anatomist seems to have objected.

The rock which disturbed this tranquil pool of acquiescence came from Egypt. It was thrown by one of those brilliant young men who from time to time take their branch of science by the coat-tails and pull them irreverently. One such man was T. H. Huxley. Another was the Australian-born Grafton Elliot Smith· In a letter to *Nature*[1] he said that Symmington's statement was nonsense. Had he not, asked Smith, heard of a brain cast? If not, this was strange as there were many in the collection in the Hunterian Museum of the Royal College of Surgeons. Although, said the writer, he had better ones in his collection at Cairo. He also thought it surprising to find that such an eminent professor of anatomy was repeating 'the time-worn fallacy' that the interior frontal convolution of the brain was known to be more highly developed in man than in the apes. Anyone aware of the true facts would advise him that in this region the ape was relatively much bigger than man. Symmington did not deign to reply.

It would be convenient to encapsulate Smith as the irreverent but brilliant young man of science, but it is perceptible that he possessed certain other disquieting attributes. He frequently sword-slashed at lesser lights with apparent conceit and superiority. He also thought himself, and was, a humorist. He reported his scientific repartee faithfully to his colleagues, with the inevitable outcome that the tail began to wag the dog.

[1] 5 November, 1903.

Smith had arrived in England from New South Wales in 1896, with an H.B. and a gold medal for his M.D. thesis on the brain of non-placental mammals, and to his credit eleven well-received papers on the cerebrum, cerebellum and olfaction in primitive mammals. He continued anatomical research at St John's College, Cambridge, lodging with Mrs Worral, an aunt and Indian Army widow who, according to his friends, talked amusingly and smoked pungent cheroots. The nephew was a great favourite with the widow who was reported to be 'unconventional' although in what way this manifested itself is not known.

A Fellow of Smith's college was the renowned anatomist, Alexander Macalister. Macalister seems to have favourably impressed his other students. Smith wrote of the don[1] that he was a very busy man but implied that his extra-mural distractions kept him so. He continued that :

'He seems to be intensely devoted to Anthropology of, I am sorry to say, the bone measuring variety and devotes all his time that is not absorbed in Early Christian History and Oriental Philology to the personal superintendence of the work in the Anatomical School.'

Not a bad start for a new arrival, even such a well-qualified one. But two months later[2] he amplified the theme, writing :

I see a good deal of Macalister. His chief anatomical interest is anthropological. If anything delights him more than inventing a new craniometric index it is the manufacture of some cacophonous name to brand it. But he is equally interested in Egyptian history, in Irish and Gaelic literature and archaeology, in the Evolution of Ecclesiastical Vestments, in the Cambridge collegiate system, in the specific identity of the Egyptian cat, and the progress of the Cambridge Presbyterian Church, among more or less (principally less) kindred subjects.

From the first Smith seems to have been unimpressed by Macalister's impersonal teaching methods, divorced as they were from any contact with a live subject. This was then the customary method of teaching anatomy. The late T. H. Huxley had been of the same opinion as Smith. In fact, the Australian

[1] 7 September, 1896.
[2] 18 November, 1896.

unashamedly confessed that he was a staunch admirer of the great man. He had been impressed in youth by Huxley's *Principles*. One wonders whether Smith fancied the Huxleian role himself.

In Smith's obituary in *The Times*[1] a colleague praised him for his 'child-like simplicity of approach to scientific trust' and said that 'his work was done in spasms, periods of idleness alternating with bursts of intense energy'. The first observation is too open to individual interpretation to be of much use and the second is certainly undetectable in his early career. Between 1896 and 1897 he published eight papers on cerebral morphology and began a descriptive catalogue of the brain collection at the Royal College of Surgeons. In 1899 he was elected Fellow of his college after three years' residence, five years' qualification being normal. Between 1900 and 1909, during which time he became the first professor of anatomy in the new government medical school at Cairo, he published fifty anatomical papers on the brain of extinct and modern mammals. While employed, with others, on the ambitious Archaeological Survey of Nubia, a part of which involved the examination of some twenty thousand prehistoric burials and the collection of 'sixty-four cases of remains', he also paid visits to the United Kingdom to take an active part in council meetings of the Anatomical Society, in Dublin in 1906, in Birmingham in 1907.

In the main, Smith's vacations were spent either in England or abroad taking part in archaeological digs, or as he termed it 'bone-grubbing'. At the Birmingham meeting he presented several communications. He recalled a month later that he:

> ... was talking on the pelvic fascia ... and no one raised a word of protest against my heresies. When I read a paper on the anatomical localization of the human cortex, Paterson got up and in a rather insolent tone asked: 'What was the use of it all?' I replied that: 'I did not think it was necessary to explain to the Anatomical Society my reasons for studying the anatomy of the human body.'

Although Smith was Boswell to his own Johnson the minutes of the meeting said the sally was 'greeted with tumultuous applause.'

[1] 2 January, 1937.

In 1907 Smith was elected to the Fellowship of the Royal Society and in 1909 he was offered the chair of anatomy at the University of Manchester, which he accepted. He was thirty-eight years of age.

Grafton Elliot Smith's impact on the teaching of anatomy at Manchester University was swift and revolutionary. Smith believed that the teaching of anatomy, the most venerable subject in the medical curriculum, needed a drastic reappraisal. The traditional dissection of the cadaver, the *tour de force* of the medical student, seemed to him to be divorced from its objective. Smith did not pioneer the use of X-ray equipment, the living model, the introduction of a live patient to demonstrate the facts of the structure and function of the body, but in 1909 such teaching methods approached innovation. Certainly few had realized their value.

The dissecting room at Manchester assumed a new spirit. Through intimate contact with the students he was extremely popular although, according to his biographers, he rated the average student's intelligence too high, and many were unable to keep pace with his mental agility. Dr Davidson Black, a Canadian Professor from a University in Toronto, who came to Manchester to do neurological work, fell under his spell. He became so interested in Smith's preoccupation with anthropology that he transferred to the study and making of human brain casts. It was reported that there was mutual understanding and affection and that this was the happiest period of Smith's life.

But Smith suffered from the kind of distractions he criticized in his mentor at Cambridge. Like Macalister, he interested himself in matters unconnected with anatomy. He investigated the origins of magic and religion, the early migrations of man and the diffusion of culture, and with ease found lively opposition to his views. That he enjoyed controversy for its own sake is illustrated by his delight in the rage which greeted his assertion that a carving at the Mayan city of Copan in the West Honduras was of an elephant. He recalled how a group of experts in Mayan archaeology afforded the spectacle of being united to prove him wrong while unable to agree amongst themselves whether the carving was of an extinct mammoth, macaw, tortoise, tapir or squid.

His enthusiasm for fun was not widely known; his brilliance was. And he used his ascendancy to belabour his adversaries.

His big opportunity came at the British Association meeting at Aberdeen in 1912 where during his address as president of Section H (Anthropology) he gave full rein to his intolerance of the attitudes of many of the assembled anthropologists and anatomists.

Concluding a lengthy harangue, he said that comparative anatomy could supply the evidence needed and its neglect was due in large measure to the singularly futile pretensions of some of the foremost anatomists who opposed Darwin's view at the British Association more than forty years before. Smith referred to Owen's contention about the *hippocampus minor* and described Charles Kingsley's ridicule as apt and justified. This, he said, served as an illustration of the nature of the discussions which distracted men's minds from the real problem.

Smith then gave his views on the evolution of man, that towards the close of the Cretaceous (some seventy million years ago) some small arboreal shrew-like creature had taken another step forward, that there was a reduction in the part of the brain occupied by the sense of smell in favour of that of vision. This enhanced sight and awakened curiosity to examine, supplied guidance for hands to perform more precise and skilled movement. Smith believed that the genius of man's intellectual preeminence was thus sown at the dawn of the Tertiary. The first primates were small, humble folk, leading unobtrusive and safe lives in trees, taking no part in the fierce competition waged below by their carnivorous and other brethren. Instead man's ancestor had cultivated equable development of senses and limbs and special development of the more intellectually useful faculties of the mind. In learning to execute with delicate precision movements to which no ape could attain, which the primitive ape-man could only attempt once his arms were completely emancipated, 'that cortical area [of the brain] which seemed to serve for the phenomenon of attention became enhanced in importance'.

He then said:

Hence the prefrontal region, where the activities of the cortex as a whole are focussed and regulated, began to grow until eventually it became the most distinctive characteristic of the human brain, gradually filling out the front of the cranium, producing the distinctly human forehead. However large the brain may be in *Homo primigenius* [Neanderthal man] his small prefrontal region is sufficient evidence of his lowly state of intelligence and the reason for his failure in the competition with the rest of mankind.

Smith lent heavily on Huxley for his hypothesis but ignored the biologist's plea for more inductive reasoning and less philosophizing. But the speaker's contribution was unique inasmuch as he rejected hypotheses which distinguished fossil men more by their differences from modern human beings than by their similarities. A number of those responsible were present.

His address was uncompromising. His allusion to twentieth-century anatomists with nineteenth-century attitudes was received with an angry growl. It must have appealed to Smith's sense of humour to be able to rib his colleagues in a formal presidential address, which by tradition was sacrosanct. But the opportunity for revenge did arise.

In the absence of a Mr Peet, Smith read the absentee's paper which proposed that megalithic monuments had originated in Egypt and had spread to Western Europe with the migration of their builders. The spread of culture by migration was a subject dear to the heart of Smith. In fact, it became an obsession. Smith incorrectly believed that all culture had a single place of origin; that no two races living in different parts of the earth could have duplicated inspiration. All culture, he argued, had to be transmitted by physical contact of one tribe with another, and on a larger scale, by one race with another. Indeed Smith could have written Peet's paper himself.

According to the report of the meeting in *Nature*[1] 'strong exception was taken to this theory which derived the round form of Western European megalithic monuments from the square Egyptian variety . . . the views of the paper were very strongly criticized'.

This description of the reception of the paper, read by Smith and reflecting his own views, was strong meat in the subdued parlance of such a journal and almost certainly meant shouting and thrown papers. Those mainly responsible, as must be suspected, were the stick-in-the-mud theorists scathingly referred to by Smith in his address. The objectors named by *Nature* were the professors Boyd Dawkins, Ridgeway, Myers and Bryce.

Amongst the other papers before the British Association that

[1] 6 September, 1912.

year was one by the forty-seven-year old anatomist and palaeontologist Professor Arthur Keith, keeper of the Hunterian collection of the Royal College of Surgeons and lately president of the
Anthropological Institute. He held the same progressive views
on the teaching of anatomy as Smith, who was six years his
junior, but they never quite hit it off. Certainly the future Piltdown controversy did not make for cordiality but it is possible
that Keith considered the Australian to be a maverick and held
himself aloof. They were dissimilar personalities. Smith was an
elocutionist. Keith spoke slowly, with the suspicion of an Aberdeen accent, slightly hesitant. He was, however, a skilful writer,
with a keen-edged style which must have made an adversary
timorous of opening a scientific journal. But there seems to have
been little malice in him, only a soft, good-humoured, occasionally testy, impatience. Smith would sneer where Keith would
gently and convincingly show the offender the error of his ways.

His arguments, nevertheless, were sometimes highly controversial and challenging. Much later, in 1931, he enraged an
entire pacifist England by referring to war as little other than
'Nature's pruning hook'.

At the Dublin meeting Keith said that recent discoveries in
the Dordogne showed that Neanderthal man was confined to a
late period in the Pleistocene, therefore we must go much further
back in time to find man's ancestral form. By the middle of the
Pleistocene at least, said Keith, long before 'Mousterian Neanderthal man' had appeared in France, modern man had appeared in
England, as proved by datable human fossils found in this
country. Keith said the most likely places where further proof of
the fact might be obtained were the Pliocene and Pleistocene
deposits of East Anglia. Particular care must be taken to watch
every quarry and excavation so that no remains were discarded
as lacking in scientific interest just because they resembled those
of modern man. Keith illustrated his lecture with a plaster cast
of the now long-forgotten Neanderthal man of Gibraltar.

This speech was delivered in Keith's usual style, without notes,
but it was in fact a curious one. It is now accepted that Neanderthal man was a comparative latecomer compared with the earlier
hominids such at *Pithecanthropus* and *Australopithecus*. But
Keith's reference to English fossils which supported this view is
inexplicable, unless he had heard a whisper of the developments
at Piltdown. There was Galley Hill man, but this fossil was
thought to belong to the Neanderthal race. And Keith had no

faith in this specimen. He certainly was not referring to the Kent's Cavern fossil.

At the same meeting, W. L. Duckworth made an ambitious claim for the Kent's Cavern jaw, forgotten since its discovery in 1867. Now Duckworth claimed that undoubtedly the jaw belonged to a Neanderthal man and was the first example to be found in this country.

Keith remained silent as Duckworth's Neanderthal man was trotted out, but after the session he told a reporter from *The Times* that he considered the whole affair ridiculous and unscientific. He told the newspaper that nobody seemed to know anything about the jaw, for example the depth in the cave floor at which the bone was found.

The outcry was immediate and intense, giving the impression that the jaw's proponents had been waiting for fifty years or so for an excuse to stage a demonstration. A dozen or more letters to *Nature*[1] said that William Pengelly had been most particular to note in his diary all the relevant particulars about the discovery of the jaw.

Keith was astounded. He said in a footnote to the correspondence that he was being misjudged. His sole object had been to draw attention to the fact that a claim that Neanderthal man had been found in Britain was supported merely by a rough sketch of a jaw which looked nothing like it. Keith said that he fully believed that Neanderthal man might one day be discovered in this country—Duckworth might even be right in regarding the Kent's Cavern jaw as such—but no discovery could be accepted unless the evidence was produced.

Then where was the famous jaw? The remains had been presented to the British Museum in 1870 where they had lain ever since. Duckworth was allowed to sketch the fragment but that was all. The museum authorities feared the hacksaw and hydrochloric acid of the enthusiasts might deprive them of the fossil altogether. Many demands were made that the bone should be produced for testing, that it should be placed on display or be made more accessible for examination. The British Museum refused.

This impasse brought an outburst-cum-puff from Hastings. J. Lewis Abbot wrote[2] :

Will you kindly allow me, as one who has made considerable

[1] 3 October, 1912.
[2] *Nature.* 5 December, 1912.

additions to our Pleistocene fauna, vertebrate and inverte-
brate, to support the appeal for the resurrection of that vast
amount of material now stored away that was obtained at
Kent's Cavern? Those of us who have paid close attention to
the subject are aware that the recorded lists give us but a poor
idea of what the cave could tell, that from the waste dumps
[Abbot's spurious Kitchen Midden Men] have been obtained
a large number of new species, and even from the lowest layers
these bones include those of man himself. In these circumstances we feel that the time has come, not only for this material to be put into competent hands, but for the caves to be
reworked on modern lines and in the light of recent research.

Keith later came out fully against the Kent's Cavern jaw,
writing that the teeth it contained differed only from those of
modern Englishmen in a high degree of wear and complete
freedom from disease. Keith was right. Abbot's plea for further
excavation of the cave was answered, but the search was un-
successful. In 1925, however, a Mr Powe, extending his garden,
dug into the face of the limestone cliff near the north entrance
of the cave and recovered fragments of a human skull. When
assembled at the Royal College of Surgeons by Keith the skull,
which was 'of the same colour and consistency' as the Neanderthal jaw, was found to be that of a modern woman.

There were fears for attendance at Dundee, for the Association's annual meeting coincided with the 14th International
Congress of Anthropology and Prehistoric Archaeology at
Geneva. They were justified. The counter-attraction proved too
much for the hoped-for guests. For French palaeontology the
congress was as a Nuremburg rally for the Nazis.

French was the official language of the congress. It had formerly been English. Of the two hundred papers presented, only
five were not of French origin. Marcellin Boule rose to state that
only twenty authenticated Neanderthal men had been discovered
and none, he said pointedly, were English. Professor Emile
Carthailac delighted the meeting with a lecture on Palaeolithic
cave murals of France and Spain, which was illustrated with
lantern slides in line and colour of paintings of bison, reindeer,
elephant and horse, and even impressions of the cave-dwellers'
hands. The Abbé H. Breuil, *the* expert on the Aurignacian flint
culture, gave a lecture on it.

Also several references were made to a new *Institut de palaeontologie humaine*. It marked, it was said, 'a new era in research pertaining to fossil men', and was international in conception. In fact, the faculty was composed of three Frenchmen and one Belgian. Delegates came from all parts of the world, including two from Australia and several from the United States, but there was no official British representative. There was, however, one Englishman present. Reginald Smith of the British Museum asked whether there was a resemblance between the flints found in the chalk of his native country and those of Aurignac.

There was yet another sensational Gallic find. *The Times*[1] gave an account of a remarkable discovery by Count Begouen and his son of clay animal figures, a bull and cow bison, in a cave at Ariège, where three months previously Palaeolithic murals had come to light. The floor of the gallery was found to be impressed with about fifty human heel-marks 'suggesting ritual dances and observances similar to those of the present-day natives of Australia and Africa'. A large number of engraved pieces of bone and ivory depicting animals were also recovered.

The one bright spot for English prehistorians was the result of a visit to England by 'the Professor Abbé Breuil, the greatest authority on Aurignacian remains', according to *Nature*. As a consequence, Professor W. J. Sollas and the abbé departed from Oxford for a tour of caves in the region of Gower, Wales. Both were hopeful of finding wall paintings. A halt was first made at Swansea to examine a collection of flints found at Paviland (Wales). These were identified by Breuil as Upper Aurignacian, some proto-Solutrean. Thus heartened the pair began their systematic search, beginning with the caves of Paviland in the west, working eastwards. As hope began to wane, said *Nature*, as cave after cave failed to yield any signs of paintings, as they entered Bacon's Hole at the extreme eastward end of the search, some colour was seen on the right-hand wall. Closer examination revealed ten bright red bands arranged in a vertical series, perhaps a foot in length. The stalagmite which tapestried the wall completely sealed the red pigment so that it could not be removed by rubbing. Breuil, an enthusiastic little man who closely resembled an advertisement for Gauloises, said that a similar arrangement of bands, but only eight, had been found at the end of the Great Gallery in the Font de Gaunna, Dordogne.

British human palaeontology had to be content with this

[1] 31 October, 1912.

superior wall decoration and a small rattle of disputed human fossils. Eoliths, however, were being found in greater numbers. At this point *Nature*,[1] after the obituaries, announced in *Item 8* of *Notes* that :

Remains of a human skull and mandible, considered to belong to the early Pleistocene period, have been discovered by Mr Charles Dawson in a gravel-deposit in the basin of the River Ouse, north of Lewes, Sussex. Much interest has been aroused in the specimen owing to the exactitude with which its geological age is said to have been fixed, and it will form the subject of a paper by Mr Dawson and Dr Smith Woodward to be read before the Geological Society on 18 December [1912].

One week later, on 12 December, *Nature* reported at greater length :

The fossil human skull and mandible to be described by Mr Charles Dawson and Dr Arthur Smith Woodward as we go to press is the most important discovery of its kind hitherto made in England. The specimen was found in circumstances which seem to leave no doubt of its geological age, and the characters it shows are themselves sufficient to denote its extreme antiquity. It [the remains] was met with in a gravel which was deposited by the River Ouse near Piltdown Common, Fletching, Sussex, at a time when the river level flowed at a level eighty feet above its present course. Although the basin of the stream is now within the Weald and far removed from the chalk, the gravel consists of iron-stained flints closely resembling those well-known in gravel deposits on the downs and among these are many waterworn eoliths identical with those found on the chalk plateau near Ightham, Kent. With the flints were discovered two fragments of the molar tooth of a Pliocene elephant and a waterworn cusp of the molar of a mastodon. The gravel therefore is partly made up of the remains of a Pliocene land-deposit. The teeth of hippopotamus, beaver and horse, and part of the antler of red deer were also found, with several unabraded early Palaeolithic implements. The latter seem to determine the gravel as Lower Pleistocene. The human remains, which are in the same

[1] 5 December, 1912.

mineralised condition as the associated fragments of the other mammals, comprise the greater part of the braincase and one mandibular ramus which lacks the upper portion of the symphysis . . . the bones [of the skull] are nearly twice the normal thickness . . . the brain capacity is about 1,700 cc. . . . The forehead is much steeper than in the Neanderthal type, with only a feeble brow ridge; and the back of the skull is remarkably low and broad, indicating an ape-shaped neck. The mandible . . . is identical in form with that of a young chimpanzee, showing even the characteristically simian inwardly curved flange of bone at the lower border of the retaining symphysis. The two molars preserved are of the human pattern, but completely long and narrow. At least one very low type of man with a high forehead was therefore in existence in Western Europe long before the low-browed Neanderthal man became widely spread in this region. Dr Smith Woodward accordingly inclines to the theory that the Neanderthal race was a degenerate offshoot of early man while surviving modern man may have arisen directly from the primitive source of which the Piltdown skull provides the first discovered evidence.

As can be seen, not only was it asserted that Piltdown man was far older than Neanderthal man, it was immediately proposed that Neanderthal man was a freak, that the only real ancestor of modern man was represented by the remains found in Sussex. British palaeontology rubbed its hands with pleasure.

Chapter 11

A FUGITIVE FROM the surge of French anti-clericalism which aided fossil man's acceptance by the *Académie* was a novice of the Society of Jesus, Marie-Joseph Pierre Teilhard de Chardin. This enmity had driven the Society's scholars from France and Teilhard de Chardin had been dispatched first to Egypt, then to the Channel Islands, to continue his training.

In 1909, at the age of eighteen, Teilhard de Chardin was at the Society's scholasticate at Ore Place, an ugly, red-brick edifice on the hill above Hastings. The student's days were spent in the study of theology, a subject which he found boring. His extramural activities sustained him, however, and he seems to have been delighted by all he saw of Sussex.

Teilhard de Chardin wrote home to describe Hastings as the *'Cannes de l'Angleterre'*. His letters to the family home, three kilometres from the village of Orcines, near Clermont, in the Massif Central, bubbled with accounts of elegant Eastbourne, of Winchelsea, Wadhurst, Bodiam, Camber, Rye, Folkestone, Hythe, of snails and whisky at Battle Fair, of Selsey and Chichester. But Teilhard de Chardin's primary interest was the geology of the chalk of the Sussex Weald, which was notable for the fossil remains of iguanadons and other saurians.

Evidently geology was not a new interest. As a boy he had collected pebbles and geological curios. When a juvenile at the Jesuit college of Notre Dame de Mongré at Villefranche-sur-Saône, this preoccupation, coupled with the Society's claim to teach the santification of science by religion and the service of religion by science, led him to his vocation. At the college he was rated brilliant but distracted. He attained first place in examinations without exertion but as geology had no place in the curriculum distinction did not impress him. A tutor, Henri Bremond, wrote of Teilhard de Chardin[1] that:

Thirty years ago one of my classical pupils was a little fellow from Auvergne, very intelligent, first in every subject, but

[1] Les Nouvelles Littéraires. 11 January, 1951.

disconcertingly well-behaved. The most backward and thick-skulled members of the class occasionally came alive, their eyes would light up when they were given something more thrilling to read and something more exciting to do. But he, never; and it was only a long time afterwards that I learnt the secret of his seeming indifference. Transporting his mind far away from us was another, a jealous and absorbing passion—*Stones*.

This was written when Teilhard de Chardin had an international reputation as a discoverer of Peking man and Piltdown man, and so there is a strong possibility that the recollection has benefited from hindsight. It is certain, however, that the student won but one prize for religious knowledge. His tutor's memory is possibly defective in one particular: the priest seems never to have been 'little'. He had the stature of his father, indeed both his parents, for his mother was a tall woman. A local farmer once remarked: 'I just met one of the little Teilhards—eight years old and not more than six feet tall.'

Teilhard de Chardin and a fellow student at Ore Place, Felix Pelletier, embarked, as a relaxation from the austerity of the theological instruction, on a self-imposed archaeological survey of Sussex. No doubt not a small part of the appeal was the freedom to wander about the English countryside. The religious persecution in France meant that even the sight of clericals provoked animosity, and civilian clothes had to be worn for safety. On 31 May, 1909, he wrote to his father of a new friendship:

...I have made the acquaintance of a local geologist, Mr Dawson, in amusing circumstances. Visiting a local quarry near here [Hastings], we were astonished to see the manager prick up his ears when we talked to him of fossils. He had just discovered a huge bone of the pelvis of an iguanodon, and had [received] a telegram from Mr Dawson announcing his intention to visit the quarry. I have learnt since that the iguanodon was found pretty well intact, bit by bit, and that the fragments are being packed in a case to be sent to the British Museum. Mr Dawson turned up while we were still on the spot, and immediately came up to us with a happy air, saying: "Geologists?" He lives at Newhaven, but he may be

able to help us. At least we shall have someone we can inform
about anything which is too big to manage ourselves.[1]

There is evidence that this meeting was not accidental. Arthur
Smith Woodward[2] recounted how Dawson had learned of the
visits of the Frenchmen from the quarrymen. Dawson rewarded
the quarrymen for fossils brought to his attention. If Dawson
wished, wrote Woodward, they would be glad to prevent these
'poachers' from entering the quarry. Woodward concluded this
anecdote with :

> Mr Dawson, with characteristic generosity and scientific zeal,
> replied that the workmen should rather welcome his fellow
> collectors, and he himself would give them the 'tips' of which
> they felt deprived. At the same time he asked about the cus-
> tomary days and hours of the Frenchmen's visits and soon
> made an opportunity to meet them in the quarries.

Woodward's interpretation of Dawson's direction to the workmen is possibly too generous. The part-time scrabblings of the
Frenchmen could in no way be as productive of fossils as full-
time quarrying. His offer to reward the workmen for directing
their attention to finds would also be too much open to abuse
and fiction, the poverty, even starvation level, of the quarry em-
ployees being well known. It is also an inescapable conclusion
that Woodward came to hear of this generosity from Dawson
himself. But Woodward always spoke well of Dawson. Their
friendship was of long standing.

Charles Dawson, one of two sons of a barrister-at-law, was
born at Fulkeith Hall, Lancashire, but the family moved to
St Leonards-on-Sea, Sussex, while he was still a boy. His life
followed a typical pattern : a boyhood passion for archaeology,
then geology. He was guided by a keen amateur, S. H. Beckles,
F.R.S., his schoolmaster at the Royal Academy, Gosport. In
1885, at the very early age of twenty-one, Dawson was elected
to the Fellowship of the Geological Society. The previous year
at Society meetings he had met Woodward, his lifelong scientific
mentor, then a recently entered second-class assistant in the
Geological Department at the British Museum, South Kensington, London. Woodward wrote of Dawson in an obituary[3] that :

[1] Robert Speaight: *Teilhard de Chardin : A Biography*, 1967.
[2] *The Earliest Englishman*. Watts & Co. London, 1948.
[3] *Geological Magazine*, 3. 1916.

He [Dawson] had a restless mind, ever alert to note anything unusual; and he was never satisfied until he had exhausted all means to solve and understand any problem which presented itself. He was a delightful colleague in scientific research, always cheerful, hopeful and overflowing with enthusiasm.

The only thing to be said for death is that one cannot be spoiled by one's obituaries, but in this case the praise is genuine. Dawson appears to have been generally liked. Arthur Keith wrote in his journal[1]: 'Charles Dawson comes to see me. A clever, level-headed man.' In his autobiography Keith wrote also of this first meeting: 'We had a pleasant hour together. His open, honest nature and his wide knowledge endeared him to me . . .' Teilhard de Chardin wrote of Dawson as '. . . methodical and enthusiastic' and said he was 'big, genial and enthusiastic . . .' An obituary in the *Hastings and East Sussex Naturalist* said of Dawson that he was:

> . . . always cheerful, hopeful and overflowing with enthusiasm. The premature loss of his inspiring and genial presence is indeed a great sorrow to his large circle of devoted friends.

The oft-quoted enthusiasm for his hobby is amply illustrated in the variety of Dawson's output. Keith described him as 'the lawyer-antiquarian' and 'the exemplar of the English country amateur'. Dawson discovered natural gas at Heathfield, Sussex. The gas was used to illuminate the Geological Society meeting[2] to which the paper was presented, and Heathfield railway station thereafter. He exhibited a 'Toad in the Hole'—a fossil toad in a flint nodule—to the Linnean Society[3]. His private collection, purchased by the Hastings Museum after his death, included flint implements, bone objects, antique glass bottles, a cast-iron statuette said to be Roman, a Norman 'prickspur', and an anvil dated 1515.

Dawson published *Dene Holes and their Makers, A List of Wealden and Purbeck Wealden Fossils,* both in 1898, *A Description of the Battle of Beachy Head* (1899), *The Services of the*

[1] 28 January, 1913.
[2] 18 June, 1898.
[3] 18 April, 1901.

Barons of the Cinque Ports at the Coronation of the Kings and Queens of England (1901), *Sussex Ironwork and Pottery* (1902), *The Restoration of the Bayeux Tapestry* (1907), and a two-volume work, *The History of Hastings Castle* (1909). Professionally Dawson had a legal practice at Uckfield. He was also clerk to the magistrates of the Uckfield Petty Sessional Division, and to the Uckfield Urban Council. He was Steward of the manors of Netherfield and Cauwes and from 1898 of Barkham, three miles from Uckfield. From 1905, however, the year of Dawson's marriage, there is a perceptible dimming of Dawson's interest in his legal affairs in favour of his hobby. The bride was Mrs Hélène Postlethwaite, an attractive widow with a son. The Dawsons took up residence at Castle Lodge, which nestled in the ruins of the Angevin castle at Lewes.

Dawson befriended Teilhard de Chardin, introduced him to the Geological Society, and assisted him to make his first big discovery.

Dawson had been an honorary collector — a somewhat nebulous title—for the British Museum for some thirty years. During this time he had contributed three new species of iguanodon —a large extinct reptile—and one species of *Plagiaulax,* a small fossil mammal. A species of iguanodon and the *Plagiaulax* had been named in his honour. At a meeting of the Geological Society on 22 March, 1911, which was little less than a public testimonial to Dawson, Woodward played the declaimer. He described how Dawson, since learning of Professor O. C. Marsh's discovery of early mammal bones in the grit of Wyoming, Kansas, over twenty years before, had searched similar deposits in Sussex. This was a search, said Woodward, of painstaking persistence and self-sacrifice. There was prolonged applause.

Dawson rose and thanked the speaker for his kind encouragement and willing readiness to assist in the identification of specimens. He said that during the last two years he had been favoured with the skill and assistance of Teilhard de Chardin and Felix Pelletier, to both of whom the ultimate success of the search was due.

Later in that year, in November, the partnership was further rewarded when A. C. Seward, professor of botany at Cambridge, gave more news of the activities of Dawson, Teilhard de Chardin and Pelletier to the Society. Commenting on a collection of fossil plants submitted to him by Dawson for examination, he said that although several of the specimens had been previously re-

corded, two had not. The result was *Lycopidites teilhard*
Salaginella dawsoni.

Teilhard de Chardin described Arthur Smith Woodward as
'a little man, with grizzled hair, very hale and hearty, but ex-
ternally rather cold'. He had come to the British Museum at
eighteen years of age highly recommended by Professor W. Boyd
Dawkins, his principal at Owens College, Manchester, as 'the best
student in Geology and Palaeontology of his year'.[1]

Like Dawson, Woodward came from the North of England
but he was the son of a Macclesfield silk-dyer and therefore
lower in the social order. Educated at a local grammar school,
Woodward launched into scientific authorship at the age of
eleven with an account of a holiday in North Wales which included an appendix on the natural history and geology of the
area. Two years later he printed this on his own press, producing
a small *octavo* volume of about thirty pages.

Woodward went to Owens College to read chemistry but
under the influence of Boyd Dawkins he soon turned to palaeontology. His success in competing for the post at the British
Museum was despite the wishes of the keeper, Dr Henry Woodward, who not only had another candidate in mind but for some
obscure reason disliked the idea of another unrelated Woodward in
his department. Woodward's rapid transfer to paid employment
was for reasons of finance rather than aspiration. He continued
to educate himself at evening classes at King's College, London.

As Teilhard de Chardin seemed never to have looked small,
Woodward had neglected to look young. He is always recollected
as an intensely busy man, completely without humour, a devoted
researcher and describer in his chosen field of fossil fishes, a
field in which he became an international authority and probably
the greatest palaeoichthyologist of his time. He was elected to the
Geological Society on the same day and at the same early age
as Charles Dawson. Henceforth the Proceedings of the Society
seldom fail to mention him in some particular.

In 1896 he was already being referred to as 'an accomplished
palaeontologist of the vertebrates' and credited with more than
a hundred papers on fossil fishes. In that year he was awarded
the Royal Society's Lyell medal. In 1898 he was elected to the
council of the Society, which he relentlessly papered; on a new
species of *Aerolepsis*, and the jaw of *Ptychodus* in 1903, on the
fossil fishes of New South Wales (1905), on a new species of

[1] Letter to British Museum. 21 April, 1882.

Chimeroid fish (1905), on the Cretaceous of Bahia and on a new dinosaur from Lossiemouth, Scotland (1907).

As vice-president of the Society in 1908 Woodward read a paper by the recently deceased Sir John Evans on Palaeolithic flints and proposed an amendment which would admit ladies to the Geological Society. From 1914 to 1916 he was president.

At the museum he was promoted assistant keeper in 1892. From 1898 to 1901 was spent preparing a catalogue of the fossil fishes in the collection. In the latter year he became keeper and remained in this position until his retirement in 1924.

On 24 February, 1912, Woodward received a letter from his old friend about the find in a very old Pleistocene bed between Uckfield and Crowborough, at Barkham Manor. Dawson wrote that he had found part of a human skull 'which would rival Heidelberg man'. He invited Woodward down to Sussex, adding that a fellow antiquary, Edgar Willet, would drive them by motor car from Uckfield to the site. Woodward replied that he would come down to Sussex as soon as he could. In the meantime he counselled discretion. On 24 March Dawson wrote, however, that : 'The roads leading to it [Piltdown] are impassable and excavation is out of the question'. In the winter the mud roads about Piltdown were churned into deep, water-filled ruts. The pit itself, as a contemporary photograph shows,[1] was often completely submerged. On 26 March two Piltdown specimens arrived at the museum by post. One, Dawson thought, could be part of a hippopotamus tooth; the other was to him a mystery. Woodward replied that Dawson had correctly attributed the tooth. The other specimen was merely a fragment of ironstone. On 28 March Dawson wrote that he would take care 'that no one sees the piece of skull who has any knowledge of the subject and leave it to you. On second thought I have decided to wait until you and I can go over by ourselves to look at the bed of gravel. It is not very far to walk from Uckfield . . .'

Woodward does not seem to have considered the developments at Piltdown warranted an urgent visit. In April he went to Germany to examine dinosaur bones. Dawson announced by letter on the 23 May he was coming up to London, and would bring the Piltdown specimens to South Kensington on the following day, Friday, probably after lunch.

The meeting took place, as Woodward soberly wrote later,[2]

[1] At British Museum of Natural History, South Kensington.
[2] *The Earliest Englishman.*

'to talk about them [the discoveries] and to learn whether his conclusions were justifiable'.

According to Dawson,[1] however, his entry into the office was scarcely commonplace. Dawson produced the piece of skull with a flourish, remarking: 'How's that for Heidelberg?' The lawyer did explain the reason for this remark. The recent discovery of the massive skull-less jaw in the sand-pit at Maur suggested to Dawson that the thick Piltdown skull bones might have common ownership. In this article Dawson told how he came to make the find. At the end of the last century, he thought, he had gone to Piltdown to preside at the Court Baron at Barkham Manor. While awaiting the customary dinner given to the tenants of the Manor, Dawson strolled outside. His attention was at once attracted by some iron-stained gravel unusual in the district. It reminded Dawson of some Tertiary gravel he had seen in Kent. He also remembered that in the view of geologists there were no flint-bearing gravels in the central area of the Weald; such gravels finished some three or four miles north of the South Downs in the Ouse valley. He was therefore surprised when on enquiry he was informed that the gravel had been dug on the nearby farm and had been used to repair roads for as long as anyone could remember.

Dawson said that he was glad when the dinner finished so that he could visit the pit, where he found two farm hands digging. On enquiry the men explained that they had never yet found any fossil bones. Dawson 'specially charged the workmen to keep a lookout'. Since then Dawson had made occasional visits to the pit but it was worked according to the requirements of road repair.

On one of these visits, however, a labourer handed Dawson a portion of human cranium of unusual thickness. At first this thickness was the only point of interest, according to Dawson, but he at once made a long and fruitless search. Soon afterwards he spent a whole day at the pit in the company of a friend, A. Woodhead, but the bed appeared to be 'unfossiliferous'. Many pieces of dark-brown ironstone raised false alarms and the wetness of the season hampered the search.

'It was not until several years later' that Dawson, when looking over the rain-washed spoil heaps, found a second and larger piece of the skull, and soon afterwards he found the portion of hippopotamus tooth.

[1] *The Hastings and East Sussex Naturalist*, 2:2. 25 March, 1913.

Despite Woodward's quoted enthusiasm, Dawson had to write an ultimatum on 27 May. He said that the pit was now dried out and :

'Next Saturday (2 June) I am going to have a dig at the gravel bed and Fr Teilhard de Chardin[1] will be with me. He is quite safe. Will you be able to join us?' Teilhard de Chardin, who breakfasted that fateful morning with the Dawsons at their home 'perched among the ruins of the castle', wrote[2] that at 10 a.m. he and Dawson set out for Uckfield where they were joined by Professor Woodward.

We embarked [he wrote] in a motor car, with the elements of a picnic, which took us three miles across Uckfield Park and deposited us at the place where the hunt was on. This was a stretch of grass, four or five metres in width, beside a wooded glade leading to a farm. Under this grass there was a layer a pebbles, about fifty centimetres thick, which they are digging up, bit by bit, for road-mending. A man was there to shift the earth for us.[3] Armed with spades and sieves, etc., we worked away for hours and eventually with success. Dawson unearthed a fragment of the famous human skull—he had already found three other pieces—[according to Dawson's account, so far only two pieces of skull had been recovered, plus the piece of hippopotamus molar]—and I myself laid hands on the fragment of an elephant's [*Elephas planifrons*] molar. This find considerably enhanced my reputation with Woodward, who jumped on the piece with the eagerness of a boy and I could see all the fire which his apparent coldness conceals. I had to leave before the others in order to catch my train. This first tooth of an elephant impressed me in the way another man is impressed by bringing down his first snipe.

According to Woodward both he and Dawson were fully occupied with 'ordinary duties'. Weekends and occasional holidays only could be spared for the task. He said that this was probably an advantage because the detection of fossil bone and teeth stained brown in a dark-coloured gravel, full of bits of ironstone and brown flints, necessitated a close and slow examination of every fragment. Only one labourer could be employed

[1] He was ordained on 24 August, 1911.
[2] 3 June, 1912.
[3] Probably Venus Hargreaves, a labourer.

on the heavy digging as each spadeful had to be passed through a sieve by the expert. The residue in the sieve was piled aside in 'spoil heaps' which were re-examined after the natural washing by rain made the task easier. The gravel was spread thinly over the ground so that mid-week rain prepared it for the weekend search.

Woodward said that Dawson obtained permission to explore the gravel pit from Robert Kenward of Barkham Manor without telling him what the search was about. The clandestine activities of that first weekend's dig excited much local curiosity. The Piltdown police constable appeared at Dawson's office on the following Monday and reported to him as clerk to the magistrates that 'three toffs, two of them from London, had been digging like mad in the gravel at Barkham, and nobody could make out what they were up to'. The embarrassed Dawson had 'calmly and quietly' explained that there were interesting flints in the neighbourhood and perhaps the men were merely harmless enthusiasts. The lawyer used the occasion to enrol the constable, explaining where flints might be found on his beat, and asking him to report any he might find. The digging then continued undisturbed until winter flooding of the pit prevented further work.

Woodward described the further finds thus:

In one heap of soft material rejected by the [farm] workmen we found three pieces of the right parietal bone of the human skull—one piece on three successive days. These fragments fitted together perfectly. After much inspection which prevented my discarding it as a piece of ironstone, I found in another heap an important fragment [of skull] which fitted the broken edge of the occipital bone and gave us the line of contact with the left parietal bone [found by Dawson]. Finally on a warm evening after an afternoon's vain search, Mr Dawson was exploring some untouched remnants of the original gravel at the bottom of the pit, when we both saw the human lower jaw fly out in front of the pick-shaped end of the [geological] hammer which he was using. Thus was recovered the most remarkable portion of the fossil which we were collecting. It had evidently been missed by the workmen because the little patch of gravel in which it occurred was covered with water at the time of year when they had reached it. On different days we also picked up three undoubted flint implements, besides several eoliths, and fragments of a tooth of an elephant, teeth of a beaver, and one much-rolled tooth of a mastodon—the first to be discovered in a river gravel in Europe. On the surface of an adjacent field we found a piece of antler of a red deer and a tooth of a horse, both fossilized, which we supposed to have been thrown over the hedge by the workmen.

As Woodward commented, 'we met with enough success to publish the first account of our discoveries in December'.

Woodward refers to the secrecy of the Piltdown dig as a matter of course. No scientific worker at that time would have thought any explanation was necessary. Certainly any premature publicity would cause damaging public intrusion at such an excavation. But the discoverer feared the public far less than his professional colleagues. He feared carefully rehearsed evidence in rebuttal. Past experience would have shown him that any claims for such a find would be highly controversial. Therefore the fewer that knew about the discovery the better its chances of success in the debate which would inevitably follow.

How big then was this select band? Certainly A. Woodhead, Dawson's friend and an original searcher, was a member. Almost definitely another would have been Edgar Willet, the amateur chauffeur. Then, of course, there was Teilhard de Chardin, possibly Felix Pelletier, the priest's archaeological companion, and Woodward himself. As the dig progressed this number increased to include F. O. Barlow, an expert plaster-cast maker at the British Museum's anthropological section under Woodward, and another museum employee, W. P. Pycraft, an authority on dentition and head of the museum's anthropological section under Woodward. Then the help was enlisted of the Australian anatomist, Grafton Elliot Smith, who had made a special study of fossil men, and lastly Sir Ray Lankester.

Certainly Lankester's support had been sought either by Woodward or Dawson for he threw a heavy hint to J. Reid Moir, the leading amateur authority on eoliths, in an undated letter (according to Moir, Lankester never dated personal letters) which said:

... It seems possible that it [the Piltdown remains] is our Pliocene Man—the maker of rostro-carinate flints [eoliths]! At any rate if they [the anti-eolith cadre] say to us "you say we call in vague, unknown agencies such as torrents and pressure to produce these flints by natural force, but you are in the same position of calling in a hypothetical man. You have no other evidence that such a man was there!" Now we can say "Here he is." It is wonderful that, after so many years, man's bones should turn up in a gravel. I do not despair now of you finding a sub-Crag human cranium and lower jaw. You must keep this dark for a month or so yet as the discoverers will not be ready to publish before that lapse of time and more will be found some day in the same place.

This letter, quoted by Moir (*ibid*), has a certain interest as the recipient himself had just alleged that he had found such a fossil human near Ipswich, Suffolk. It had not stood a chance, however, as the remains were accompanied by Roman pottery.

The *Manchester Guardian*[1] was the first to break the news of the Piltdown discovery to the public at large. Under the headlines 'The Earliest Man? A skull "millions of years" old. One of the most important of our time' the newspaper reported :

In spite of the secrecy of the authorities who are in possession of the relics the news is leaking out and is causing great excitement among scientists, although there are very few even among geologists and anthropologists who have any first-hand information.

The report continued inaccurately that the skull belonged to the same age as the Heidelberg 'skull' and resembled the Neanderthal specimen 'but belongs to a much lower and more primitive type of mankind'. It commented that the experts would not venture an opinion but probably the man represented by the new skull lived millions of years ago, well before Galley Hill man, even before the recently discovered Ipswich skull (J. Reid Moir's find). The newspaper deliberated that as the human bones had been discovered with the remains of extinct animals it was possible that he had met his end 'while following his prey'. The report claimed that the search for the 'missing link' had been narrowed by the Sussex discovery although Eugene Dubois' *Pithecanthropus erectus* (Java man) might be mentioned in this respect. It concluded that 'other links are still missing'. *The Times*[2] carried the following note :

[1] 21 November, 1912.
[2] 23 November, 1912.

Excavations in Sussex by an anthropological student have brought to light the fragments of a human skull. The skull, said by the experts to be that of a Palaeolithic man, is the earliest undoubted evidence of man in this country. A detailed description of this and other discoveries will be presented at a meeting of the Geological Society to be held on 18 December. The skull would appear to carry anthropological knowledge back to a much more remote date than the human skeleton discovered by Mr J. Reid Moir in the Ipswich district last year.

By its restraint this report was more accurate apart from the error that Dawson was a student of anthropology. This incorrect association is unimportant other than as evidence that the source of the report was neither Dawson nor Woodward. J. Lewis Abbot claimed later that he had pointed out the antique gravel at Piltdown to Dawson and he would have been a likely suspect apart from the vaunting of the Ipswich find, which might indicate Reid Moir or Lankester. Many people later made claims that they knew of the Piltdown discovery, even that they knew of the fraud from the outset,[1] but as none of these thought it necessary to come forward before it was detected some forty years later one must doubt the veracity of such statements.

On 18 December, 1912, at Burlington House, London, the offices of the Geological Society, Piltdown man made his public debut. It is traditional that no meeting before or since attracted such attention and attendance. Arthur Keith described the meeting that evening as 'crowded and excited'. *The Times*[2] said 'there was great interest and it was attended by geologists from many parts of the country'.

On a small raised dais at the end of the hall sat Dawson and Woodward. On a table between the discoveries was a plaster reconstruction of the skull; the 'missing link' between man and his ape ancestors. F. O. Barlow had given him a ferocious but cheerfully encouraging look, the patchwork of deep red of the fragments of the skull so far discovered shown up by the white of those absent but provided by Woodward and Barlow.

Dawson spoke first. It is alleged that within a few words he had talked himself into trouble; that he carefully avoided stating the year when he was handed the first piece of skull by the

[1] See J. S. Weiner. *The Piltdown Forgery*. Oxford, 1955.
[2] 19 December, 1912.

workman. On the discovery that Piltdown man was nothing more than a forgery the omission of this detail was interpreted as just one example of the cunning of Dawson, in this case an attempt to cover his nefarious activities with a veil of confusion.

The official paper[1], as published in the Geological Society's quarterly journal,[2] is the usual source work for Dawson's alleged sin of omission. The paper merely quotes Dawson as saying that he was walking along the farm road close to Piltdown Common when he noticed that the road had been mended with some peculiar brown flints which he thought were unusual in the district. He then says :

> *Upon one of my subsequent visits* [my italics] one of the workmen handed me a small portion of an unusually thick human parietal [side] bone ... It was not until some years later, in the autumn of 1911, on a visit to the spot, that I picked up, among the rain-washed spoil heaps of the gravel pit, another and larger piece.

Writing of the discovery in 1945 the now totally blind Woodward merely quotes the official publication, adding the detail that on this *subsequent* occasion the workmen handed Dawson what they thought was 'a piece of coconut'. He also picked out from Dawson's account in the *Hastings and East Sussex Naturalist* the statement that the lawyer's attention had been drawn to the gravel at 'about the beginning of the present century'. In fact Dawson did supply the missing detail.

A reporter from *The Times* at the Geological Society meeting quotes Dawson as saying that 'four years ago' (that is 1908) he was walking near Piltdown when he observed some workmen digging gravel for farm roads. On this occasion one of the workmen gave him the fragment of skull. The report continues that during that last winter (which would be 1911) Dawson was fortunate enough to retrieve two more fragments.

It seems, therefore, that the missing detail was deleted from the official paper before publication the following March. The Geological Society talk was delivered from notes and not from the official paper, which was not published until the next year.

[1] C. Dawson and A. S. Woodward. 1913. 'On the Discovery of a Palaeolithic Human Skull and Mandible in a Flint-bearing Gravel overlying the Wealden at Piltdown (Fletching), Sussex.'

[2] 69 : 1913, pp. 117–51.

Certainly Dawson, and Woodward for that matter, made a mistake, but surely it is not an incriminating one, as is normally suggested.

Dawson told the meeting that Woodward considered the human remains of such importance that as soon as the floods had subsided at the end of May attempts would be made to discover the remaining fragments. By September sufficient fragments of the skull had been recovered for a reconstruction to be made. Dawson said that the diggings had also produced bone fragments of two species of primitive elephant, a hippopotamus, red deer, horse and beaver, and numerous flint implements of a 'very primitive type'.

While the search was in progress Dawson had thoroughly examined the geology of the neighbourhood and the position of the gravel proved to be of great antiquity. The gravel rested on an old land surface over which the Ouse used to flow. Since the gravel was deposited the Ouse had deepened along its seaward valley by sixty to eighty feet. Dawson concluded that the human remains and some of the fossil mammals were of the early Ice Age. The other animal remains were probably older and belonged to the late Pliocene; they had somehow been washed naturally into the gravels.

The flint implements, said Dawson, were of two kinds. The most recent were Pre-Chellean; the others belonged to the class known as eoliths on which, he said, there was much debate as to whether they were of human authorship or not.

Woodward told the meeting that, with the aid of Barlow, he had been able to restore the skull. It had proved different from any class hitherto met with in France, Belgium or Germany. It had the steep forehead of modern man with scarcely any brow ridges. In fact the only external appearance of antiquity, it seemed to Woodward, was the position of the occiput, which showed that the attitude of the neck was like that of an ape. The most striking feature of the skull was the thickness of the bone, said Woodward. It was twice as thick as that of modern man, even thicker than that of the negro and Australian 'black'. It was well known, said Woodward, that the skulls of negroes and 'blacks' were far thicker than any ape's.[1]

[1] In his book Woodward mused that this thickness could have been the result of exposure to sun and air. He quoted Herodotus (Book III, Thalia) that Egyptians have shaved heads from childhood but Persians wear hats to such effect that battlefield skulls of the latter could be

Then Woodward turned to the most sensational part of Pilt-down man—the jaw. It differed markedly from that of man and, he said, 'agreed exactly' with that of a young chimpanzee. The jaw, however, still retained two molar teeth with crowns which displayed 'a marked regular flattening such as has never been observed among apes, though it is occasionally met with in low types of men'. 'If the molars were removed', said Woodward, 'it would be impossible to detect the jaw was human at all.'

Woodward reached his main conclusion. All cavemen (the Neanderthals), he said, were characterized by low foreheads and very prominent brow ridges resembling those of a fully grown modern ape. But the Piltdown specimen was proved by the antique gravel to be much older than the cavemen. Woodward found it very interesting to note that the new skull was very similar in shape to that of a very young chimpanzee while the skull had the brows of a fully-grown animal.[1] He was inclined, therefore, to the theory that the caveman was an offshoot of early man that had probably become extinct. Modern man, said Woodward, might have derived directly from the primitive source represented by the Piltdown skull. Woodward was sure that Piltdown man was a hitherto undetected genus and proposed therefore that his discoverer should be honoured by naming the specimen *Eoanthropus dawsoni*, the Dawn man of Dawson.

The next speaker was Grafton Elliot Smith. From the context of the paper it is clear that he said something but its exact nature is not known. His main findings were in the form of an appendix to the printed paper published the following March. The

---

fractured with a single pebble while those of the former could scarcely be fractured by striking them with a stone. Woodward enlarged this view to include the 'spongy texture' of the Piltdown skull which would give resistance to heavy blows. He consulted Dr. R. S. Shattock, Royal College of Surgeons, who 'repeatedly' examined the fragments to assure himself the skull was not diseased.

[1] This is a reference to the then widely held opinion that the embryo of a descendant resembled the adult of its evolutionary ancestor. This theory of recapitulation is now known to be false. Embryonic stages of descendants are generally the repetition of corresponding embryonic stages of the ancestor. There are, however, instances in insects, verte-brates and man where the adult descendant resembles the ancestor in youth. This type of descent is known as paedomorphosis, or 'Peter Pan' evolution, because the youthful characters of the ancestor are present in the descendant which appears not to have grown up.

appendix said that Smith's observations were upon a cranial cast submitted to him by Woodward.

To his first sight the brain seemed to resemble the well-known Palaeolithic brain-casts, especially those of Gibraltar (Neanderthal) and La Quina. Taking all the features into consideration, Smith regarded the Piltdown specimen 'as being the most primitive and most simian human brain so far recorded; one, moreover, such as might reasonably have been expected to have been associated with the mandible which so definitely indicates the zoological rank of its original possessor'.

Smith said the apparent paradox of the association of a simian jaw with a human brain was not surprising 'to anyone familiar with recent research upon the evolution of man'. In the process of evolving from ape to man 'the superficial area of the cerebral cortex must necessarily be tripled . . . The growth of the brain preceded the refinement of the features and the somatic characters in general.'

In the discussion which followed Sir Ray Lankester seems to have done some verbal fencing. He said that the part of the jaw which connected it to the skull was quite unlike that of a human. The jaw certainly indicated something new in the remains of early man. He found it difficult to believe that the eolithic implements were of the same age as the skull, or even that the skull and jaw belonged to the same individual.

Arthur Keith, however, was more confident. Speaking from the body of the hall, he said that the discovery had fulfilled the prophecy of what the ancestor of man was likely to be. The skull was much earlier than Neanderthal Man but showed modern characters not found in that specimen. He considered that Dawson and Woodward had made a much bigger discovery than they were actually aware—they had found Pliocene man, not Pleistocene man. He had turned out to be just as the speaker had expected. Maybe, said Keith, the later of the two kinds of flint implements had made the authors think that the skull was of a later date than it really was. He did not think so. The Heidelberg jaw was of Early Pleistocene date. The Piltdown jaw, being more primitive, must belong to an earlier age—to the Pliocene.

The next speaker, W. Boyd Dawkins, could not agree. That remains of Pliocene animals were found with the skull, he said, was a pure accident. Ignoring the eoliths, which were too open to individual interpretation, said Dawkins, the other flints clearly showed that the human remains were of a later date than the Pliocene animals. Call them Chellean or Aurignacian or whatever anyone chose, he personally attached no importance to such 'sub-divisions'. He said that there was no doubt that the skull was Pleistocene but he complimented Dawson, Woodward and Smith on their exposition. He concluded that the Piltdown skull was as complete a 'missing link' as that found in Java some years ago. To anyone who doubted whether the ape's jaw was capable of formulating speech he would reply that there was no connection between making flints and this faculty.

It seems that the enthusiasm for Piltdown man was such that Charles Dawson got near to being chaired from the hall. Even in 1912 the length of the Pleistocene Epoch still had an elastic quality. The estimates varied from 150,000 to 1,500,0000 years (about 2,000,000 is correct). The consensus of opinion was for 500,000 years. But whatever the estimate, Piltdown man qualified by his primitive aspect for placement at the beginning of the Pleistocene if not earlier. His brain capacity, as estimated by Woodward, and the position of the occiput placed him neatly between man and ape. That he was capable of some sort of human reasoning was thus assured but his ape jaw postulated animal menace : the ability to defend himself with teeth if required.

The human remains were found with two groups of animal bones, which offered two datings. The earlier was the Pliocene (now termed Villafranchian) group, which consisted of primitive elephant, mastodon and rhinoceros. Then there was the later Lower-Middle Pleistocene group : beaver, red deer, hippopotamus and horse.

The flint implements were in two similar groups, the eoliths and the 'Pre-Chellean'.

Woodward was cautious. He regarded Piltdown man as of approximately the same antiquity as the Heidelberg jaw, that is Middle Pleistocene. Dawson thought that perhaps his friend erred on the side of caution. He was prepared to accept Early Pleistocene. E. T. Newton, F.R.S., who had made a special study of both the Pliocene and the Pleistocene, preferred the former, earlier period for Piltdown man. The Belgian authority Rutot did not hesitate to place the deposition of Piltdown gravel as early as the closing part of the Pliocene.

It seemed that the meeting had been amply forewarned that such a creature as *Eoanthropus* should figure somewhere in the evolution of man. T. H. Huxley had hinted as much in his lectures at the Royal Institute a half-century before and Charles Darwin had written of the progenitors of man[1] that 'the males had great canine teeth, which served them as formidable weapons'. W. L. Duckworth stood at the meeting to declare that 'the anatomy of the Piltdown skull realized largely the anticipation of students of evolution'. Arthur Keith had said as much.

At the outset, Lankester, Keith, even Woodward had reservations about the jaw. Woodward said that although the flat wear of the molars appeared to be human, only the missing eye-tooth would provide irrefutable evidence that the jaw was human. He considered that the Piltdown jaw was too long to be filled by normal human teeth and from his reconstruction he concluded that the canine must have been much larger than in modern man and separated, as in the ape, from the next tooth to the rear with a space to facilitate an interlock with the opposing large tooth of the upper jaw. He noticed, however, that the worn surfaces of the molars were remarkably flat, proving that during mastication the jaw must have been as free as that of modern man and not restricted to the ape's slight side motion. He therefore mounted the chimpanzee canine substitute so that it projected but slightly above the molars. Keith was of the opinion that the canine would be completely human in character and in a separate reconstruction he modelled the jaw so as to accommodate typically human teeth.

The French were unfortunate in that they did not have a Mark Twain to visit Piltdown during the excavations of the summer of 1913 for the diggings were overcome by the boisterousness of the 1905 *Congrès Préhistorique de France*. It seems that most of the British luminaries of geology and kindred sciences, and not a few from the Continent and the United States, were as a matter of courtesy allowed a token dig, sieve or search. Dawson and Woodward were frequently interrupted by the arrival of motor coaches laden with natural history societies. On 12 July, 1913, a visit was paid by some sixty members of the Geological Society, an excursion said to have been organized by Dawson. He could barely restrain most of this party from entering the pit. A few succeeded. Other visitors included Arthur Keith, Sir Ray Lankester, Grafton Elliot Smith, Davidson Black and Arthur Conan Doyle, the inventor of Sherlock Holmes.

Pecuniary interests became involved at Piltdown. A penny

[1] *The Descent of Man*, p. 248.

picture postcard of the diggings with the inset heads of Dawson and Woodward, entitled *Searching for the Piltdown Man*, a local confection, could be purchased at the Lamb Inn, about a mile from the site. The owner himself later succumbed, changing the name of the inn to *The Piltdown Man*. In increasing numbers the public found the pit, stared at what they knew not, and went away refreshed. Then such things impressed people to a degree which is unfashionable now.

In a contemporary photograph the diggers stare at the camera with the fixed expressions of an execution; Woodward stern, Dawson in a straw hat looking like a pork butcher. With the discoverers in the workings was a goose. According to a later commentary this bird was always present.

On Saturday, 30 August, 1913, the long sought for and vital canine tooth was recovered. Teilhard de Chardin had written home of the Woodward-Keith controversy that : 'In my opinion all these reconstructions . . . add nothing definite to the interest of the fragments. The important thing is to look for more pieces.' At intervals throughout the summer he had dug with Dawson and Woodward, staying with the Dawsons at Lewes. Teilhard de Chardin's search had been interrupted by a retreat at Ore Place but he returned that day. Woodward described the momentous find thus :

> We had washed and sieved much of the gravel, and had spread it for examination after washing by rain. We were then excavating a rather deep trench in which Father Teilhard, in black clothing, was especially energetic; and, as we thought he seemed a little exhausted, we suggested that he should leave us to do the hard labour for a time while he had comparative rest in searching the rain-washed gravel spread. Very soon he exclaimed that he had picked up the missing canine tooth, but we were incredulous, and told him we had already seen several bits of ironstone, which looked like teeth, on the spot where he stood . . . so we both left our digging to verify his discovery. There could be no doubt about it.

Woodward described how he and Dawson had spent until dusk crawling over the gravel in a vain quest for more fragments. Teilhard de Chardin after 'a few moments of excitement had returned lightheartedly to Hastings'. There was one more important discovery that season; two nasal (turbinal) bones were found by Dawson on a vertical section of gravel close to the spot where the workmen said they had found the braincase. Hoping to find the remainder of the facial bones, the lawyer dug round the bones with the blade of a pen-knife but there was no more.

The canine was all that Woodward had predicted, except that it was slightly smaller, more pointed and fitted more vertically into the Piltdown jaw. The enamel of the inner face of the tooth was completely worn away down to gum-level 'exactly as in apes'. Dawson wrote in 1915 that 'the tooth is almost identical in form to that shown in the restored cast'.[1]

All the teeth were now X-rayed. Dr A. S. Underwood, commenting on the remarkable resemblance of the canine to that of the ape used by Woodward in the text which accompanied the reproductions of the radiographs, said that the tooth was absolutely as modelled at the British Museum, that the wear, for all its unusual degree, was natural enough, and that the X-ray clearly showed a patch of secondary dentine such as was always deposited progressively with natural wear.[2] But another dental authority, C. W. Lyne, would not agree at all. He said that the canine was an immature tooth and so the degree of wear it displayed was quite out of keeping with its apparent youth.[3]

Woodward announced the discovery of the canine to the British Association meeting at Birmingham in September and then to the Geological Society. The general conclusion was that the tooth proved that Piltdown man's dentition was extremely ape-like and not similar to that of human beings as proposed by Keith. Confronted by this implacable evidence Keith climbed down, remarking rather tamely that the roots of the Piltdown teeth seemed human in type.

Having achieved partial victory Woodward strove to quiet Keith on the score of the capacity of the skull. Keith was now strongly insisting the volume of Piltdown man's brain was as large as that of modern man. He based his argument on the premise that the fossil skull was too early in the evolutionary pattern to have developed a feature common to modern skulls— the left-hand side dominating the right in size. Keith stressed that in very primitive skulls both sides are symmetrical, thus he gave the left side of the Piltdown skull similar volume to that of

[1] *The Hastings and East Sussex Naturalist*, 2: p. 182.
[2] *British Journal of Dental Science*, 56, pp. 650–2.
[3] *Proc. Roy. Soc. Med.* 9, pp. 33–62.

the right. Woodward, the fish expert, advised the human anatomist Keith that he was wrong. Make the volume of the right
side of the plaster reconstruction less than the left, he urged,
then we will be in accord.

Grafton Elliot Smith, however, attributed Keith's 'error' to
ignorance of the original specimens. In a letter to *Nature*[1] he
warned Keith not to place too much reliance on what could be
deduced from inaccurate plaster casts. Woodward, he said, had
free access to the original. Smith thought it was undesirable that
misunderstanding which arose from this simple fact should be
allowed to breed further confusion.

Despite its professed pacific intention, the letter naturally
contributed nothing toward this end. Smith aggravated Keith
further in another letter to the magazine[2] saying that he might
have been inclined to go along with Keith in the matter of skull
volume before he had seen the actual skull fragments, which he
had done recently. Now, said Smith cheekily, he was convinced
that Keith's reconstruction was impossible.

Keith was furious. He replied that Smith was doing grave injustice to both Woodward and Barlow, the plaster-cast maker.

[1] 2 October, 1913.
[2] 13 November, 1913.

The famous Piltdown gravel according to Sir Arthur Smith
Woodward. The parts of the layers that have been removed by
weathering and washing away by rivers are indicated by dotted
lines.

Key: a, Chalk, the upper part containing flints which fall on the surface
below (as indicated by arrows) when the surrounding chalky material is
washed away; b, Upper and Lower Greensand; c, Weald Clay, the
upper part of the Wealden Formation; d, Hastings Sands, etc., forming
the middle part of the Weald; P, Position of Piltdown; x, Region of
the original chalk where the men who made the eoliths lived (according
to the eolith supporters).

(From *The Earliest Englishman*. Watts & Co. London, 1948.)

Woodward was only too eager to allow anatomists to examine the Piltdown fragments. This facility had been freely extended to himself, who thought that the British Museum reconstruction was erroneous. And, said Keith, Barlow's skill had made the casts highly accurate. Keith admitted that he had given similar volumes to both sides of the skull. But by doing so, wrote Keith, he was only placing the discovered fragments in their correct anatomical position. He advised Woodward to ignore Smith and follow suit.

Smith replied[1] that Keith put a finger on his own problem when he mentioned similar volumes. Woodward had, he wrote, started off by giving the skull similar proportions but fortunately he had seen the error of his ways before the Geological Society meeting. Although the brain of Piltdown Man was a primitive form, instructed Smith, it had strong modern affinities. The skull therefore was non-symmetrical. Keith should change his views, not Woodward.

The debate on the brain volume of Piltdown man continued in this vein for the rest of the year and into the next. Keith maintained that his construction was the correct one; Smith calling him wrong and flicking out annoyances. Keith used his presidential address to the Royal Anthropological Society in January to insist that he was right, therefore the capacity of the skull was grossly underestimated. Smith argued eloquently before the Royal Society in February that the small brain of Piltdown man, although definitely human, was of a type from which had been derived those of primitive races, such as Neanderthal man, the Australian aborigine and the negro. Dubois' *Pithecanthropus*, or Java man, he argued, represented an unprogressive branch which had died out in the Pleistocene. *Eoanthropus*, Dawson's fossil man, had progressed to modern man.

Unfortunately for Smith his adversary was also at the meeting. Keith rose to state that the small brain referred to by Smith was in fact being deprived of some three hundred cubic centimetres of volume by Woodward's faulty reconstruction. Of this collision Keith wrote[2]:

I did not mince my words in pointing out the glaring errors ... It was a crowded meeting and he [Smith] and I filed out side by side. I shall never forget the angry look he gave me.

[1] *Nature*, 30 October, 1913.
[2] *An Autobiography*. London, 1950.

He must have felt that I was right for he never published his Royal Society paper and when at a later date he made a re-construction of the skull it did not differ greatly from mine.

Smith's impugnment of Keith's ability to reconstruct early human skulls resulted in a demonstration. Keith re-assembled a specimen Egyptian skull which had been carefully broken into

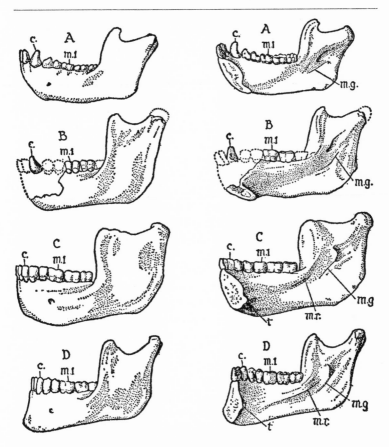

Sir Arthur Smith Woodward compares the Piltdown jaw with those of a chimpanzee, Heidelberg man and modern man.

Fig. A Young Chimpanzee; B Piltdown Man; C Heidelberg Man; D Modern Man; c. Canine tooth; m.l. First molar tooth.

(From *The Earliest Englishman.* Watts & Co. London, 1948.)

small pieces by an independent party. The reconstruction was found to be accurate to within a few cubic centimetres. This sensational feat was the talk of scientific circles for many a day.

It is hard to say who was right about the reconstruction. Keith was right inasmuch as the Piltdown skull was represented as that of an early kind of humanity. The Java skull and another found later in China showed no dissimilarities in the right and left sides of the crania. Woodward's ignorance of the subject caused him to reconstruct the Piltdown skull in line with the asymmetry of modern skulls.

In fact Woodward made another error which made the brain seem to him even smaller. As Sir Wilfrid Le Gros Clark said many years later[1] Woodward, not being a human anatomist, had mistaken a small side ridge on the roof of the Piltdown skull for the central (median) ridge not uncommon in ancient skulls. Le Gros Clark said that Keith detected this error immediately.

It is perhaps typical of Keith that he never publicly mentioned this glaring error, merely noting it in his diary. When many years later he was invited to write an introduction to the deceased Woodward's saga of Piltdown he confined himself to the admission that he had been wrong. Admitting that he had 'played the part of the stormy petrel' he said he had learned a great deal from the excavations he had recently conducted at Mount Carmel (now Israel). On his return in 1938, wrote Keith, he had 'yet again spread out in front of me the Piltdown fragments and set out to reconstruct them in the light of recent experience'. Keith continued:

I soon found myself involved in all the puzzles which I had encountered a quarter of a century earlier. The mistake I had been making all along I found to be this: I shared the common idea that the earlier the type of man, then the more symmetrical would be the left and right halves of the hemispheres of his brain. It is not until I realized that in Piltdown the left hemisphere dominated the right both in size and complexity, that the discrepant parts fell into their appropriate place. The specialization of the left half of man's brain at so early a date took me by surprise.[2]

[1] *The Exposure of the Piltdown Forgery*, Royal Institution, 20 May, 1955.
[2] Sir Arthur Keith's Foreword to *The Earliest Englishman*.

Chapter 12

THE PILTDOWN EXCAVATIONS proceeded into 1914, progress being reported to the Geological Society or the scientific journals by either Charles Dawson or Arthur Smith Woodward. So far, this season's yield had been confined to another piece of mastodon molar, and part of a rhinoceros molar which was picked up by Davidson Black on a visit to the site with Grafton Elliot Smith.

But Piltdown was by no means exhausted. Woodward was watching labourer Venus Hargreaves slashing away with a mattock under the nearby hedge when he saw splinters of bone scattered by a blow. Searching the spot with his hands Woodward pulled out 'a heavy blade of bone' covered with sticky yellow clay. When washed it was observed that one end of the bone was recently fractured. Dawson accordingly 'grubbed' with his fingers in the earth and retrieved the other half. One end had been trimmed by sharp cuts to a wedge-shaped point.

Woodward took the two pieces of bone to South Kensington where Frank Barlow 'hardened' and fitted them together. Further examination showed that although unstained the bone agreed with the high degree of mineralization of the bones from the Piltdown pit, and so must have come from there, being thrown out unnoticed by workmen seeking gravel.

The sharpened end suggested to Woodward the work of a primitive flint tool. The bone, some sixteen inches in length and four inches in diameter, was part of the thigh-bone of a fossil elephant.

Scientific speculation as to the use that Piltdown man could have made of the tool was rife but unproductive. One end seemed to have been rounded for comfortable handling and the other pointed for performing work. A groove, presumed by Woodward to be the remains of a hole of which part had broken away in antiquity, could have been threaded with a strip of skin for carrying. Woodward attached importance to this feature, concluding that as the point was sharp and showed little sign of wear, the breakage had rendered the tool useless.

On the whole, the tool suggested a stick for grubbing up roots.

The inevitable opposition to Piltdown was gaining momentum. It was not, however, claimed that he was the product of disease or relic of Russian invasion but that he was two animals. Despite Charles Darwin's prediction, the jaw, as the chief British objector, Dr. David Waterston of King's College put it, had too much of a striking resemblance to that of a chimpanzee. The teeth not only approached those of the ape in form, he said, they were in several instances identical. Associating the jaw with the skull, he said, was like articulating a chimpanzee's foot to a human leg.

The French palaeontologist Marcellin Boule was of like opinion and wrote that he 'saw no reason to regard the jaw as belonging to the man whose brain-case was deposited in the gravel where both were found'.

More robust attacks came in 1916 from the United States. Gerrit Miller, curator of mammals at the National Museum of the Smithsonian Institution, Washington, D.C., sent a chimpanzee jaw to the Geological Society recommending that it be compared with the Piltdown example. Miller wrote that the Piltdown mandible had nothing to do with the skull. It belonged, he said, to a fossil chimpanzee which must have inhabited England during the Pleistocene. From the morphology of the teeth he suspected a hitherto undetected species and named it *Pan vetus*.

On the American's attack, *Nature*[1] unfavourably commented :

If mankind had been evolved from an anthropoid stock the occurrence of a combination of human and anthropoid characteristics in earlier or dawn human forms, such as occur in *Eoanthropus*, is just what we ought to find.

At the Manchester Literary and Philosophical Society, in February 1916 Smith conducted a one-man debate on what he described as 'the new phases of controversy regarding Piltdown man'. These were, he said, that the canine tooth belonged to the upper and not the lower jaw; that the mandible belonged to a chimpanzee; that the features which differentiated the mandible from that of modern man had been exaggerated[2];

[1] 8 June, 1916.

[2] In addition to the views of Arthur Keith, Professor A. F. Dixon had told the Royal Dublin Society that the ape-like peculiarities had been over-emphasized, that the assumption of absence of chin and prognathism were not necessary.

that the canine could not have belonged to the skull and jaw because of the apparent difference in age, one authority believing it to be definitely older, another definitely younger.

Smith said he had examined all these arguments but had found no evidence to support any of them. He drew particular attention to the inference that the cranium was not sufficiently ape-like to be associated with the jaw. To this he replied that the skull revealed certain features of a more primitive nature than any known representative of the human family.

In *Man*,[1] T. E. Nuttal appealed for reason. Describing himself as a medical practitioner and student of anthropology, he said that even after a second reconstruction by Woodward there still existed a considerable discrepancy between his version and Keith's. Keith's demonstration on the Egyptian skull was impressive, his anatomical skill could not be denied but it must be admitted that his Piltdown skull erred on the large side. There could be, said Nuttal, a rational explanation for the dispute. Keith believed in the high antiquity of man, holding that he had originated in the Pliocene. If it could be proved, therefore, that such a large-skulled individual had existed in the Pleistocene Keith's views would be given strong support. Precisely the same reasoning could be applied to Woodward's view. He believed that man originated in the Pleistocene so if he could prove that at that time humans possessed but a meagre cranial capacity then his views would be upheld. Nuttal was sure that neither Keith nor Woodward would consciously allow his views to influence his reconstruction, still 'all of us, quite unconsciously, find what we desire and expect to find'. This sober reflection was somewhat spoilt by Nuttal's closing remark that he thought Keith's reconstruction was nearer reality than Woodward's.

Meanwhile, W. P. Pycraft, an ornithologist who was head of the museum's anthropology section, was countering a series of letters from Gerrit Miller. In 1917 he gave a final reply to this vexatious correspondence with the approval of Woodward, Smith, Keith, Underwood and Barlow, writing:

The jaw has peculiarities which make it human despite the fact that it presents many points of likeness to that of a chimpanzee. All supposed disharmony between the jaw and the skull is imaginary. The molar teeth are human,

[1] 17: 1917.

radiographs and the other evidence show that they differ conspicuously from the corresponding teeth of great apes.

Not one authority expressed any doubts concerning the age of the skull. Although neither hydrochloric acid nor tongue-test had been applied doubts on this score had already been stifled by scientific advance. The Geological Society's quarterly journal[1] carried the following impressive notice :

A small fragment of the skull has been weighed and tested by Mr S. A. Woodhead, M.Sc., F.I.C., Public Analyst for East Sussex and Hove, and Agricultural Analyst for East Sussex. He reports that the specific gravity of the bone (powdered) is 2.115 (water at 5 degrees C as standard). No gelatine or organic matter is present. There is a large proportion of phosphates (originally present in the bone) and a considerable proportion of iron. Silica is absent.

One wonders why the same test was not applied to the jaw bone, but it seems that such a test was never contemplated. As it was, Woodhead's criteria were worthless as later events proved.

Dawson wisely kept out of the anatomical controversy, leaving the field to Woodward, Keith and Smith. On 26 August, 1916, he died. Those familiar with the lawyer's energy were greatly shocked by his sudden demise at the age of fifty-two years. Dawson had suffered from anaemia which had suddenly turned to septicaemia. The present author was considerably mystified by the sudden death of Charles Dawson while to all appearances at the height of his vigour. Could his anaemia in any way have affected his mental faculties either partially or to a degree which would diminish his sense of responsibility? Dr Stefan Varadi, a consultant haematologist of international standing, kindly informed him that certainly the manifestations of long protracted anaemia usually are fatigue and shortness of breath. Mental capacity, however, does not suffer, except in extreme cases where there is an unsatisfactory supply of oxygen to the brain. The only exception is perhaps the so-called *pernicious* anaemia where, even in its relatively mild form, psychiatric manifestations can occur. This form of anaemia is due to lack of vitamin B_{12}, which is also an essential vitamin for

[1] 69:1913.

the normal function of the brain tissue. But if it is true that Dawson 'was renowned for his remarkable energy which persisted until the time of his death' it is unlikely that he had pernicious anaemia. Especially as all Dawson's obituaries referred to 'a protracted illness.'

Dawson certainly showed no sign of the onset of mortal disease. After Piltdown he made another discovery which Keith, if he had heard about it, would not have received too warmly. It concerned the skeletons in his Hunterian Museum at the Royal College of Surgeons.

Dawson was struck by what he described as 'the persistence of a thirteenth dorsal vertebra in certain human races which had not attracted scientific notice'. He detected this extra vertebra in the skeletons of an Arawak Indian, a Niva-Fu whale-hunter, a male and female Eskimo, and an ancient Egyptian.

Dawson attributed this phenomenon to a common factor in the lives of these races: the canoe or kayak, and the constant manipulation of the hips to maintain equilibrium, necessitating an additional muscle attachment in this region. The lawyer's findings were never published but he certainly prepared a lengthy paper on the subject. It is possible that Woodward may have advised him against publication. The manuscript for the abandoned project is still in the Geological Department's collection.

On the 24 March, 1915, Dawson was at the Royal Anthropological Institute to give a remarkable demonstration aimed at the destruction of the argument for eoliths. Eoliths had been recovered from the Piltdown pit and why Dawson, if he were the forger, should wish to cast doubt on them is inexplicable. It must have been an honest attempt to be objective about Piltdown. The lawyer had shaken pieces of common starch stained to resemble the 'old brownies' of the Kent plateau and had produced, to the intense indignation of J. Reid Moir and J. Lewis Abbot, starch 'eoliths'. He repeated the experiment before the Geological Society.

Woodward, creating a precedent, asked the artist John Cooke, R.A., what he thought Piltdown man would have looked like in life. As he commented later with evident satisfaction, Cooke, 'could not avoid making the portrait altogether human'. Dawson had smiled at the drawing and observed that 'he could match it in Sussex today'. This desire to belittle the great difference between the appearance of fossil man and modern man is not an unusual feature of the period. Indeed W. L. Duckworth once exuberantly exclaimed that if Neanderthal man entered a bar in modern dress the majority would not notice him. One marvels at the sort of person Duckworth drank with.

A better known portrait by Cooke is of the discoverers and those connected with Piltdown. Dramatically lit and seated in the centre of the group at a table littered with skulls is Keith. Standing to his left are Dawson and Woodward; to his right, Smith and Barlow. The others in the group are Lankester, Pycraft and Underwood.

Nature[1] commented that the likenesses were excellent and the composition of the group pleasing, but failed to detect a flaw. An outstanding absentee was Teilhard de Chardin. At the time of the painting he was a private soldier of France under heavy bombardment at Ypres on the Western Front.

As was the custom, Dawson's obituary was read by the president of the Geological Society and published in its quarterly journal[2]. In the circumstances it is curiously short, certainly not fulsome. J. Lewis Abbot fared far better later. Dawson had been a 'resident and contributing' member of the society for thirty years. He had given at least one financial donation to the society. The society had been preferred to others before which to announce his sensational find, the most important discovery of fossil man in Britain, indeed as far as the British were concerned, in the world. The Royal Society would have been overjoyed to have been thus favoured. Possibly the lawyer was unfortunate in his president. Alfred Harker was a 'pure' geologist, his particular interest being igneous rock and movement of the earth's crust, and he may not have cared a fig for fossil man.

The brief obituary mentioned Dawson's work in the Wealden formation and the valuable collection of reptilia deposited at the British Museum, that he was widely known in connection with his discovery of the Piltdown skull, that he had died at Lewes after a protracted illness, and that he had been a Fellow since 1885. Dawson fared much better in *Nature*[3] with a longer notice which listed all his contributions adding that 'his comparatively early death is a distinct loss to science'.

[1] 13 March, 1915.
[2] 73, p. vii.
[3] 17 August, 1916.

Woodward waited until 17 February, 1917, two years after the event, to announce sensationally that his late friend had in fact discovered a second Piltdown man. The delay is strange and indeed unkind if the modern view that Dawson's lust for glory was the reason for the forgery is correct. Nothing would have pleased the lawyer more than to pass away to the sound of acclaim.

That Woodward was secretive is beyond doubt. Keith frankly admitted that no small part of his hostility to Woodward's reconstruction of the Piltdown skull had stemmed from a resentment that the exact nature of the first discovery had been kept from him until a bare fortnight before the Geological Society meeting in 1912. He could not quite understand why Dawson had taken the fragments to the British Museum instead of, in his opinion, more correctly to the Royal College of Surgeons.[1]

In his paper on Piltdown Man II[2] Woodward said that in the joint paper of 1913 Dawson had shown that the characteristic Piltdown brown flints could be traced in the ploughed fields of the district. One large field, about two miles from Piltdown, had especially attracted Dawson's attention. Both he and Dawson had examined this field several times during the spring and autumn of 1914 without success. But during the winter the farmworkers had raked the stones from the field and piled them in heaps, making the task easier. Woodward stated:

'Early in 1915 he [Dawson] was so fortunate to find here two well-fossilized pieces of human skull and a molar tooth, which he immediately recognized as belonging to at least one more individual of *Eoanthropus dawsoni*.' Shortly afterwards in the same ground, continued Woodward, 'a friend' found part of a lower molar of a species of fossil rhinoceros, as highly mineralized as the Piltdown specimen.

In this casual way did Woodward announce the second search, the discovery of the second Piltdown Man and the participation of an unnamed friend at the new site. The effect was tremendous. Most of the doubters of Piltdown I went over to the believers. The new human molar and skull fragments proved beyond doubt the correct association of skull and jaw at Piltdown. No coincidence of nature could have brought the bones of a man and an ape together at two separate sites.

[1] *An Autobiography*, pp. 324–5, 1950.
[2] *Q.J.G.S.* lxxiii part i. 1917.

Woodward's view was the correct one and David Waterston and Gerrit Miller were wrong.

After Dawson's death Woodward continued his search at Piltdown alone. In 1917 *Nature*[1] noted that :

> During the past season Dr Smith Woodward has spent six weeks, partly in association with Professor Grafton Elliot Smith and Major C. Ashburnham, exploring the Piltdown gravel. Although a large amount of undisturbed material was sifted and carefully examined round the periphery of the pit in which the original discovery of *Eoanthropus* was made, nothing was found but one unimportant fragment of the tibia of a deer.

Surprisingly, there was no further mention of the Piltdown II site. Woodward wrote[2] that later he opened a series of pits along the other side of the hedge in the field adjacent to the original Piltdown site. At times he was helped by Grafton Elliot Smith, Professors W. T. Gordon and Barclay Smith, and others. The searchers began 'close to the spot where the skull was found, and worked in both directions from this place'. The work was slow because of the overlying loam being deeper here and the efforts 'were all in vain'. He mentioned that in later years (on retirement from the British Museum in 1924 Woodward went to live at Hill Place, Sussex, to be near his beloved Piltdown) the new owner of Barkham Manor, D. Kerr, dug some of the gravel at a spot near the farmyard, allowing him to watch the labourers. Only a 'pot-boiler' was recovered. As Woodward commented picturesquely, 'the search was now outside the eddy which brought the scientific treasure to its resting place'. Nothing more was found at Piltdown.

Sure evidence that minds were changed by Piltdown II came after the end of the war. In the second edition of Marcellin Boule's book[3] the former antagonist of the one-creature theory now accepted that the skull and jaw belonged to the same individual. Not so his countryman Ernest Robert Lenoir who wrote that '. . . This curious bone enjoyed a period of great notoriety but since the American mammalologist [Gerrit] Miller in two very serious papers of 1915 and 1918

[1] 13 September.
[2] *The Earliest Englishman*, p. 13.
[3] *Les Hommes Fossiles*. 1921.

showed that Smith Woodward's fossil was only the remnant
of an anthropoid, silence has gradually descended on this find.'[1]
Lenoir must have been hard of hearing.

In the United States Professors Henry Fairfield Osborn and W.
K. Gregory left Gerrit Miller to his opinion of duality. Osborn,
according to his own account,[2] was converted on Sunday, 24
July, 1921. Possibly he had been placed in the right frame of
mind by a visit to Westminster Abbey. He described how on
that day 'Smith Woodward produced from an old fire-proof
safe these few precious fragments of one of the original Britons
... preserved in this manner from the bombs thrown by
German aviators.' Osborn was reminded of the opening words
of a prayer of college days by his professor of logic at Prince-
ton : 'Paradoxical as it may appear O Lord, it is nevertheless
true . . .' He explained the relevance by adding:

> We have to be reminded over and over again that nature is
> full of paradoxes and that the order of the Universe is not
> the human order; that we should expect the unexpected and
> prepare to discover new paradoxes.

Gerrit Miller watched his support dwindle. He ironically
contrasted this conversion on sight of the holy relics with the
effect on Professor Ales Hrdlička. Hrdlička said[3] that thanks
to the courtesy of Woodward he was able to submit the original
lower jaw to a detailed examination. He found there was 'a
feeling of strong incongruity' and that to 'connect the shapely
wholly normal Piltdown jaw with the gross, heavy Piltdown
skull into the same individual seems very difficult'. He pre-
empted scientific opinion by thirty years when he also said of
the Piltdown II discovery that :

> The additional molar tooth of the Piltdown remains is in
> every respect so much like the first molar of the Piltdown
> jaw that its procedure from the same jaw seems certain, and
> it would seem probable that the account of it being dis-
> covered at a considerable distance away might be mistaken.
> The tooth agrees with the jaw perfectly, not only in dimen-
> sions and every morphological character, but also in degree

[1] *Quid de l'homme?* p. 77. Paris, 1934.
[2] *Natural History*, 21, pp. 581–582, 590. February, 1922.
[3] *Am. Journ. of Phys. Anthrop.* 5: pp. 337–347. December, 1922.

and kind of wear. A duplication of all this in two distinct individuals would be almost impossible.

Miller commented[1] that Hrdlička's suggestion that there had been a mistake met with no response. Miller too wondered whether some misunderstanding had arisen from the sudden death of Dawson. He wrote :

In thinking about it we must remember that Dawson personally described the circumstances of both the earlier finds [skull and jaw] but the last set of discoveries was announced after his death and unaccompanied by direct word from him.

Hrdlička found it impossible to believe that the skull and jaw had been supplied by the same creature. It is possible that his scepticism sprang from recent experience. Searching amongst the National Museum collection in 1913 he had encountered two human skulls discovered in 1857, both of supposed vast antiquity. The skulls, encrusted with lime stalagmite containing charcoal and shells, were attributed to a Pliocene deposit in Calavaras County, California. But after removing the incrustation Hrdlička found that the skulls were entirely modern, almost certainly North American Indian. Shortly afterwards he encountered a report of a third skull discovered in 1856 by a goldminer named Mattison at Table Mountain, Calavaras County, California. J. D. Whitney, State Geologist of California, had removed the incrustation and sent the skull to Harvard where this too was found to be typical of the North American Indian. Hrdlička quite rightly suspected all three skulls were a hoax at the expense of the goldminer Mattison.

Arthur Keith remarked of this discovery[2] that it 'made about as much sense as finding an aeroplane in a church crypt that had been bricked up since Elizabethan times'. In 1919 Hrdlička went further. Discussing the finds of supposed fossil man in North and South America[3] he discounted all of them completely as the remains of American Indians and intentional burials. He added the useful warning :

[1] *Smithsonian Report for 1928*. Washington, 1929.
[2] *Antiquity of Man*, Vol. 2: xxiv.
[3] *Bureau of American Ethnology, Bulletin 66*.

... those in whose work credulity and fancy have no part and who possess sufficiently hard-earned experience in these matters, can be convinced of geologically ancient man in America only by facts that will make all conscientious doubt on the subject impossible. As chances of peculiar associations of human bones and artefacts are infinite therefore anthropology must be called on again and again to pass judgement on claims of the antiquity of such objects. But burden of proof lies with those who urge such claims, they must show clear, conclusive evidence. Our colleagues in collateral branches of science will be sincerely thanked for every genuine help they can give anthropology but they should not clog our hands.

Chapter 13

PILTDOWN MAN DID not entirely absorb Charles Dawson or monopolize the time of the professionals Woodward, Keith and Smith. Each continued to pursue his line of interest, indeed it might be profitably speculated that the Piltdown discoveries were used as a cart in which to push the individual's theories.

Woodward, when not at the British Museum, was either on some scientific project overseas or in attendance at the Geological Society as contributor, officer or president. The Proceedings of the Society show his diversity of output: *On Mammal Teeth* (with Dawson and Teilhard de Chardin) (1912); *Fish Remains of the Upper Devonian* (1913); *On an Engraving of a Horse on a Bone from Sherborne School* and *On the Lower Jaw of Dryopithecus* (1914); *Presidential Address on Fossil Fishes* (1915); and *On an Archaeopteryx* (1918).

Woodward had a further surprise for the Society in 1915 which dramatically supported the find at Piltdown. He showed his audience lantern slides of a reconstruction of a human skull brought to the notice of the British Association meeting at Sydney, Australia, in 1914. According to Woodward the skull had been recovered from a river deposit on a sheep station at Talgai, Queensland, together with the remains of large extinct Pleistocene marsupials. The skull was 'typically human' and 'of primitive Australian type' but the strangest feature was its large canine teeth which interlocked, like those of an ape, and precisely like those of Piltdown man. The lantern slides had been loaned by Grafton Elliot Smith who had visited his homeland.

This was not the first British appearance of the Talgai skull. In February of that year (1915) Smith had shown the slides to the Manchester Literary and Philosophical Society, asserting that the important discovery proved that man had reached Australia when the great fossil marsupials were still living. In *Nature*[1] Smith wrote that the fossil man was of sufficient antiquity to be placed in the last ice epoch of the northern hemi-

[1] 196, 1915.

sphere, commenting: 'The presence of the skull might seem to explain how Australia, with its marsupials, had invaders, like the dingo' which 'had no more right here than the Germans had in Belgium'. The skull, he said, 'was worth its weight in gold'.

In 1917 the Australian Professor Arthur Smith of Sydney University, one of the original describers at the Association meeting[1], and elder brother of Grafton Elliot Smith, increased the size of the teeth. He said they were the largest so far discovered. He mentioned that the skull was more primitive than any hitherto described except Piltdown in the 'great squareness and enormous size of the palate and teeth'. The fact that the brain-cage had already reached the stage of the modern aborigine was, he said, further confirmation of the view that the brain had first acquired human status, the facial features coming afterwards.

Another describer of the Talgai skull had been Charles Dawson[2] who was in no doubt that the skull bore a close resemblance to Piltdown man. He said that:

A curious and somewhat swift confirmation has occurred with respect to this subject of interlocking canines from an an unexpected source ... Numerous skulls had been unearthed from various parts all over the colony and forwarded to [visiting British Association] scientists for examination. One from Darling Downs, Eastern Australia had cranial features typically those of the Australian aboriginal, but the upper canine tooth was very large and prominent and bearing traces in its wear that it must have interlocked with its lower canine tooth.

Dawson went on to explain that the lower jaw was missing but added the surprising details that Grafton Elliot Smith had informed him that the place nearest to where the skull was found was 'by curious coincidence called Pilton, so to avoid confusion it was decided to call it the Darling Downs skull.'

The confirmation of the Talgai skull was not only 'curious' and 'somewhat swift'; it was also timely. If such a fossil man had inhabited Australia in the Pleistocene then considerable support was lent to the Piltdown example. There is a curious lack

[1] *Proc. Royal Soc. of Queensland.* 4 October, 1917.
[2] *Proceedings of Hastings and Sussex Natural History Society.* 1915.

of emphasis on the real facts surrounding the Australian Pilt-down man. Nobody but Dawson mentioned that the lower jaw was missing in the Talgai specimen and so as supporting evidence it was not so impressive as it at first seemed. Moreover, Arthur Smith innocently announced in *Nature*[1] that the Talgai skull had in fact been found some thirty-one years before by a stock-man on Talgai station, and so its attribution to a Pleistocene deposit must be purely conjectural and the statement that it was found in the company of Pleistocene fauna is highly suspect. A later reconstruction of the skull revealed that it had been some-what misinterpreted, the teeth being nowhere near as large as had been originally suggested. The skull was found to be well within the type-range of the modern aboriginal. The Talgai skull is possibly of fair antiquity. It might even be Upper Pleistocene, although most authorities put it much later. But one may well question whether the original interpretations were entirely free from the desire to establish firmly evidence for Piltdown man at the expense of fact.

No doubt Woodward would have been only too glad to for-sake the contentious sphere of fossil man and return to his old love—fossil fishes. The trouble over his reconstruction of Pilt-down man must have revealed to him his shortcomings as a human anatomist. But his position at the British Museum made a withdrawal impossible. As luck would have it the next fossil man to be thrust under his nose was highly puzzling.

Although the remains, discovered in Rhodesia in 1921, possessed a Neanderthal skull, the limb bones lacked the curva-ture normally associated with the European specimens. But the foramen magnum (a kind of cable entry for the nervous system in the base of the skull) was so far back that a slouching atti-tude was certain. A baffled Woodward confined his involvement to a bald description in *Nature*[2] suggesting a new species—*Homo rhodesiensis* (Rhodesian man). He then passed the buck to the bird-man W. P. Pycraft. Pycraft was as perplexed as Wood-ward—but then came inspiration. He reconstructed the hip bone to give the fossil a forward lean. Thus was born *Cyphanthropus* ('Stooping Man').

Neither description was well received. There were loud asser-tions that Rhodesian man was in fact made up of two men—

[1] 9 September, 1915.
[2] 108. 1921.

Homo sapiens (body bones) and Neanderthal man (skull). Pycraft was hotly criticized over the hip reconstruction. Woodward must have cursed the day that Rhodesian man came to South Kensington. He left Pycraft to haggle and withdrew from the controversy—only to be dragged into another.

In 1922 A. Leslie Armstrong described two harpoon heads found by him and another, a Mr Morfield, in a pit in a peat bed at Hornsea, East Yorkshire. These, he said, showed definite features belonging to the Maglemosian culture. The Maglemosians were a Mesolithic hunting people, adapted to a river and shore life in the forestation of the full Boreal times about 8,000 to 10,000 B.P. (Before the Present). Their relics have been detected over an area extending from Northern Europe to the East Baltic. These include equipment for tree-felling, carpentry, fishing and fowling, and carved bone implements. Armstrong considered the harpoons to be evidence of the Maglemosians in eastern England. He offered the harpoons to the Hull Museum only to be told by the curator, T. Sheppard, that the find was impossible. He questioned the authenticity of the implements, implying that Armstrong had made them himself. Sheppard said that no other find of the kind had been recorded even though this culture had been closely watched for. It was unbelievable that the harpoons could have remained so sharp if they had weathered at least 7,000 years of geological and climatic onslaught.

Also there was, said Sheppard, a discrepancy in the account of the find. Morfield, the owner and finder of one harpoon, had said that he found his specimen at a depth of fourteen feet. Allowing for natural erosion of the bed since the time they were said to have been buried of, say, ten feet, this made the depth of the peat in which the harpoons were said to have been discovered to be some twenty-four feet. There was no peat bed on the coast of Yorkshire of even a quarter of this thickness.

In reply Armstrong had said his harpoon was not in fact found in a peat bed but in boulder clay at the base of the peat. But Sheppard found his explanation highly unsatisfactory.

A. C. Haddon, Miles Burkitt and J. E. Marr, all of Cambridge University, had examined the Hornsea harpoons, comparing them with four authenticated examples from Kunda, Estonia. In type, mineralized condition, even workmanship of the harpoon barbs, they were identical. Sheppard would not have this, and the matter was referred to the Royal Anthropological Institute which formed a committee which included Woodward to look further into the matter.

Armstrong and Sheppard were called before the committee and questioned 'minutely' on the harpoons. Morfield had recently died. The committee reported that in general 'there was no evidence against their genuineness'. There was, however, one curious feature, the workmanship on the harpoon barbs suggested that they were the work of one individual though they were found some four miles apart. One wonders whether the bogus flints of Moulin Quignon came to mind for the committee added that there were no Maglemosian harpoons in the British museums from which they could have been copied. The committee said that Sheppard appeared to have strong grounds for doubting the authenticity of the specimens but 'the evidence on which his [Sheppard's] judgement was based was no longer available'.

With this intriguing innuendo the report ended. But the finds are now accepted as evidence that the Maglemosians lived on the Yorkshire coast. Miss D. A. E. Garrod wrote to *Man*[1] that she had been informed by Abbé H. Breuil that similar harpoons had recently been found at Béthune, Tuberguy, Pas de Calais and La Heine in north-western France and at Ninone, Belgium. Such a find in eastern England, she said, was therefore likely.

Grafton Elliot Smith had enlivened the British Association meeting in 1912 with his reading of the paper on the single origin of the megaliths of Egypt and Britain. He had neglected no opportunity to sound the migrational drum ever since.

Smith lectured the British Association in 1917 on the matter. He said that man's mental and moral attitudes were largely determined not only by primitive instincts which he shared with his simian ancestors but by the conscious and unconscious influence of the tradition amidst which he had grown up. At no stage in his career had he acquired the highly complex and specialized instincts which, for example, impelled him, unprompted, to build megalithic monuments, or invent the story of the Deluge, independently of others doing the same arbitrary things. Smith urged that these facts seemed to emphasize how confusing was the word 'age' and they revealed 'how

[1] 24, p. 48.

devoid of foundation was the mis-named evolutionary theory that claimed that all phases of culture were just natural stages through which every people has passed in virtue of the operation of the blind forces of an arbitrary and inevitable process of evolution'.

At the British Association the following year[1] he regarded the changes from one flint culture to the next as definite breaks in continuity, the Aurignacian, Solutrean, and Magdalenian cultures, for example, representing successive waves of immigration by representatives of *Homo sapiens.*

He took the view that the idea of domesticating animals spread in this way from one source. Smith considered that the primeval source of humanity was North America.

In an essay[2] he traced the primates from an origin in America across the Eocene land-bridges, eastward to Europe and Africa and with somewhat less certainty westward to Asia. Each step towards modern man, he said, must have had a single local origin. Later, when psychological factors came into play, there may have been a transmission of culture with a minimum transmission of race, only those features being accepted for which the recipients were, in a sense, already prepared. As there was no sign that evolution had produced in different areas indentical forms by different routes, so there was no reason to suppose that cultures could have arisen as spontaneous, sporadic creations of the human intellect independently and simultaneously in different parts of the world. He added that as the frontal region of the brain was the last to reach full development in the child, so the precursors of present-day man were also deficient in this region.

Smith's main contribution to the war effort was an investigation into the causes and treatment of shell-shock. Keith made strident statements on science in war.

Keith had found out about the Gibraltar skull affair for he wrote to the editor of *Nature* in 1914,[3] on the subject 'Soldiers as Anthropologists', that a certain Major Collins, whilst engaged in trenching operations in the Boer War, had collected enough material for a paper on the prehistoric stone implements of South Africa; that this soldier's interest in anthropology did not interfere with his duties was evident for he had won the

[1] *Proc. B.A.* vii. 1918.
[2] *The Evolution of Man.* Oxford, 1918.
[3] 10 December.

D.S.O. Such a letter was pointless except as a direct warning to the incumbent at the War Office that Science would not tolerate a repetition of the situation which had led to Broome's expulsion from the army because of his interest in prehistory. No doubt all this was lost on Earl Kitchener of Khartoum who was involved in matters of greater concern than fossicking soldiery. He did not subscribe to the journal; his one hobby was the collection of china. He had once, however, received a sharp note from Queen Victoria for permitting his soldiers to play football with the skull of the Mahdi.

At the British Scientific Products Exhibition, London, in 1918, Keith pointed out that physicists and laboratory workers were of the greatest value in war, rather than medical men in hospitals, since they discovered scientific instruments, iodine for dressing wounds, X-ray, and so on. He remarked that it used to be said that wars were won on the playing fields of Eton, but in future they would be won in the country's laboratories. This platitude was no doubt highly acceptable to the manufacturers of scientific equipment but it could be faulted on humanitarian grounds as he was told in no uncertain terms by the Red Cross. It is as a writer and writer on writers that Arthur Keith was known. As the country's foremost anatomist with a special inclination towards anthropology he was in a good position to review articles written by human palaeontologists. He had no need, as Huxley had said of scientific reviewers, to imitate the Ethiopians and 'cut steaks from the ox that carries them'.

As officer and one-time president of the Royal Anthropological Institute, Keith had the run of that body's publication *Man*. His lengthy reviews of scientific works must have made their authors grind their teeth. By way of footnotes he demolished any complaints. Of Fred G. Wright's *The Origin and Antiquity of Man*[1] he remarked that there was little that threw light on this 'origin', and that the writer refused to accept what had happened in the past as a clue to what happened in the present. The most outstanding example of this was his opinion that woman was the result of direct creation. Keith said that Wright seemed to have as much faith in miracles as he did in science.

The following year, however, Keith published the first edition of his *The Antiquity of Man* but Wright, on being given the chance of getting his own back, seems to have been too aware of Keith's authority and his attacks are qualified with flattery.

[1] *Man*, 13:58, p. 116.

Wright urged that Keith ought to have been more cautious than to apply dates obtained from the examination of human skulls to the reconstruction of the Piltdown jaw which the reviewer thought was that of an animal. He said that Keith rightly admitted the possibility that the cranium and the jaw could have belonged to different individuals, then he 'left the stable ground of biological experience for that treacherous country in which reign the co-efficients of chance and argued well and ingeniously for the mandible belonging to the cranium'. He said his reconstruction of the Piltdown cranium was nearer the mark than 'the first ill-fated construction [Woodward's]'.

Keith neglected to reply. He may have felt that to do so in the circumstances was improper. In any case the review brought a letter from Grafton Elliot Smith who did not at all care for the reference to the first construction. In a highly technical reply he pointed out that 'with all its admitted faults' it was a closer approximation than any of the reconstructions for which Keith had been responsible. Smith concluded that 'this was a fact, the truth of which any anatomist who carefully examines the specimens and the whole literature of the dispute can convince himself'.

The next anthropologist to feel the Keithian ruler was Professor Wood-Jones, a professional colleague of Smith at Manchester. Wood-Jones theorized that man could be the ancestor of the anthropoid ape.[1] The orthodox view held that the common ancestor of man and ape was the small tree-dwelling *tarsius*. Not a few authorities at this time had begun to question this and reason that man, because of his refinement, had branched out from the main stem of evolution first, that the branching of the *tarsius* had come later, hence the more primitive ape. In complete contradiction to man's usual lack of humility in these matters it was also held by some authorities that as the ape was highly specialized for arboreal life he was the progressive phylum. Man, the ground-ape, they argued, was non-progressive, even degenerate.

Commenting on the Wood-Jones hypothesis, Keith congratulated the author on clearing away minor evolutionary difficulties by substituting major ones.[2] He said that there could be no progress in anatomy, any more than in cultural anthropology,

[1] *The Problem of Man's Ancestry*. London, 1918.
[2] *Nature*, 101. 1918.

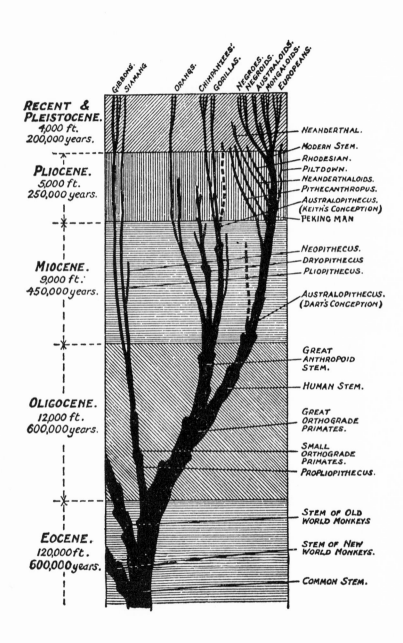

GIBBONS. SIAMANG. ORANGS. CHIMPANZEES. GORILLAS. NEGROES. NEGROIDS. AUSTRALOIDS. MONGALOIDS. EUROPEANS.

RECENT &
PLEISTOCENE.
4,000 ft.
200,000 years.

PLIOCENE.
5,000 ft.
250,000 years.

MIOCENE.
9,000 ft.
450,000 years.

OLIGOCENE.
12,000 ft.
600,000 years.

EOCENE.
120,000 ft.
600,000 years.

NEANDERTHAL.
MODERN STEM.
RHODESIAN.
PILTDOWN.
NEANDERTHALOIDS.
PITHECANTHROPUS.
AUSTRALOPITHECUS.
(KEITH'S CONCEPTION)
PEKING MAN

NEOPITHECUS.
DRYOPITHECUS.
PLIOPITHECUS.

AUSTRALOPITHECUS.
(DART'S CONCEPTION)

GREAT
ANTHROPOID
STEM.

HUMAN STEM.

GREAT
ORTHOGRADE
PRIMATES.

SMALL
ORTHOGRADE
PRIMATES.
PROPLIOPITHECUS.

STEM OF OLD
WORLD MONKEYS

STEM OF NEW
WORLD MONKEYS.

COMMON STEM.

unless it was presumed until proved to be contrary that similarity and identity of custom presuppose a common origin.

Keith did, however, pick a formidable enemy in W. J. Sollas,
professor of geology and palaeontology at Oxford University.
This enmity was of long standing. Keith constantly railed
against certain geologists who, he said, were completely un-
interested in helping the anatomist to supply dates for
human fossils. The leader of this faction, thought Keith, was
Sollas.

Sollas argued[1] that Europe had once been inhabited by Eskimos and that this race had migrated north in the wake of the
retreating ice of the last glaciation. He based his theory on a
skull found at Chancelade which he considered displayed Eskimo
features to a marked degree, particularly in its broad cheekbones. Keith said that he had seen the skull in question and
although it possessed a few superficial resemblances to the Eskimo
'it was as European in its essential characters as those of the
people of England and France today'. Keith concluded that he
feared 'Professor Sollas' most cherished and most fascinating
theories may have to be scrapped before another edition is
called for, which, if truth is to be served and deserts rewarded,
should be soon'.

Sollas did not suffer this attack in silence.[2] He could cite no
better authority on the subject than the Professor Abbé H.
Breuil 'who of all anatomists was best competent to speak on

[1] *Ancient Hunters and their Modern Representatives,* 3rd Edition.
London, 1924.
[2] *Man,* 14, 1924, p. 189.

Sir Arthur Keith's placement of Piltdown man in 1931. He is
shown as a branch which left the main stem of evolution in
the Pliocene. Dart's Australopithecus was an anthropoid and a
non-starter.

Another interesting point is that the Keithian 'tree' shows that
he considers that negroes left the main stem of evolution in rather
the same way as the other variants of the human species. Note
the alarming discrepancy in the length of the geological periods.

(From *New Discoveries Relating to the Antiquity of Man.*
London, 1931.)

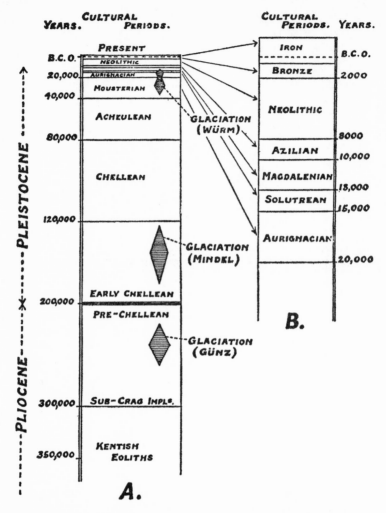

Sir Arthur Keith's view of the dates of flint cultures A. B shows an amplification of scale A. The scales show highly erroneous placement of the great glaciations and grossly underestimated durations for the Pleistocene and Pliocene. The Riss glaciation is undetected. Keith continually railed at geologists, particularly Professor W. J. Sollas, for their lack of enterprise in dating geological deposits.

(*New Discoveries Relating to the Antiquity of Man.* London, 1931.)

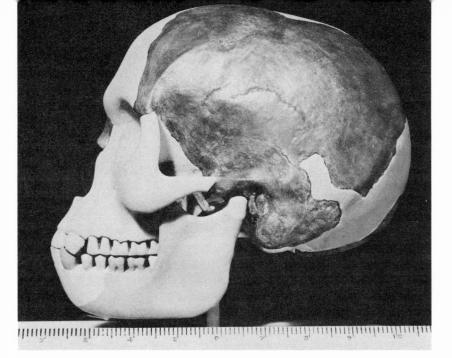

'Piltdown man' (*Eoanthropus dawsoni*). The dark portions were bones found at Piltdown, Sussex. The white portions are of plaster and were contributed by the British Museum of Natural History, South Kensington, London.

A comparison of skulls in descending order of refinement from front to back: Modern man (Caucasian); Neanderthal Man (Generalised); Peking Man (adult); Gorilla.

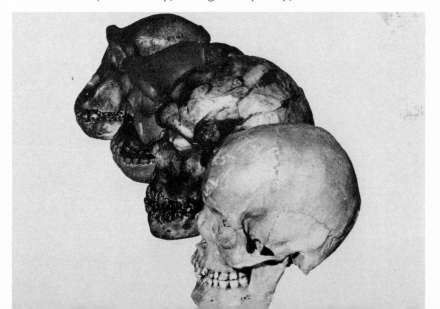

The Piltdown Men: (*Left to right*) *Front Row*: W. P. Pycraft, Arthur Keith, A. S. Underwood, Ray Lankester.

Back Row: F. O. Barlow, Grafton Elliot Smith, Charles Dawson and Arthur Smith Woodward. John Cooke, R.A., rather tactlessly shows Keith measuring the skull of 'Piltdown man' under the direction of Smith. Teilhard de Chardin is absent on war service.

the subject'. Breuil had written : 'Dr Testut has clearly shown
the resemblance of the Chancelade skeleton to those of the
Eastern Eskimos . . . there is an array of facts in favour of the
existence of an actual relationship, which is so admirably confirmed by the Chancelade skeleton'. By quoting another who
was quoting another, Sollas considered the matter satisfactorily
settled. He concluded : 'I think I have now dealt with the
matter of the review; on its manner I cannot comment, for *le
style c'est l'homme.*'

Sollas reiterated his view, to spite Keith further, in an article
on the subject in *Man.*[1] He wrote that the ancestors of some at
least of the Magdalenian people were to be found among the
existing races of the arctic region, particularly those with large
brains and Mongoloid features. Testut, he said, had unexpec-
tedly arrived at this conclusion in 1889 when he said that the
skulls that most resembled those of Chancelade were those of
the Eskimos. The only doubter of this theory was Sir Arthur
Keith (knighted in 1921 for services to science), who had written in his *Antiquity* that Chancelade man was of a true European racial kind. This was nonsense.

The Chancelade skull, wrote Sollas, represented the European
during the closing phases of 'the Ice Age' and was marked by
the Magdalenian flint culture. Keith had also stated that the
Chancelade nose was long and straight but had added that the
bridge was broken away so that its degree of prominence was
unknown. But Testut had said that when found the Chancelade
nose bone was complete but this had been broken later when
the cast was being made and had been lost. It was very narrow
and strongly bent to the left side and inflected so as to curve
forwards and upwards until it approached the horizontal. This,
said Sollas, fits the description of most Eskimos. Keith could not
avoid the admission that the skull face was very wide and on
this feature Chancelade man had the 'misfortune' to be assigned
by him to a Mongoloid race. The question, however, said Sollas,
was not whether the Chancelade skull was Mongoloid or
not but whether Chancelade man was an Eskimo. Keith
considered that the angle of the jaw was inconsistent with his
being an Eskimo but any assessment of this was unreliable for
the owner of the Chancelade mandible must have received a
terrible blow on the head during his life which fractured the
skull. Testut had cited the case of a similar blow experienced

[1] 25:90, p. 157.

by a coachman whose horses had run away with him. The coachman had succumbed to his injury but Chancelade man, 'without medical assistance', had survived because of his splendid vitality.

Keith replied[1] that he welcomed the views of such a distinguished professor of geology on anatomical matters. He considered that brain size was not relevant to the issue, as people living in France before Chancelade were renowned for the size of the brain, for example, the Cro-Magnons. In fact Chancelade had more in common with the Cro-Magnons than with any known form of Eskimo. He regarded him as at one with the people of 'the so-called white races'. Sollas regarded him as a Mongol, the particular race he had chosen being the Eskimo. How could the matter be settled? 'By mere stroke of the eye.' Keith said he had been familiar with this procedure for over half a century, and Sollas even longer.

> We became anthropologists [he said] as soon as we could distinguish one race from another. As boys we had no need of callipers, nor indices, nor any mathematical procedure in identifying different breeds of dogs. The same method applied when out in the world and meeting diverse races of mankind. Some racial types were less well-marked than others but fortunately the Eskimo had a most sharply characterized form of human skull ... Sollas seems to think that when a craniologist has a skull of unknown history in his hands, he sits down and measures its angles and calculates its indices and then sets out to search for a skull possessing similar angles and indices. Craniologists, I am glad to think, still have a trace of humour as well as common sense left to them; they do not stop strangers in the street to see if they are negro, Mongol or Caucasian. I do not believe that even Sollas does this ... the cast of eye is sufficient for diagnosis of making racial identification of man or skull.

Keith said that it was ungallant of Sollas to throw the entire onus of mistaking Chancelade man for an Eskimo on the late Professor Testut. He said that it must be remembered that anthropologists of Testut's time believed races and cultures spread together (this is a heavy dig at Grafton Elliot Smith). Had it not been for the similarity of the cultures no one would

[1] *Man*, 25:98, p. 186.

have seen any resemblance between the races. Keith said that in racial diagnosis the nose bones were a more reliable guide than any other. The Chancelade nose bone had broken away but its roots were still in place and such a kind had never been seen in any Eskimo. Chancelade man had a large nose of a moderate width; such dimensions not only occurred in the Eskimo but in Europeans, especially in certain parts of France. Anatole France had such a nose but he bore no resemblance to an Eskimo. But Sollas would never be convinced. If Chancelade man was not an Eskimo then the whole pyramid that he had reared came tumbling down. In such circumstances it was too much to expect him to be impartial.

Professor Karl Pearson[1] tried to mediate. He thought the difference of opinion stemmed from the fact that Chancelade man had elements of modernity lacking in existing Eskimos, but he also had certain Eskimo features not present in modern man. Keith had said that 'a cast of eye' and an intimate knowledge of skulls of the races of mankind were essential qualifications of the craniologist. Pearson agreed with this view but the results of such a doctrine would seem to be that when two craniologists disagreed the only way to measure their authority would be by counting the number of skulls each had held in their hands. 'Is there not a touch of the mediaeval schoolman in this doctrine?' he asked.

Sollas replied[2] that ever since Testut's masterly description of the Chancelade skull was published in 1889, eminent anatomists had all agreed on his close relationship to the Eskimo. From what Keith had said he was beginning to fancy his Chancelade skull must be different from the one known to Sollas.

W. E. (later Sir) Le Gros Clark, a future execrator of Piltdown man, also interceded. He said that in 1920[3] he had published the result of a study of Eskimo skulls from old graves in Greenland. He had compared the contours with those of the Chancelade skull and there was no doubt that there were remarkable resemblances but there were also obvious differences, certainly enough to preclude a conclusive answer.

But Keith dropped the matter, possibly considering that Sollas' remarks about the different skulls might be taken as a

[1] *Man*, 26:27, 1926, p. 46
[2] *Man*, 26:40, p. 168.
[3] *Roy. Anthrop. Inst. Jour.* 50. 1920.

capitulation or at least as a signal that he did not want to argue any more. This debate is an example of the kind which engaged the minds of two of the most distinguished scientists in Britain. Who was right? The present author can but quote an extract on Cro-Magnons from the authoritative *Guide to Fossil Man*[1] that:

> . . . the Chancelade remains have been likened to the skeletons of modern Eskimos. . . . Whether or not these are valid distinctions it is apparent that the European Upper Palaeolithic men exhibited a wide range of variation.

Jacquetta Hawkes, writing in 1963[2] of the culture of south-western France during the Upper Palaeolithic, said Chancelade man could be singled out as one of those responsible for:

> . . . creating the last and most brilliant Upper Palaeolithic culture of south-western France . . . whose skull is universally admitted to have Eskimoid affinities in its vertical sides, pointed keel, and somewhat broad cheek bones. Although the old view that this race withdrew northwards in the wake of the ice after the last glaciation to form the ancestors of the modern Eskimo has now been much blown upon, it may have an element of truth in it. There seems no reason to deny that Chancelade man may have been involved in both the genetical and cultural inheritance of the Eskimo peoples.

A footnote is added:

> The majority of anthropologists today reject the view that an affinity exists between the Chancelade type and the Eskimo . . . Nor is there any longer much support for the argument in favour of a connection between the late Upper Palaeolithic Magdalenian culture in western and central Europe and the Eskimo. All the available ethnographic and archaeological data testify to ties linking the forebears of the Eskimo with the Asiatic and American continents, not with western Europe.

Keith continued his disruptive reviews but he devoted more

[1] Michael H. Day. Cassell 1965.
[2] *Prehistory and the Beginnings of Civilization, Vol I*. George Allen & Unwin.

time to his *Antiquity*, which was published in 1925 as a two-volume work; a revised edition came out in 1929, and another, as *New Discoveries*, in 1931. It says much for the skill of Keith that he was able to write on his highly technical subject in a way that could be understood by the educated public without recourse to the 'Up jumped Baby Bunny' style thought fit for laymen by his professional colleagues. Another example of this rare talent was Sir Ray Lankester, and to a certain extent Grafton Elliot Smith, although the latter was also prone to unnecessary simplification.

Keith did, however, take time off to stamp on a claim for a South American anthropoid ape. The New World is completely devoid of this type of ape. The claim was made by a Dr Montandon on ten-year-old evidence. Writing in 1929[1] Keith said that he had heard about this so-called discovery. A Dr de Loys and a party were camping in jungle west of Venezuela when noises caused them to arm themselves with branches. Two animals, thought at first to be bears, 'behaving shamelessly by defecating into their hands as they advanced, had halted and threw their excrement at the invaders'. The company shot one, a female; the other, presumably a male, had made off. Keith wrote that de Loys had made no notes of the characteristics of the animals at the time and his recollections were somewhat vague. He simply mentioned that the animal had no tail. There was a photograph of the deceased animal seated on a box of unknown size which gave no indication of scale. The identification was further complicated by the abandonment of the animal's skin and skull when the party encountered hardship. Nonetheless Dr Montandon, ten years afterwards, was asserting that a new race of anthropoids had been discovered in South America and had named it *Ameranthropoides loysi*. Keith said the object on the box looked like a spider monkey. He concluded :

> Thus we fear that the latest discovery which ascribes to South America a higher or lower kind of anthropoid ape, is doomed to go the way of so many others which have been announced from that continent. Since the beginning of this century there have been many alleged discoveries of such human ancestors but all have been proved to be other than this.

Keith had another interest which was as dear to his heart

[1] *Man,* 29, p. 135.

as his reviews or his writing. As president of the British Association in 1927 he had appealed for the preservation of Downe
House, Kent, nineteen miles from London, where Charles Darwin had lived for forty years and had written his *Origin* and
Descent. He had died there in 1882.

Keith was successful. The property was purchased by Sir
Buckstone Brown, F.R.C.S., who transferred it to the Association
with endowment funds for its maintenance and preservation
'for all time'. Later Brown endowed a building on an estate near
Downe for use as an experimental surgical unit. On retirement
Keith went to live there as Master of Buckstone Brown Institute
where he continued surgical research. In his appeal Keith told
the British Association of Downe's additional claim to fame. He
said : 'We know now that as Darwin sat in his study at
Downe, there lay hidden at Piltdown, in Sussex, not thirty miles
distant . . .'

D R K. A. H E B E R E R was an example of that type of anthropologist which Arthur Keith said did not exist. He actually measured human skulls. In 1902 he had embarked on the task of measuring the skulls of live citizens of Peking, North China. He published a monograph on his findings.

Heberer also searched Chinese pharmacists' shops for fossil bones. Known locally as 'Dragon's bones' the fossils, when powdered and swallowed, were said to have remarkable medical qualities beside which today's penicillin seems pallid.

The results of Heberer's search were sent to Professor Max Schlosser at the University of Munich. He reported in 1903 that amongst the collection was the upper left molar of either a man or an anthropoid ape of a hitherto unknown genus. Schlosser recommended that anyone who might enjoy the privilege of carrying out palaeontological investigations in China should search for the remains of a new fossil ape or a Tertiary or Early Pleistocene human.

This advice seems to have been the starting point of what for the next twenty-four years became the preoccupation of any palaeontologist who visited the country. But it was an unrewarded task. The 'Dragon's bone' collectors, sensing competition, were non-committal about where in China they had been obtained. The pharmacists freely sold the fossils at a high price but said that as far as they were concerned the bones came from Heaven.

In 1916, however, the Chinese Department of Commerce invited Dr J. Gunnar Andersson, a former director of the Swedish Geological Survey, to administer similar work in China. The aim was an estimate of the country's mineral resources. Feeling that such a vast undertaking would deter the most zealous and ambitious geologist, the Chinese government added the inducement that part of the general activities of the survey would include the establishment of a museum of geology and palaeontology. Although the local authorities might have been aware of their country's palaeontological promise they must have been quite unprepared for its furtherance at the cost of the country's economic expansion.

The survey had not been in progress for more than a few months when Andersson decided that the programme could not be carried out without devoting some attention to the geology of the Western Hills, about twenty-five miles to the south-west of Peking. The Chinese were mystified by this attention. Here were the quarries of the 'white jade' and limestone, and the coalfields. The geology of this sector was well-known. But it was no coincidence that another feature of the Western Hills was a red clay, the soil which had been found in the roots of the molar described by Schlosser.

Andersson began his hunt at Chikushan, some thirty miles south of Peking, but with no immediate success. Two years later, it is said as the result of overhearing by chance workmen's conversation which informed him that 'Dragon's bones' could be found in plenty nearby, Andersson transferred operations to a limestone cliff near Choukoutien village. Within a short time he had found pieces of quartz quite foreign to the area. He is reported as saying (to whom is not known): 'This is primitive man'. Grafton Elliot Smith[1] reported the words in a less dramatic and more explicit form as: 'In this spot lies primitive man. All we have to do is find him.' The Nanking government thought otherwise and intimated that the survey was suffering in the interests of foreign palaeontology. Anderson was told to confine his attention to geology. An appeal was made to Stockholm and the industrialist Ivar Kreuger provided an endowment which enabled the importation of a young German geologist, Dr Otto Zdansky, to continue the search in place of Andersson.

The archaeology of parts of China was by no means a closed book particularly to France. Père Emil Licent of the Society of Jesus had been at Tientsin since 1914 and was a regular correspondent of Marcellin Boule and the omnipresent Abbé Breuil. The fossils he sent Boule were in the main turned over for examination to Père Teilhard de Chardin.

In 1923 Teilhard de Chardin arrived in China. For two years past Emil Licent had been pressing him to come to the country to help with his collection and take part in an expedition to the interior. The priest disembarked at Shanghai and proceeded to Tientsin by train; two soldiers to each coach to ward off attacks by bandits.

[1] *The Search for Man's Ancestors.* London, 1931.

The visitor wore several hats. His visit was sponsored by the Paris *Musée de Science*, which had the backing of the *Ministère de l'Instruction Publique*, the *Académie des Sciences* and the *Institut de paléontologie humaine*. By prior agreement any important discoveries were to go to the *Musée* in Paris, and duplicates to Licent's *Musée Hoang-ho-Pai-ho*, a wing of the *École des Hautes Études* in Tientsin.

Teilhard de Chardin was unimpressed by his archaeological colleague and fellow Jesuit Licent, who was touchy and quick-tempered and whose palaeontological work suffered from the distraction of a vast and chaotic collection of butterflies and moths. It is a mystery how the relationship of this ill-matched pair survived a 900-mile journey to Kansu province, which marches with Tibet to the west and Mongolia to the north. In addition to the threat of bandit attacks there was a plague of some deadly fever. Teilhard de Chardin reported dead bodies at numerous villages.

It seems, however, that safe passage was guaranteed by General Ma-Fou-Sian, mandarin and war lord, various lesser mandarins providing escorts *en route* for the caravan of six carts drawn by oxen. By the return to Tientsin in September 1924, after a journey worthy of Burton or Speke, the pair had collected fifteen packing cases of animal fossils and, according to Teilhard de Chardin, found traces of the ashes of two Palaeolithic hearths. Nevertheless, it appears, that the visitor was glad to return to Paris.

By 1926 Otto Zdansky had collected a large assemblage of fossil bones at Choukoutien but as there were no reference works in China which would enable an exact identification of the remains he returned to the University of Uppsala, where he devoted the summer of that year to the task.

Mingled with faunal fragments were two molars 'of human type'. But Zdansky was cautious, writing[1] that he was convinced that the evidence of the teeth was 'wholly inadequate to venture any far reaching conclusion regarding the extremely meagre material described, and which, I think, cannot be more closely identified than *Homo sapiens*. I find I am credited in certain quarters with the discovery of "Peking Man" (*vide* the daily newspapers); my purpose here is only to make it clear that my discovery of these teeth (which are of Quaternary age) should

[1] *Bull. Geol. Surv. China* 1927, Vol. 5, Nos. 3–4.

be regarded as decidedly interesting, but not of epoch-making importance.'

But whether he liked it or not Zdansky was becoming the reluctant toast of palaeontology. On 22 October, 1926, Grafton Elliot Smith's old associate at Manchester University, Dr Davidson Black, now professor of anatomy at the Peking Union Medical College, had made a 'confidential announcement' about the find of the human teeth to a scientific congress attended by Edwin Aintree, the then secretary to the Rockefeller Foundation.

It might be thought that an open secret would be as safe in Peking as anywhere but it appears that nothing was further from the case. The scientific congress was attended by delegates from Australia, New Zealand, the United States and France, with rounds of cocktail parties, intellectual conversation and 'rose-scented wine' which reminded Teilhard de Chardin of Paris. (The priest had returned to China for the conference.)

To this was added the pomp of a visit by the Crown Prince of Sweden. Indeed there was an element of Grand Guignol. There was political chaos and no central government. Although the Chinese Nationalists were in peaceful occupation of the city, the Chinese Communists were at its outskirts. There was even an 'interventionist' Russian armoured train in Peking Station. Feints at both sides were mounted by General Ma-Fou-Sian's private horde and bandits appeared like tumblers at a circus when the excitement seemed about to flag. Despite the unsettled state of the country and the military operations which for a time threatened Peking, two native representatives of the Chinese Geological Survey, Wong Wen-hao and V. K. Ting, appeared at Choukoutien to take over operations.

On 27 October, 1927, Dr Birger Bohlin, another Swede, financed this time by the Rockefeller Foundation, found a third molar at Choukoutien. Arthur Keith adds the detail that the tooth was rushed to Peking by 'jinrikisha', a drive of some thirty-seven miles through country infested with 'soldier bandits'. It was on the strength of this discovery that Davidson Black astounded the scientific world in December by the announcement of the discovery of a new fossil man, naming him 'Peking Man' (*Sinanthropus pekinensis*).

This spectacular feat, based as it was on a single tooth, got a mixed reception. Grafton Elliot Smith commended Black for his courageous decision. Keith said it was audacious and ran the risk of egregious blunder. Boule said, however, that Black had been more or less obliged to make such a bold claim to support his previous one. Black in his description[1] seemed to have no doubts about Peking Man. He said the tooth could not be attributed to any race of known species of mankind, living or extinct. So much did it differ from other molar teeth, it represented not only a new species but a new genus. He believed the tooth belonged to a child of eight years old and that it was derived from the same jaw as the lower premolar discovered by Zdansky.

The following year Birger Bohlin, with two new arrivals at Choukoutien, C. C. Young and Pei Wen-Chung, found fragments of two jaws and braincases. In April 1929 a renewal of the Rockefeller Foundation grant enabled a section named the Cenozoic Research Laboratory to be set up; this was established in Lockhart Hall, a building formerly belonging to the London Missionary Society. Davidson Black became honorary director, C. C. Young his assistant and palaeontologist, and Pei Wen-Chung was placed in charge of field work. Teilhard de Chardin was appointed adviser and collaborator.

Teilhard de Chardin's continued presence in China with but short breaks from 1926 onwards, despite his chronic homesickness, was the result of conflict between his personal beliefs and those of his Church. In 1922 he had been invited by a fellow Jesuit, a professor of dogmatic theory, to prepare a paper indicating ways in which original sin might be represented to those unsatisfied with its official formulation. Teilhard de Chardin did no more than undertake a mental exercise by attempting an explanation of a doctrine he did not dispute. He wrote that original sin was a kind of necessary flaw in the universe.

But the paper found its way to Rome, and via Cardinal Merry de Val and the General of Jesuits, Father Ledochowski, back to the priest's Provincial at Lyons. The memory of the Modernist witch-hunt was still fresh in the mind of Père Costa de Beauregard[2] and Teilhard de Chardin was asked to promise neither to say nor to write anything against the traditional position of the Church in the matter of original sin.[3] A glimpse

[1] *Palae. Sinica,* 1927, Vol. II.

[2] Modernism was the tendency to diminish the stature of Christ. Père George Tyrell S.J., its advocate, was excommunicated and a number of books on the subject, including Henri Bergson's *L'Evolution Créatrice,* were placed on the *Index Librorum Prohibitorum.*

[3] Père Henri Lubac, S. J. *L'Obéisance du Père Teilhard de Chardin.* Paris, 1967.

of Teilhard de Chardin's dissent was contained in a letter[1] to a Jesuit friend, Père August Valensin. He wrote :

'In a kind of way I no longer have confidence in the exterior manifestations of the Church. I believe that through it the Divine influence will continue to reach me, but I no longer have much belief in the immediate and tangible nature of official directions and decisions. Some people feel happy in the visible Church, but for my own part I think I shall be happy to die in order to be free of it—and to find our Lord outside of it.'

There is an account of Teilhard de Chardin's appearance at this time of exile. Henry de Montfried said :[2]

... his long face, forceful and finely drawn; the features emphasized by premature lines, looked as though carved out of tough wood. There was a lively twinkle in his eye; humour too, but no hint of irony; forbearing and kind.

That excellent narrator Leonard Cottrell, a historian who has done for Egyptology what the late Gavin Maxwell did for the otter, has so rightly commented[3] on the number of times archaeological searches have been rewarded just as the searcher was about to give up in despair. In 1873 Heinrich Schliemann was about to pay off his workers when he discovered at 'Homer's Troy' what he thought was the fair Helen's jewellery. Howard Carter's six-year quest in the Valley of Kings had reached the end of its last season when Tutankhamen's Tomb came to light in 1922. And it was so with Peking man.

The 1929 winter was fast approaching. W. C. Pei dismissed the labour force on 2 December. Late that afternoon he walked to the excavations at the foot of the Choukoutien escarpment and probed into the sand with his yard-stick, exposing the smooth dome of a skull embedded in cave travertine. According to George Barbour[4] he loosened the block containing the skull with a hammer and chisel and 'saw at once that the top of the cranium was larger than any ape so far unearthed'. A battery of candles from the village store gave just enough light

[1] 10 January, 1926.

[2] Robert Speaight. *Teilhard de Chardin: A Biography.* London, 1967.

[3] *The Bull of Minos,* 2nd Edition. Evans, 1962.

[4] *In the Field with Teilhard de Chardin.* Herder and Herder. New York, 1965.

for a time exposure of the skull *in situ*. He carried the skull back to his room with care. He got another photograph of his prize wrapped in burlap soaked with flour paste, and balanced above three braziers so that it could dry out during the night. By dawn he was able to set out for Peking without fear of shedding fragments on the road. Pei wrapped the treasure in his soiled linen, bargained with a rickshaw puller, and set out for the city, his precious bundle between his feet, hidden by the long skirt of his Chinese scholar's gown. Pei covered the thirty-five miles safely and delivered his trophy to Davidson Black at the Peking Union Medical College well before dusk.

Of this skull Grafton Elliot Smith wrote :

There can be no doubt that just as the finding of the jaws [*sic*] in 1928 suggested the possibility of the same kinship with the Piltdown man, the skull in 1929 caused opinion to swing in the other direction, and suggested a nearer kinship with *Pithecanthropus* [Java man].

Black published his scientific description of the find in 1930 but an earlier announcement was made to the Press. *The Times'* correspondent in Peking, under the headline 'Early Man in China : Pre-Neanderthal Skull Found', wrote[1] :

At an open meeting of the Geological Society of China on 28 December the closely guarded details of the finding in North China of the skull of a man hundreds of thousands of years old were officially revealed. The discovery was claimed to be the most important of its kind. The credit for the actual discovery goes to a young Chinese geologist, Mr W. C. Pei. The skull belongs to an entirely new genus, known to science as *Sinanthropus pekinensis* and is definitely placed above Java man in brain capacity but below Neanderthal man. The skull is considered to antedate that of Neanderthal and held to be nearer the genus *Homo* than either Piltdown or Java. Although not the 'missing link' in the popular sense, the Peking man has been described here as a cousin to the dawn ancestor of man [Piltdown], and estimates of the age of the skull vary greatly. Dr [A. W.] Grabau, adviser to the China Geological Society, states that the Peking man lived at the beginning of the Quaternary,

[1] 30 December, 1929.

and gives his age as 1,000,000 years, but Père Teilhard de Chardin, president of the Geological Society of France, and also adviser to the Chinese Survey, favours an estimate of 400,000 to 500,000 years . . . [Modern estimates agree with Teilhard's.]

Arthur Keith wrote in *New Discoveries*, on the evidence of the teeth, that the owner must have been as distinctive as *Pithecanthropus erectus* and *Eoanthropus dawsoni*. In his next chapter, however, on the discovery of the skull, he amended this to say that it closely resembled *Pithecanthropus*. He left his original statement unaltered, he said, 'so that readers could see for themselves how the methods of anthropologists are fallible'.

Grafton Elliot Smith wrote that Black had hoped that by prompt publication of his find and wide circulation of manuscript reports he would avoid misunderstandings 'such as those that marred the discussion of previous fossil men but despite these precautions eminent palaeontologists in Germany [possibly Weidenreich—an expatriate] and France [Boule] are already claiming that *Sinanthropus* belongs to the genus *Pithecanthropus*. In America there is the suggestion that *Sinanthropus* is merely a Far Eastern example of Neanderthal man. Others believe the Chinese fossils are not human at all.'

An obviously angry Marcellin Boule had in fact put it more forcibly, writing that: 'Black, who had felt justified in forging the term *Sinanthropus* to designate one tooth, was naturally concerned to legitimise this creation when he had to describe a skull-cap. It is now quite evident by studying Black's table of measurements, the differences between *Pithecanthropus* and *Sinanthropus*, far from possessing generic value, are less than variations recorded within the very natural specific groups of Neanderthal. Correctly the Choukoutien fossils should be called, until there is proof to the contrary, *Pithecanthropus pekinensis*.'

Old Eugene Dubois, not seeing any resemblance at all, resented this allusion. He said that only his *Pithecanthropus* justified the name 'ape-man' and that *Sinanthropus* belonged to the Neanderthal race and was in fact a primitive type of *Homo sapiens*.

Smith wrote in 1931 that he could see an analogy, 'though it is not identical' to the Piltdown jaw. He regarded it as evidence in support of the claim that the Piltdown skull and

jaw were part of the same individual. He said that features of
the *Sinanthropus* jaw suggested the possibility that the fossil
man of China 'might be more nearly akin to the Early Pleistocene man of Piltdown rather than Java man'. The *Sinanthropus*
braincase had many features unknown to both *Eoanthropus*
and *Pithecanthropus* and threw a great deal of light on their
common ancestor. He continued :

> In studying early man's remains it is always very important
> to search for tools and implements to mark a particular
> phase of industry. It was a very significant phenomenon
> that during the last three years there was no trace of imple-
> ments.

The absence of tools, concluded Smith, was no coincidence.
Sinanthropus was at too early a stage of development to have
begun to shape stones. He added that 'it was impossible to state
whether he had perishable tools such as wood, although it was
probable with his type of brain he would have had sticks as
means of defence and of obtaining food either by digging or
killing animals'.

This statement was an amalgam of oversight and peculiar
reasoning. Smith himself had quoted Andersson's remark on
the discovery of the pieces of quartz. These certainly came into
the eolith category. If *Sinanthropus* was akin to the tool-making
Piltdown man, why was it significant that no tools had been
discovered at Choukoutien?

Now the discoveries came quickly. Under the directorship
of Pei more skulls and bones were brought to light. By 1935
the material attributed to Peking man was eight more or less
complete braincases, a dozen fragments of lower jaws, two
fragments of humeri and radius, one semi-lunar bone and four
ungual phalanges. According to the German authority Franz
Weidenreich, the discovered population of Choukoutien was
represented by the remains of ten children, two adolescents and
twelve adults, men and women. By 1939 this had risen to
thirty-eight individuals, fifteen being either children or adolescents. There were ashes, implying the use of fire, and evidence
of bone and stone tool industries.

The Abbé Breuil wrote that *Sinanthropus* must have been
able to kindle fire and must have done so frequently, he used bone
implements and he worked stone 'just as much as the palaeolithics

of the West'. In spite of the skull, he said, which closely resembled that of *Pithecanthropus*, he was not merely an ape-man but a human, with an ingenious mind capable of inventing, and hands sufficiently adroit to fashion, tools and weapons.

But Boule condemned such conclusions, writing that 'in order to give *Sinanthropus* human status the anatomists leant on the archaeologists and the archaeologists on the anatomists'. The palaeontologist, he urged, must consider the circumstances of the deposit and the unvarying nature of the *Sinanthropus* remains. How could an almost complete lack of 'long bones' be explained?

Franz Weidenreich had a sensational answer. The *Sinanthropus* skulls, he said, were brought to the cave by hunters who chiefly attacked women and children and chose heads as spoils or trophies. He proposed that these hunters were superior beings, probably the usurping *Homo sapiens*. He thought the stone tools were by no means primitive—many of their features were not present in the tools belonging to the Upper Palaeolithic discovered in France. This sophistication, however, was thought by Weidenreich to support his argument that there had been a superior race present at Choukoutien. Boule entirely agreed. He argued, remarkably, that no one could contest this theory by asking why no remains of the *Homo sapiens* oppressors had been found in the cave. Such were not necessary, said Boule, as in Western Europe there were grottoes and caves rich in Palaeolithic implements in which no *Homo sapiens* remains had been found. So the Choukoutien remains must be 'a mere hunter's prey' and *Sinanthropus* was no more than an animal exploited for food.

In the light of this reasoning it must be wondered how any implement could be attributed to any human fossil. A fractious authority could always introduce a higher cannibal which could despoil, leave his tools and then vanish without trace.

Sir Wilfrid Le Gros Clark[1], however, wrote that there was no evidence to support the assumption of this superior being and that Peking man was well able to develop the Choukoutien culture. In spite of his low average cranial capacity, some individuals found in the cave came within the normal range of *Homo sapiens*. His findings were also based on the discoveries by Dr G. H. R. von Koenigswald from 1936 to 1939 of more Java men which were so closely akin to the Chinese fossils it

[1] *Fossil Evidence for Human Evolution*. Chicago, 1955.

is now presumed that the vast differences Black saw between *Sinanthropus* and *Pithecanthropus* were due in the main to his enthusiasm for a new genus. Even the title *Pithecanthropus* has now been rejected in favour of *Homo erectus*—a mere species of the genus *Homo* to which modern man belongs.

In his discussion of the Choukoutien fossils Le Gros Clark said carefully that the modern assumptions had to be based on the plaster casts and the reports made at the time. He had good reason. After the death of Davidson Black in 1936, according to one account from silicosis caused by dust from drilling the fragments from their mineral covering, the control of the Central Cenozoic Laboratory passed to Dr Franz Weidenreich. The excavations continued into the occupation until 1941 when increased interference by a far more tangible usurper than that erroneously postulated by Boule—the Japanese—made further work at the site impossible.

By this time, however, Weidenreich had already departed for the United States with a set of plaster casts. The original fossils remained at the Peking Union Medical College. What happened next is uncertain. Evidently Wong Wen-hao decided to send the bones to Weidenreich in America and obtained the co-operation of the American, Dr Henry Houghton, director of the Medical College. The bones were crated and taken to the United States Embassy which itself was in the throes of departure from China. The crates have never been heard of since. What is certain, however, is that today the Chinese People's Republic blames the United States for the loss.

Work at the site was resumed under the Chinese Republic in 1959. On 6 July of that year a fragment of another mandible was discovered. The close of the scientific description of the jaw[1] contains the following not too subtle indictment :

As the world famous *Sinanthropus* remains uncovered before the liberation were all disappeared during World War II while in American hands at Peking this new *Sinanthropus* discovery is of especial value.

Carleton S. Coon[2] stated that all the *Sinanthropus* material was lost in an accident as a result of military action while being transferred from Peking to the S. S. *President Harrison*. W.

[1] *Vertebrata Palasiatica*. Peking, 1959, p. 169.
[2] *Origin of Races*. London, 1963.

Howells[1] supplies the further information that the fossils were given to a Colonel Ashurst who commanded the U.S. Marine detachment at the embassy. The remains left Peking by train at 5 a.m. on 5 December, 1941, and arrived at the port of Ching-wangtao two days later. The crates passed from the control of the Marines when they were interned by the Japanese.

[1] *Mankind in the Making*. London, 1960.

Chapter 15

THE SECOND DECADE of the twentieth century had be-gun with four contenders for the title of ancestor to modern man. These were Neanderthal, Java, Heidelberg and Piltdown. The problem seemed insoluble and many and bitter were the debates between those who favoured one as the direct ancestor of modern man and those who would not have him in the family at any price.

The ape-jawed Piltdown man seems to have been the favourite. His ferocious jaw was overlooked because of his noble forehead. Indeed his intellectual prowess, it was thought, saved him from annihilation. As Neanderthal man and his kind had sat in caves scowling helplessly at the glaciers, the superior intel-lect of Piltdown man had caused him to take off southwards to warmer climes. Neanderthal man and his Java cousin had perished of cold and starvation. By his survival Piltdown man had become our ancestor.

But then had come Peking man, another silent witness to the uniqueness of the Sussex fossil. The debate which ensued was in its later stages coeval with another of greater implications. Indeed it cast a shadow over *Sinanthropus*. The real missing link, so its discoverer claimed, had been found at last.

In 1922 Dr Raymond Dart had arrived in South Africa to take up the chair of anatomy in the University of Witwatersrand. Dart was a former assistant in Sydney of Grafton Elliot Smith's brother, Arthur. World War I had brought him to England in the army medical corps. After the war Dart worked under the great Grafton Elliot Smith at University College, London. Dart fully admits[1] that this was the fulfilment of a student dream. He had never forgotten the lecture on fossil men de-livered by Smith to the British Association in Sydney in 1914.

There can be no doubt that Dart was fascinated by his dis-tinguished countryman. He wrote that Smith was 'tall, ruddy-complexioned with immaculate white hair . . . the complete anti-thesis of the woolly-minded genius of fiction. Elliot Smith with

[1] *Adventures with the Missing Link.* Hamish Hamilton, 1959.

all his brilliance, in every sense, was a man of the world, a great *raconteur* and popular with his colleagues and assistants who could usually rely on him to attend and enliven their daily tea parties.'

Dart also recollects the comparatively sombre Sir Arthur Keith and the professor of anatomy at the Royal College of Surgeons remembered him. Keith recommended Dart for the Witwatersrand chair but with slight misgivings, writing in his autobiography in 1950 that he had done so with 'a certain degree of trepidation. Of his [Dart's] powers of intellect and imagination there could be no question; what rather frightened me was his flightiness, his scorn for accepted opinion, the unorthodoxy of his outlook.'

Dart stood in awe of these contemporary giants of anatomy and prehistory. He was also overshadowed by them. Not many years had elapsed before he sought escape from the Olympian aura. He found it at Witwatersrand.

Within three years of his arrival in South Africa Dart had fully justified Keith's fears. Miss Josephine Salmons, a student demonstrator in Dart's department, while on a social visit to the home of a mine-owner, E. G. Izard, was shown a skull of a fossil baboon which had been blasted out of fifty feet of limestone in a quarry at Taungs, some eighty miles north of Kimberley.

The skull was new to Dart and he asked a colleague, Dr R. B. Young, who coincidently was planning a study of the Taungs quarry, to keep an eye open for similar examples. Young returned with a box of samples amongst which Dart found a natural cast in limestone of the left side and mandible of some sort of anthropoid. Further chipping of the limestone revealed an almost complete skeletal face.

In Dart's view this was clearly no baboon, and no anthropoid, living or fossil, had ever been encountered in this area. The anthropoids were confined to forestation and jungle. But what impressed Dart most was the size of the brain suggested by the skull. Dart considered that this creature was immature, possibly of some six years of age, but the brain cast suggested a cranial capacity of some 300 cc., certainly approaching that of an adult chimpanzee. Dart saw other striking features. The flat skull bore no eyebrow ridges and the teeth, Dart thought, were decidedly human in pattern.

The present writer has been unable to discover whether it

was ever Dart's intention to inform the British Museum's Natural History department at South Kensington, London. A fellow discoverer of *Australopithecus* (Southern ape), as the fossil was named by Dart, Dr Robert Broom, felt that this neglect of a time-honoured custom was at the root of the initial anger at Dart's claim. The discoverer certainly played his cards badly but through no fault of his own. Dart prepared a scientific description of *Australopithecus* for *Nature*. Unfortunately the editor of the South African newspaper *Star*, B. G. Paver, had got wind of the story. In exchange for a promise not to publish before the description appeared in *Nature* Dart gave Paver full information on the find and photographs. But the editor of *Nature* tarried while he canvassed opinions about Dart's claims from expert anatomists such as Arthur Keith. The result was a cabled ultimatum from Paver to *Nature*. He said that he could not hold the story beyond the evening of 3 February. Pressure was once more put on Keith who told the editor of *Nature* to go ahead. But by the time it did, on 7 February, it was too late. The *Star* had beaten *Nature* to the punch by four days.

As is usual with popular treatment of scientific subjects lengthy reflection was sacrificed on the altar of impact and sensation. Dart's find was hailed in the *Star* as the one and only missing link, and only Dart knew what he was talking about. London journalism, indeed that of the entire Western world, took up the cry. The real missing link had been found at last. Scientific opinion, particularly that of Sir Arthur Smith Woodward (knighted in 1924) and his colleagues at South Kensington, was caught napping. Poor Woodward had officially retired but was still in attendance at the museum. He thought that Dart had stolen a march on him and was trying to sneak a fossil man in under his nose. Forgetting his own caution over Piltdown Woodward thought that this was carrying secrecy too far and told the besieging journalists so.

The news was first broken in England by *The Times*[1]. The report said that *Australopithecus* was a creature neither anthropoid nor human in form or brain power. Only two weeks before, said the newspaper, Sir Arthur Keith had said that Rhodesian man was in the direct line of human ascent but maybe the new discovery would cause this view to be modified. The following day the newspaper went further, saying that 'many times the unearthing of a primitive skull has been hailed as the missing

[1] 4 February, 1925.

link but Grafton Elliot Smith had told a reporter that if Dart's discovery lived up to his description then such a creature had now been discovered'. Smith had told *The Times*:

> An interesting point which emerges is that the discovery [of *Australopithecus*] supports Darwin's theory that Africa was probably the home of the human family. That view has not been favourably regarded by many writers though I have always inclined to that view·

It is a pity that nobody asked Smith how he equated this inclination with his views on human migration from its source in the Near East or Asia. It will also be noted that Darwin was mercilessly used to support any proposition in hand. His *Descent of Man,* being a comprehensive review of evidence both for and against a particular proposition, readily lent itself to such subversion. Like Dr Johnson, Darwin can be reliably quoted as saying almost anything about everything. In the case of Dubois he could be cited as preferring the East for the origin of man, now he was being quoted as being in favour of Africa. In fact he had mentioned both continents.

In the next report in *The Times*[1] Dart was announcing that thousands of fossil *Australopithecines* had probably been unearthed at Taungs and thrown away. Gone with the lime, he said, to destruction at the Natal sugar refineries or the carbide works at Germiston. Dart said he had been informed that 'a very good complete skeleton' had been blasted out of the limestone and thrown on the quarry dump. We must, urged Dart, watch every deposit in future.

But what claims had Dart actually made for *Australopithecus*? The long-awaited *Nature* article appeared at last on 7 February. It lived up to its promise. Dart wrote that in the past the search for the missing link had overlooked one thing—incentive. What had possessed the evolving ape to leave his four-footed mode of progression and walk erect?

'For the production of man,' Dart reasoned, 'something was needed to sharpen wits and quicken intellect—in fact a more open veldt country [rather than jungle] where competition was keenest between swiftness and stealth and where quickness of the mind and movement were so important for the preservation of the species.'

[1] 6 February, 1925.

Dart continued that no country in the world more abounded with ferocious animals than South Africa, and he quoted Darwin as saying so. The great biologist, said Dart, had used the expression 'wild' but he meant to imply ferocity. In Dart's opinion these ferocious predators, when combined with the vast open veldt country around Taungs, where there was only occasional forested shelter, and a shortage of water, had heightened the 'bitter animal competition'. At Taungs, wrote Dart, a swift-moving, fast-thinking anthropoid had evolved. This was the birth of mankind. His name was *Australopithecus*.

Dart received many congratulatory telegrams. One was from General J. C. Smuts who at the time was being snubbed politically and had chosen natural history as a subject with which to kill time. Another came from his old mentor, Grafton Elliot Smith. Sir Arthur Keith did not oblige, merely writing in his journal (1925) that he thought the so-called *Australopithecus* seemed more akin to ape than to man. At first he was inclined to leave statements to the press to Smith, but a few days later he told the reporters that 'Dart was not likely to be led astray. If he has thoroughly examined the skull we are prepared to accept his decision.'

In fact 'they' were not. In a combined rejoinder to Dart's claim for *Australopithecus* which was published in the next issue of *Nature*[1] Keith set the tone. He wrote that he had found it easy to enlarge Dart's profile drawings of *Australopithecus* to adult size. The result seemed to him to belong to the same sub-family as the chimpanzee and the gorilla. It was, he wrote, nearly akin to both. Sir Arthur Smith Woodward, who had examined photographs of the fossil, found that he could see nothing in the orbits, nasal bones and canine teeth nearer to those of humans than those displayed by the skull of a modern young chimpanzee. Professor W. L. Duckworth thought that Dart's claims were entirely unjustified. Even Grafton Elliot Smith turned a shoulder on his disciple. He said he did not disagree with Dart but he required more proof than had been supplied so far.

He enlarged his theme in a lecture at University College in May which was fully reported in *The Times*. He said that although *Australopithecus* had been classed as the missing link it was not one of the 'significant' links for which science had been searching. It was unmistakably an ape, nearly akin to those still living in Africa. He added:

[1] 14 February, 1925.

It is unfortunate that Dart had no access to skulls of infant chimpanzees, gorillas or orang-utans of an age corresponding to that of the Taungs skull for had such material been available he would have realized that the posture and poise of the head, the shape of the jaws, and many details of the nose, face and cranium on which he relied for proof of his contention that *Australopithecus* was nearly akin to man, were essentially identical with the conditions met in the infant gorilla and chimpanzee.

Professor R. von Virchow was now dead so his usual greeting of 'microcephalic idiot' was wanting in the case of *Australopithecus*. But Professor A. Robinson in a lecture in Edinburgh did dismiss the fossil as the distorted skull of a chimpanzee.

With scientific rejection of *Australopithecus* came world-wide derision for Dart. The music-hall comedians substituted *Australopithecus* jokes for mother-in-law anecdotes. In London the *Morning Post* ran witty commentaries about the South African find. Readers were invited to contribute 'epitaphs' to mark the demise of *Australopithecus* 'in not more than six lines of verse or sixty of prose'.

One ran :

> Here lies a man, who was an ape,
> Nature, grown weary of his shape,
> Conceived and carried out the plan
> By which the ape is now the man.

The winning contribution was :

> Speechless with half-human leer,
> Lies a monster hidden here,
> Yet here, read backwards, beauty lies,
> And here the wisdom of the wise.

Most newspapers carried a cable from New York which read:

Professor Dart's theory that the Taungs skull is a missing link has evidently not convinced the legislature of Tennessee, the governor of which state has signed an 'Anti-Evolution Bill' which forbids the teaching of any theory contrary to the Biblical story of the Creation, and that man has descended from the lower orders. Similar legislation which is at present before other state legislatures marks the growth of a strict Biblicist movement represented by so-called fundamentalist churches whose leading propagandist is the silver-tongued orator, William Jennings Bryan.

At Witwatersrand Dart received threatening letters. One said that he was sitting on the brink of the eternal abyss of flame and would later 'roast in the general fires of Hell'. Another hoped his 'heresy would be punished by being unblessed with a family which looks like this hideous monster with the hideous name'. A letter to the editor of the *Sunday Times* under the heading 'Hammer and Taungs' from 'A Plain but Sane Woman' asked Dart 'how he could become a traitor to his Creator?' 'What', asked the plain woman, 'does your Master [Satan] pay you for trying to undermine God's word? Or do you not know his wages?'

The South African government nonetheless invited Dart to exhibit *Australopithecus* at the country's pavilion at the British Empire Exhibition held at Wembley, near London, in the summer of 1925. Dart also prepared a chart to explain in simple terms the place of *Australopithecus* in the evolution of mankind. He placed his fossil as a direct ancestor of *Pithecanthropus* (Peking man) and related Rhodesian man to Heidelberg and Neanderthal. The caption read: 'AFRICA: THE CRADLE OF HUMANITY'.

When he saw it Keith was immensely upset. He issued a statement to the press saying: 'The famous Taungs skull is not that of the missing link between ape and man.' He followed this up with a lengthy letter to *Nature* which firmly rejected *Australopithecus*. He wrote:

Professor Dart has described it [*Australopithecus*] as representing an 'extinct race of apes intermediate between the living anthropoids and man' . . . The skull is that of a young anthropoid ape—one which was in its fourth year of growth, a child—and showing so many points of affinity with the two living African anthropoids, the gorilla and chimpanzee.

Keith found that the development of the jaw and face showed a certain refinement not met with in the modern anthropoids, indeed it showed human traits, but *Australopithecus* had occurred much too late in prehistory to have any place in man's ancestry.

But Dart had his supporters, one of whom was the American sceptic Dr Ales Hrdlička. In 1925 Hrdlička had set out on a world-wide palaeontological survey, visiting sites in India (Siwalik) where *Ramapithecus,* an early hominid with anthropoid affinities, had been discovered, Java, China and then Taungs. He examined the *Australopithecus* skull and declared for Dart. But later in London he seems to have fallen under the spell of Keith and Smith and said before the Royal Anthropological Society that the relationship of the Taungs fossil with mankind could only be determined 'when the specimen is well identified'.

In 1931 Dart realized that the only chance for *Australopithecus* was a direct confrontation with his adversaries in London. With the fossil in a wooden box carried by his wife Dora, who could be relied on not to lose it, Dart arrived in England and immediately got in touch with Smith, Keith and Woodward. All three gave him an enthusiastic reception but it was misleading. They only wanted to tell him about *Sinanthropus.*

Smith, however, gave Dart a chance. Smith had recently returned from Choukoutien and was engaged by the Zoological Society in London to speak on the Chinese fossil on the evening of 17 February. 'Will you come as my guest—and bring your Taungs baby with you?' Dart joyfully agreed.

The evening was a disaster. Woodward was in the chair and Smith was at his best. Playing the audience like a harp he gave a scintillating account of *Sinanthropus.* With lantern slides he showed how the Chinese fossil was confirmation of but different from Java Man. Eloquently Smith described how it was strongly suspected that *Sinanthropus* was a cannibal because of the numerous cracked skulls and split bones which had been encountered at Choukoutien—and how he was sufficiently advanced to know how to make fire. Smith sat down to resounding applause. After a brief introduction Dart was thrown to the lions.

At once Dart knew that this audience, after imbibing the heady wine of Smith's oratory, was not an ideal one before which to vindicate his claims for *Australopithecus.* He was no speaker. He described his own performance as 'pitiful' and 'fumbling'. The look of polite attention on the assembled fourscore faces became fixed. As Dart feared, it was an anti-climax.

A feeble rattle of applause greeted him when he resumed his seat.

Smith who, according to Dart, sensed his guest's disappointment, invited Dart to dine the following evening at the Royal Society Club. He was placed on the left of the famous physicist Sir Charles Boys. Dart reported that he was well received but he decided to return to South Africa.

Dart left his fossil with Smith, who persuaded F. O. Barlow of the British Museum to make some plaster casts. Dora, who had collected the skull from Smith's Hampstead home, left it in a taxi. Smith spent until four the following morning on the telephone attempting vainly to trace the whereabouts of *Australopithecus*. The cabby, however, had handed the box in at Fulham police station.

It is traditional that poor Dart, defeated and dejected, followed the cue of Dubois and retired into obscurity with his fossil. Dart hotly denies this and with justification· The scepticism and anger which met his claims for *Australopithecus* in some strange way had brought distinction to his university. Dart detected a change in the attitude of his colleagues. In the year of the discovery he was elected Dean of the Faculty of Medicine. That same year he was invited to become president of the South African Association for the Advancement of Science and a Fellow of the Royal Society of South Africa.

Robert Broom was one of the most tireless palaeontologists of all time. His work on the extinct reptiles of the Karoo drew the attention of J. C. Smuts who by now had become premier. Broom was offered the post of curator of palaeontology at the Museum of the Transvaal; his real task, however, was to find another *Australopithecus* for though Dart had continued his search at Taungs he had had no further success. In 1936, within a few weeks of commencing operations at a limeworks at Sterkfontein, a few miles west of Johannesburg, Broom brought one to light. But because of differing anatomical features the new discovery was named *Australopithecus transvaalensis*. He later changed this to *Plesianthropus* (near apeman).

Other discoveries followed rapidly. Some more *Australopithecines* came to light at Sterkfontein, others at the nearby quarries of Kromdraai and Swartkraans. But because of their size these later finds were attributed not only to a different species but a new genus. They became *Paranthropus robustus* (robust apeman) and *Paranthropus cressidens* (larger ape-man).

The search was interrupted by World War II but was resumed in 1947. In this year Dart's persistence was rewarded at
Makapansgat, 120 miles north of Pretoria. The new fossil was
thought to have used fire, as some charred sticks were found
along with the bones in the newly-revealed limestone cave. Dart
therefore gave him the title *Australopithecus prometheus.* In
1959 Professor L. S. Leakey found *Zinjanthropus*—Nutcracker
Man—so called because of a suspected but absent enormous jaw.
This has not been found, however. Nutcracker man was found
in Tanzania, 2,000 miles north of Taungs, but there is no doubt
about his *Australopithecus* affinities. In this area *Australopithecines* are today being discovered in abundance.

The peculiarities that gave rise to the generic and specific
names of these fossils are still the subject of much debate. But
all the *Australopithecines* have in common features which justify
to an amazing degree the claims made by Dart in 1925.

Australopithecus has a long face which protrudes in a
snout, a steeply slanted forehead, ape-like lower jaw and human-
type dentition. The brain of an adult varies with the individual
from 450 cc. to 650 cc.[1] The foramen magnum, the cable
entry by which the skull is articulated with the top of the spine,
is distinctly further forward than that of the chimpanzee or
gorilla. This suggests that *Australopithecus* held his head up-
right and could walk erect.

Adult individuals come in two sizes. At Taungs, Sterkfontein
and Makapansgat, he is the size of a modern adult pygmy, about
five feet tall, and weighs just less than a hundred pounds. At
Kromdraai and Swartkraans, however, he is a much more im-
posing individual, both taller and heavier, well within the full-
size human range in height and weighing about one hundred and
fifty pounds; this of course is another species of *Australopithecus.*

There were once three main views as to the place of *Australopithecus* in evolution. First, that he is a true anthropoid allied to
the chimpanzee or gorilla with certain features curiously like those
of man. Second, that he is a hominid, his resemblances to man
being far too numerous to be explained other than by a direct
relationship; in this view if he is not man's direct ancestor then
he is very closely allied to the first men, a collateral branch to

[1] For brain size comparison: apes, such as gibbon, orang-utan, chimpanzee, gorilla—100-700 cc.; ape-men, Java and Peking—750-1,250 cc.;
Neanderthal Man or Neanderthaloids—1,050-1,750 cc.; modern man
(normal)—1,750-2,350 cc.

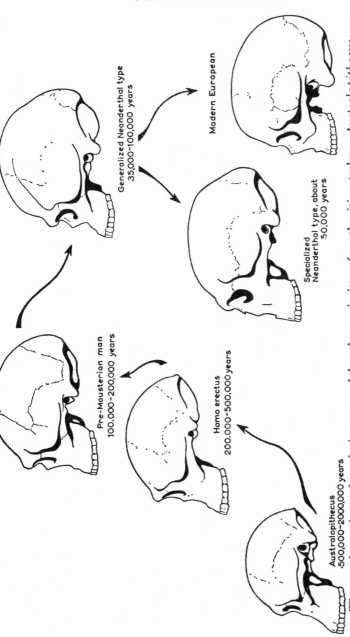

Modern European

Generalized Neanderthal type
35,000-100,000 years

Specialized
Neanderthal type, about
50,000 years

Pre-Mousterian man
100,000-200,000 years

Homo erectus
200,000-500,000 years

Australopithecus
500,000-2,000,000 years

The modern view of evolution agreed by the majority of authorities today. *Australopithecus* plays the part of Piltdown Man. The specialized type of Neanderthal man occupies Piltdown man's later position before the Sussex fossil's final dismissal from the fossil catalogue in 1953. (From *History of the Primates*, 9th edition. Sir Wilfrid Le Gros Clark, British Museum, 1965.)

that of human stock, which died out without issue. Third, that he represents a group of anthropoids in the process of evolving towards humanity which, however, never actually crossed the threshold into humanity; the promise of his erect-walking and high brain capacity being unfulfilled.

That *Australopithecus* could walk erect is now generally accepted. But how erect and for how long is highly debatable. Sir Wilfrid Le Gros Clark suggests that his posture would be something less than human. S. L. Washburn feels that he only rose to two feet when running and reverted to all fours as soon as possible.

The degree of erectness is an important issue and has far-reaching implications. If the creature could stand, this would free his hands to use pebbles as tools or even to fashion them.

When Dart found *Australopithecus prometheus* in 1947, by naming him such he made an extravagant claim. He never actually found evidence of fire or ashes to support it. But he went further. He said that *Australopithecus prometheus* was a hunter of small mammals for food. His weapons, claimed Dart, were stones and chipped bones.

This claim was not made idly. The *Australopithecus* remains were found in the company of a large number of baboon skulls. Forty-eight out of fifty-two of these skulls show impact fracture. Le Gros Clark agrees that the kind of fracture is consistent with well-directed blows from an implement of some kind. He finds it difficult to offer a more likely explanation. If *Australopithecus* was in fact a missile-throwing hunter, this certainly suggests a skill not possessed by anthropoid apes. Killing by use of weapons is the prerogative of the human race.

The American Carleton S. Coon, however, has suggested that this evidence has been misinterpreted. As in the case of *Sinanthropus* he considers that *Australopithecus* was more likely to be the hunted than the hunter. Coon based his theory on the statistics revealed by the total animal remains found with the fossil at Makapansgat. Ninety-two per cent were antelope of various species, one point seven were baboons and two point six were those of the *Australopithecines* themselves. Coon reasoned that if the fossil had been the resident of the limestone cave, or even a cannibal as some authorities had suggested, then his bones would have been present in a greater proportion.

It was a former student of Dart, his successor at Witwatersrand, G. W. H. Schepers, who claimed to have found evidence that *Australopithecus* hunted his own kind for the pot. Inside the skull of a *Paranthropus robustus* at Kromdraai was a large pebble which apparently had driven the bone before it into the cavity.

> The presence of this rock is evidence suggestive that the claims that have been previously made that the *Homunculi* as represented by the *Australopithecoid* and *Plesianthropoid* [derived from *Plesianthropus,* Broom's later name for *Australopithecus transvaalensis*] fossils were skilled enough to employ missiles for defensive, offensive and predator purposes.

Unfortunately Schepers' paper merely heaped coals on the fire of the hunted versus the hunter controversy. Could *Australopithecus* then really have been the victim of some superior race as suggested by Coon? As in the case of *Sinanthropus* there are no remains of a later and more sophisticated race to support this contention, and modern stratigraphical dating strongly suggests that *Australopithecus* seems to have existed over a vast space of time, from five and a half million to one and a half million years B.P. Tools have been found dating back two and a half million years, well in the range of *Australopithecus.*

It is certain that something or someone was flaking crude pebble tools in *Australopithecus* territory in the later period of his existence. At Makapansgat seventeen pebble tools were found just above the layer of *Australopithecus* bones. Two pieces of rock in the same layer at Kromdraai seem to have been shaped. Definite worked pebbles have been found in the same layer as *Australopithecus* teeth at Sterkfontein. It seems definite that at least one species of *Australopithecus* was a toolmaker.

Chapter 16

IN ADDITION TO more *Australopithecus,* and *Pithecan-thropus* from both China and Java, the thirties offered a proliferation of Neanderthalers from Tabun and Magharet es-Skuhl on Mount Carmel, Palestine (now Israel). The remains were excavated from caves in the side of the mountain by a joint expedition of the British School of Archaeology, Jerusalem, and the American School of Prehistoric Research. These discoveries proved that the Neanderthalers were not the monopoly of Europe and demonstrated the truth of the archaeological saw that the number of discoveries of fossil men is directly proportional to the number of *Homo sapiens* in the area.

The Mount Carmel finds were a revelation. The Neanderthalers appeared in a range of forms from the slow-thinker of the Neander valley to a highly-evolved near-*Homo sapiens*. Here was strong evidence that early *Homo sapiens* had inter-bred with Neanderthal man. True *Homo sapiens* remains were in fact found on Mount Carmel.

To the present author at least Neanderthal man has a certain mordant appeal. Despite his cannibalism as displayed by the discovery of ten butchered adults and children at Krapina in 1904, he had many human attributes; the sustenance and ritual burial of the crippled Neanderthal man at La Chapelle-aux-Saints, for example. There is overwhelming evidence that Neanderthal man existed as a contemporary of *Homo sapiens* for about one hundred thousand years, and it comes as a shock therefore, when it is realized that Neanderthal man must have been hounded out of existence by *Homo sapiens*.

Neanderthal man divides into two main morphological groups. The earlier and what is called 'generalized' kind (35,000–100,000 B.P.) were gradually replaced by a different type of 'specialized' Neanderthaloid. It seems likely, therefore, that the later group were in fact reversions, the victims of a terrible kind of oppression which it is difficult for the modern

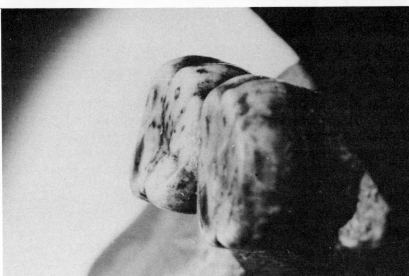

Piltdown man's jaw now attributed to a 500-year-old orang-utan.

Modern opinion is strong for the proposition that the jaw 'hinge' (lymphoid process) was artificially broken away to remove evidence of its ape origin and its unsuitability for fitting into the Piltdown cranium.

The fossil elephant thigh-bone implement from Piltdown. Marks of a modern steel blade used to sharpen the point escaped notice until 1948, and their implication until 1953.

Far right: the Piltdown molars showing the non-alignment of the flat crowns. This unnatural placement cried out for notice in 1912 but oddly escaped attention for some forty years.

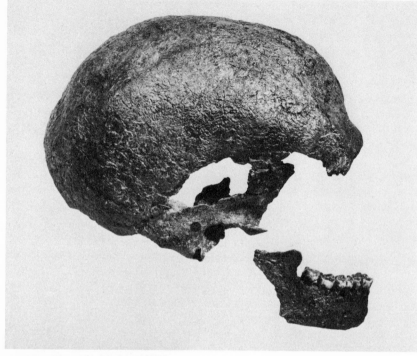

The skull and fragment of jaw of Galley Hill man—Britain's 'Neanderthal man'—now thought to be a recently-buried woman. The eyebrow ridges hailed as prominent and characteristic of Neanderthal man are well within the range of modern man. The curvature of the limb bones was caused by posthumous deformation after deliberate inhumation.

An 'eolith' from Piltdown, Sussex. Whether human workmanship—ancient or modern—was employed is conjectural.

mind to visualize. It might even be possible that early *Homo sapiens* were the cannibals of Krapina, although the present author takes full responsibility for this theory.

There was, however, an entirely different kind of find in July 1933 at Steinheim, Germany, which scientific opinion is having difficulty placing. The skull shows strong features of both Neanderthal and *Homo sapiens*. Sir Wilfrid Le Gros Clark proposed in 1955 that Steinheim man is ancestral to both. But more recently (1958) Dr J. S. Weiner has said that he represents a stage leading to *Homo sapiens* and that both Rhodesian man and the Neanderthalers arose from a different and more primitive source, this being represented by the owner of the Heidelberg jaw. Present authorities find this doubtful.

The year 1933 was also notable for a complaint from the president of the Geological Society that Europe had too long been the holy ground of geological terminology with serious consequences for the rest of the world. Sir Thomas Henry Holland said that no geological classification could have world-wide application and that we should have to be content to examine each area of the earth independently and wait for evidence which would establish coincidence between the records. It was becoming obvious to Holland that the practical effects of the ebb and flow of the Pleistocene varied from total to none at all and that the arbitrary naming of the world's geological periods by a European standard was leading to widespread chaos and misunderstanding. Too often journalism was making stock of 'paradoxical' stories of drowned fossil men being recovered from desert areas such as Timbuctu 300 miles from the nearest sea, when obviously this area had been flooded by the pluvials caused by the northern ice.

Two years later another fossil man was discovered in England. Fear of the tumult which normally followed such finds bore fruit in the dilemma which faced the finder. Dr Alvan T. Marston, a dentist, had for the past two years regularly visited a gravel pit at Swanscombe, Kent, not far from Galley Hill. He was alone on Sunday, 29 June, 1935, when he noticed a piece of bone sticking out of the gravel. Knowing the ritual penalties for unwitnessed archaeology, Marston hesitated. If he left the bone in the gravel while he went to get an independent witness there was a likelihood that it would be reburied by the shifting gravel. If he removed it before it was witnessed or photographed then there was more than an even chance that the site would be disputed.

Marston hit on a peculiar compromise. He removed the bone, a piece of skull, and marked the spot with a stone wrapped in a handkerchief. On his way out of the pit, however, Marston encountered a mechanic working on the crushing plant. He returned with the man and showed him the handkerchief. The witness must have thought Marston had lost his mind. Marston then made a sketch of the spot and posted a notice asking quarry-men to watch for further fragments, returning to the site the following day to take a photograph. As it happened the account of the find was not disputed but one wonders what would have been the fate of this evidence if it had.

Marston wrote to H. Dewey of the Geological Survey announcing the find of a human occipital bone 'in good condition' and that the remainder 'had a very good chance of turning up'. He spent the week-ends of the next few months searching the gravel until March the following year when he and his son John uncovered a second piece of skull. Leaving his son to mount guard Marston sought and returned with a local chemist with a camera.

Marston exhibited his fossil at the 1936 meeting of the British Association at Norwich. The implements found at the site in the past were identified by Abbé H. Breuil as Acheulean. The faunal remains, representing in all twenty-six species of extinct animals, including wolf, straight-tusked elephant, lion, rhinoceros, horse, red, fallow and giant deer, placed the deposit at the Middle Pleistocene (*Mindel-Riss* or Penultimate Interglacial), which corresponded perfectly with the flint culture. In his paper Marston said:

> I might as well say here and now that both Sir Arthur Keith and Sir Arthur Smith Woodward have already made a cursory examination of the [human] bones and whereas Keith said it was *Homo sapiens* closely resembling Piltdown, Smith Woodward believed it Neanderthal and expressed the hope that when more was found that the bones would prove to be Heidelberg.

Marston himself believed that the Swanscombe skull was not much later than Piltdown; that it might even be earlier. It certainly wasn't Neanderthal, he said, although it might be Heidelberg.

In justice to its important contribution to palaeontology in 1936 a memorial was unveiled at Piltdown at the site of the famous gravel. This event was not unprecedented. Although the Neanderthal cave was no longer in existence, indeed the entire valley had been transformed by limestone quarrying, the area had been proclaimed a National Park. The Piltdown gravel presented similar difficulty for the original bed had been excavated away.

The memorial—a monolith of Yorkshire stone—was unveiled on 22 July by Sir Arthur Keith at the invitation of Sir Arthur Smith Woodward. The engraved words read 'Here in the old river gravel Mr Charles Dawson, F.S.A., found the fossil skull of Piltdown, 1912-1914'.

Teilhard de Chardin was still in China and could not be present. Keith and Woodward were the only English survivors of the Piltdown band. Sir Grafton Elliot Smith (knighted in 1934) had died on New Year's Day the previous year. He had spent the last four years of his life incapacitated by a stroke.

Keith made a brief oration to the small crowd of thirty. He said that Dawson had given them the 'entrance to a long past world of humanity such as never had been dreamed of, and had assembled evidence which carried the history of Sussex back to a period to which geologists assigned a duration from half a million to a million years . . . Professional men took their hats off to the amateur, Mr Charles Dawson, solicitor and antiquarian. They did well to permanently link Mr Dawson's name with this picturesque corner of Sussex and the scene of the discovery.' He added that Dawson should be considered in the same light as the French 'lock-keeper', Boucher de Perthes.

The monument was erected by private subscription, which included a donation from the American convert, H. Fairfield Osborne. General E. G. Godfrey-Fausett, on behalf of the Sussex Archaeological Society, offered to take over the task of the up-keep of the monument. But this was considered unnecessary and the generosity was declined with thanks.

Possibly the unveiling at Piltdown prompted Keith to make amends to his dead adversary. That year he began a lengthy 'resurvey' of the Piltdown skull,[1] saying that after many trials over the last six months he wished to withdraw from the argument and that he was inclined to accept Smith's views on the dissimilar proportions of both sides of the skull.

On another matter, he said that geologists agreed that the Swanscombe skull belonged to the latter end of *Mindel-Riss* Interglacial and therefore the fossil was much older than all the

[1] *Journ. Anat.*, Vol. LXXIII. Oct. 1938, Jan. 1939.

Neanderthal remains found in Europe, excepting the Heidelberg jaw which he regarded as early Neanderthal stock attributable to the *Gunz-Mindel* Interglacial. Piltdown man was attributable, in his opinion, to an early phase of the same Interglacial. He said that if we hadn't discovered Piltdown man we should have been content to assign Swanscombe man to modern *Homo sapiens*, but it was probably more correct to regard Swanscombe as a later member of the Piltdown phylum but greatly changed by the immense interval of time between them. He thought that while *Pithecanthropus* was being evolved in the East, the totally different Piltdown man was in existence in the West. The Western type continued to survive and change until the Middle Pleistocene, resulting in Swanscombe man.

In 1941 a debate of a new kind took place at the Geological Society. In his address the president, P. G. H. Boswell, dealt with the Society's declining membership. His point was taken up in a general discussion on 'the Function and Practice' of the society. Professor Trueman thought that recruitment had definitely been affected by what Boswell had called 'a lack of public awareness'. He felt that the society's journal should contain subjects of a more general nature. He also raised the question of concessions to members of allied societies and institutes and a reduced subscription for overseas members.

In the light of this Sir Arthur Smith Woodward, as Foreign Secretary, might not have been the right man to seek overseas enthusiasm. Advanced in age he was now totally blind. Within two years he would be dead, having dictated from memory— which Keith assures us was as strong and active as ever—his last work and final tribute to Piltdown man, *The Earliest Englishman*, his preoccupation for over thirty years.

Dr A. J. Bull, however, assigned the decline to different reasons. He said the membership of kindred societies had increased in the last two years. What was needed was the framing of a more progressive policy, that the society should adjust itself to modern conditions. Professor Cox agreed. He thought that public interest might be stimulated by the more practical applications of geology such as ore deposits, oil geology and geophysical prospecting. Sir Lewis Fermor said that 'if geology really was in the dumps in Britain the best thing to do was to have an earthquake'. Fenner meant a seismic disturbance—but in a different sense his statement was prophetic.

Cox's proposal of a broader scope was adopted. In 1943 Dr

A. H. Lewis of the Imperial Chemical Industry's research station at Jealott's Hole read a paper on the relationship between sub-soil and health.[1] On the geological side, said Lewis, much remained to be done, for example, on the fluorine content of soil. Talking of fluoresis, he said, nearly a hundred years ago Owen Rees had read a paper to the society which had drawn attention to the fact that whereas the fluorine content of recent bones is negligible, fossil bones long buried in the earth might contain up to ten or fifteen per cent. The work of Rees was followed in 1873 by the French chemist A. Carnot who showed that fossil bones acquire an increasing fluorine content with increasing age until they are almost transformed into fluorapatite. The average proportion of fluorapatite in modern bones was 0.058 per cent; in Pleistocene fossils 0.33; Tertiary 0.62; Mesozoic 0.91 and Palaeozoic 0.99.

Dr Kenneth Page Oakley of the British Museum, in a written contribution, agreed but said the progressive increase in the fluorine content of bones with increasing geological age was directly concerned with the amount of fluorine present in the deposit in which they were found. It was a statistical law, he said, and not applicable to individual specimens. The correct figure could, Oakley said, be arrived at by averaging the deter-minations made on specimens from a number of geological deposits. He thought, however, it would be an advantage for the fluorine content of fossil human bones to be determined as a routine measure. Although a negative result, he suggested, would not be proof that a bone was recent, a high fluorine content would be strong evidence of antiquity 'in case of doubt arising'.

The following year Sir Arthur Smith Woodward died, aged eighty, at his home at Hill Place, Sussex. It is just as well, for the results of the fluorination paper would have killed him. The presence of fluorine in fossil bones and its application to geo-logical dating requires some further explanation.

The test developed by Oakley depends on the fact that a fossil buried in a porous deposit such as gravel absorbs fluoride ions present in the soil and part of its substance converts into a stable compound—fluorapatite. The longer the fossil remains in the deposit the greater the amount of fluorine it will contain. Chemical analysis of a bone sample will give an approximate indication of its antiquity. The test, however, has an inherent flaw. The amount of fluorine passed into the bone is directly

[1] *Q.J.G.S.* 99–100, p. xii.

proportional to the fluorine content of the soil water of the deposit. Nevertheless, the test can indicate a later intrusion of fossil bone by revealing a discrepancy between the fluorine content of the various bones in the deposit. There is another snag. A human fossil was a rare and highly valued commodity. He would definitely have to be strongly suspect before any museum would allow a sample to be taken from him for testing.

A. T. Marston, the discoverer of Swanscombe man, became a constant adversary of the Sussex fossil; not on the grounds of falsity but through conviction that priority in age should be given to his Swanscombe skull. In a discussion following a paper on the Swanscombe fossil presented to the Royal Anthropological Society in 1937[1] an unnamed contributor had deprecated the fact that Dawson had used a potassium bichromate solution to harden the Piltdown cranial fragments. Woodward noted in his account, *The Earliest Englishman* : 'The colour of the pieces which were first discovered was altered a little by Mr Dawson when he dipped them in a solution of bichromate of potash in the mistaken idea that this would harden them.'[2]

The implications of this hardening had been lost on Marston until he recovered a piece of ox pelvis during a visit to Piltdown and immersed it in a similar solution. The colour of the bone had been changed from grey to the dark-chocolate brown which characterized the Piltdown skull and mandible. Marston now complained that it was on the grounds of the chocolate colour that Dr A. T. Hopwood had concluded that the human fossil belonged to the older group of fauna. He argued that Piltdown man might have belonged to the later faunal group.

Marston was also impressed by an almost unnoticed report in 1925 by F. H. Edmonds of the Geological Survey. Edmonds wrote that the Piltdown gravel was not one hundred and twenty feet above sea level as Charles Dawson had told the meeting in 1912 but only one hundred and two feet. This sensibly reduced the antiquity of the gravel.

By July 1947 not only had Marston come to doubt the extreme antiquity of the Piltdown remains but he also embraced the earlier theory that the jaw was that of a fossil anthropoid ape, a view, it may be recalled, held by a number of anatomists at the time of the discovery and after. Marston was of the opinion that

[1] *Journ. of Royal Anthrop. Inst.* Vol. xvii.
[2] The statement appears also in *Recent Progress in the Study of Early Man. Rep. Brit. Assoc.* London, 100, p. 129–142.

the mandible and canine tooth were much earlier than the skull. This was amply demonstrated, he said, by the survival of the delicate turbinal bones found by Dawson. The skull, he urged, must be considered to be comparatively modern.

Oakley was developing his fluorine test. The root of a sheep's molar from the top-soil of Barnfield gravel pit, Kent, possessed a fluorine content of 0.1 per cent; a modern human skull from Swanscombe, Kent, 0.1; a modern human skull from Northfleet, Kent, 0.2; a human skull from chalky soil said to contain Romano-British pottery at Northfleet. 0.3; a human tibia from a Saxon grave, Northfleet, 0.05.

Oakley now claimed his first victim. He tested the bones of Galley Hill man—skull 0.3; mandible 0.4; right tibia 0.4; fragment of limb bone 0.4; left femur 0.2. As a result Galley Hill Man came off the Middle Pleistocene pedestal on which he had stood for fifty years. He was well below the 2.0 required for this age in Kent. He was even well below the 1.0 required for the Upper Pleistocene. He was in fact a comparatively recent interment.[1]

It well might be wondered how Galley Hill man came to possess 'prominent superciliary ridges' which qualified him in some people's eyes for the Neanderthal category. These are in fact quite faint and his supporters' enthusiasm for an early dating must have enhanced their size in their imagination. The curved limb bones owe their Neanderthal character to the rigours of burial. Galley Hill man was attributed to our present era—the Holocene; one authority says it is comparatively recent. He is certainly no fossil.

Next Oakley applied the test to Swanscombe man. The Swanscombe animal bones produced a high average of 2.0 per cent. It must not be thought that there was any doubt about the Middle Pleistocene date of these specimens but Oakley was ascertaining a standard against which to check the human remains. Then came the turn of the skull : parietal 2.0; occipital 1.9. Swanscombe man passed with flying colours.

On 14 July, 1949, there was another Marston paper before the Royal Anthropological Institute. Although Swanscombe man was genuine, he was still considered a late arrival compared to Piltdown man. Marston called for justice. He said that Piltdown man was even later than Neanderthal man. His brain, he said,

[1] *A Reconsideration of the Galley Hill Skeleton.* Bull. of B.M. (Natural History) Geology 1 no. 2 (1949).

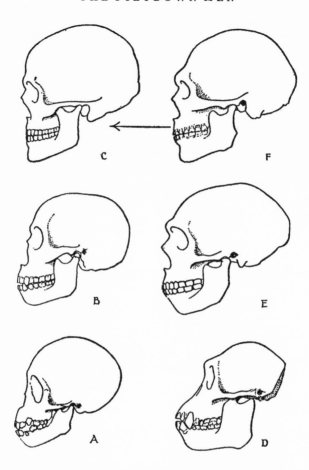

Sir Arthur Smith Woodward pushes Piltdown man out of the line of human evolution. He comments that he now considers Predmost man (Aurignacian) to be directly ancestral to man via Neanderthal man. He uses the skull of a young chimpanzee (A) to illustrate what our original ape ancestors were like, another reference to the spurious 'Peter Pan' theory of evolution. Peking man (*Homo erectus*) does not figure at all.

Key: A, Young chimpanzee; B, Piltdown man; C, Modern man (Ainu of Japan); D, Adult gorilla; E. Neanderthal man; F, Predmost man (Aurignacian).

(From *The Earliest Englishman*. Watts & Co. London, 1948.)

possessed the characters of modern man and he was in no sense
a Lower Palaeolithic fossil as was supposed. He said that it had
been clearly established (by himself) that the ape jaw and canine
had nothing to do with the skull. They had been found separ-
ately and any association was unclear and misleading. He
passionately concluded:

> It is clear that many mistakes have been made concerning
> Piltdown man—many mistakes by many highly qualified and
> highly placed men. To err is human and none of these men
> have been divine. Let the mistake be recognized. The fluorine
> test seems to have opened up a new field of enquiry; let it be
> applied to the Piltdown remains; let us know what light it
> throws as to whether they are pre-*Wurm* or post-*Wurm* in
> age.

Oakley did. On 14 December, 1949, he announced his finding
to the Geological Society:

> The fluorine (and phosphate) content of every available bone
> and tooth from Piltdown has now been tested by Dr C. R.
> Hoskins of the Government Laboratory. All those undoubtedly
> of the Lower Pleistocene group (beaver, red deer, horse) proved
> to contain 2.3 per cent fluorine, whilst those of the post-
> Villafranchian fossils (primitive elephant, mastodon, rhino-
> ceros) [almost certainly of several ages] the fluorine content
> ranged from 0.1—1.5 per cent. The *Eoanthropus* material,
> including all the scattered cranial fragments, the jaw and
> canine tooth, and the remains of the second skull found two
> miles away showed little fluorine (average 0.2 per cent).

In his conclusions Oakley made one other observation which
later assumed great importance. He said that during the drilling
of the teeth to win dentine for the chemical analysis, he noticed
that below the ferruginous surface stain the dentine was pure
white, apparently no more altered than 'new teeth from the soil'.

What then had the fluorine test proved? The oldest mammal
bones contained less fluorine than the later ones, in fact suggesting that the Piltdown deposit was a hotchpotch of faunal remains.
Of the supposed human remains Oakley wrote in 1950[1]:

[1] 'New Evidence on the Antiquity of Piltdown Man'. *Nature* 165.

The results of the fluorine test have considerably increased the probability that the [Piltdown] mandible and cranium represent the same creature. The relatively late date indicated by the summary of evidence suggests moreover that Piltdown man, far from being an early primitive type, may have been a late specialized hominid which evolved in comparative isolation. In this case the peculiarities of the mandible and the excessive thickness of the cranium might well be interpreted as secondary or gerontic developments.

This then was the final verdict. Piltdown man was too recent to be considered in the line of evolution that led to man. If he was Villafranchian or even Lower Pleistocene it was reasonable that his kind might have developed into modern man, but his low fluorine appeared to push him well up into the Pleistocene and such a great change in so short a period was impossible. But he was still thought to be a valid fossil man. Who could say what might happen to a tribe of hominids isolated by ice for hundreds of thousands of years? Darwin himself had suggested that under severe conditions over long periods such specializations were possible. But by far the greatest consideration was that a deliberate deception on such a grand scale was not to be contemplated. In fact Piltdown man's displacement, if given time, would have started a new round of debates on his place in nature. The jaw matched the skull in fluorine content admirably, thus confounding Marston with his own argument. This error is explainable inasmuch as the fluorine test still could not be employed with anything like high accuracy. That there was still no suspicion of fraud is demonstrated by a move that year to perpetuate the Piltdown gravel as a national monument.

A new thirty-two-foot-long section of the gravel was opened up in 1950 with the intention of providing a 'witness section'. The gravel recovered was carefully sifted by H. A. Toombs, Kenneth Oakley and a Mr Rixon but no bones, teeth or implements were found. The problem now confronting the Nature Conservancy was how to protect the section in a bed subject to flooding. It was solved according to Toombs[1] by bricking it in save for a couple of small glass doors through which the famous gravel could be seen. A concrete path led to the Yorkshire stone monument and the whole area of some sixty feet square was enclosed by a fence of chestnut paling. The report concluded

[1] *The South-Eastern Naturalist and Antiquary*, Vol. LVII, 1952.

that in the enclosure west of the hedge there was no sign that the gravel had been disturbed. This left about two hundred and thirty square yards for later excavation when time and money became available. As the gravel was an average eighteen inches deep this would yield over a hundred cubic yards of gravel— 'many months work if proper care is taken'. The site was generously given to the nation to be a permanent geological monument by W. F. Lutyon of Barkham Manor.

There was another hair-raising insinuation about Piltdown man late that year.[1] F. H. Edmonds, the author of the 1925 paper on the height of the Piltdown gravel, confessed he was perplexed. The older group of Piltdown animals, he said, were alleged to have been washed from a Pliocene deposit somewhere in the Weald. Edmonds thought there must be some misunderstanding. There was no Pliocene land deposit in the entire Weald which could have produced them. The only local Pliocene beds were marine in origin and lay above the five-hundred-foot contour line.

Another attack on Piltdown man came from the United States in 1951. This quoted the arguments made twenty years before by Ales Hrdlička.[2] M. F. Ashley Montagu of the department of anthropology of Rutgers University said that he had examined the skull and mandible that year and he had noticed a striking disparity. The cranial bones of Piltdown I and II were extraordinarily thick when compared with the mandible. He knew of no skull which showed this disparity, not even the 'enormous' *Australopithecine* skulls or that of a gorilla. In both these instances the mandible was as thick as the skull.

Ashley Montagu said that to support Piltdown man's jaw it had been argued that no fossil ape had ever been found in England. This was untrue for the remains of two Pleistocene anthropoids had been described by Sir Richard Owen in 1845 and Dr Hunter in 1908. And so, concluded Montagu, 'the occurrence of an anthropoid mandible with the skull of a fossil man as late as the Middle Pleistocene is a possibility somewhat less remarkable than it has hitherto appeared'.

Alvan T. Marston did better. His argument was the same as Montagu's but he accompanied it with a demonstration which must have stirred at least a few anatomical minds in the right direction. But none has ever acknowledged it. In a massive

[1] *Q.J.G.S.* 106.

[2] *Journ. Phy. Anthrop.* Vol. 6, No. 4. NS, 1951.

article in the *British Medical Journal*[1] accompanied by illustrative photographs Marston explained how he had inserted a model of the Piltdown canine into the socket of a female orangutan jaw. With figures and diagrams he demonstrated that the canine was an immature tooth 'belonging to a young adult ape'. He insisted that the Piltdown skull was modern, and repeated his theory of the modernity of the fragile turbinal bones. He said that even though the fluorine test had shown that the canine and jaw were the same age they were both incompatible with the skull. He had examined copies of the original Piltdown X-rays of the jaw. These had revealed a typical anthropoid bone structure. The skull, he said, was of a person who could not have been less than forty years of age. So he could not have been the owner of such an immature third molar and canine. Marston concluded:

The writer hopes his readers are fully convinced that a complete case has been made out for the final rejection of the Piltdown mandible and canine tooth as being human and as having belonged to the Piltdown skull.

[1] Vol. XCII, No. 1. 1 July, 1952.

Chapter 17

IN JULY 1953 AN international congress of palaeontologists, under the auspices of the Wenner-Gren Foundation, was held in London. The world's fossil men were put up, admired and set down again. But, according to Dr J. S. Weiner, Piltdown man got barely a mention. He did not fit in. He was a piece of jig-saw puzzle; the right colour but the wrong shape.

But at a dinner attended by, amongst others, Weiner, Dr Kenneth Oakley and Profesor Wilfrid Le Gros Clark he was mentioned. Oakley remarked to the American Professor S. L. Washburn that because of the sudden death of Charles Dawson the British Museum had no exact record of the spot where Piltdown II had been found. The remark transported Weiner into a post-prandial review of the Piltdown discovery, which outlasted his return to Oxford. He wrote later[1] that the lack of precise information was distinctly puzzling. Piltdown II had convinced many doubters that Piltdown I was a valid fossil man; that he wasn't just a chance association of a human skull with an animal jaw. Such an association might conceivably occur once by chance, but twice was impossible. As a lawyer, Weiner thought, Dawson should not have been prone to slipshod archaeological methods. Weiner considered that maybe Sir Arthur Smith Woodward had been informed of the precise location of Piltdown II but somehow this important detail had gone unrecorded. It seems to have gone undetected that Woodward had visited Piltdown II (see page 145).

Nevertheless, it was Dawson's supposed neglect which led Weiner's thoughts to range over wider issues.

Weiner then realized with 'astonishment' that there were only two theories about Piltdown man. First, that he was one individual as proclaimed by Woodward. Second, that he was two creatures. Neither theory being satisfactory, he thought, the riddle might be reduced to simpler terms if he concentrated on the two-creature theory. Assuming two creatures, if both had not got together in the Sussex pit by some whim of nature, could they have got there

[1] *The Piltdown Forgery.* Oxford, 1955.

by human agency? Could someone by mischance or error have dropped the ape jaw in a deposit occupied by a human fossil? But this accidental intrusion seemed impossible. It would have to have been repeated at Piltdown II. The inevitable outcome of Weiner's cogitation was an advance to the horrifying view of deliberate placement in the gravel.

It was possibly at this juncture that the whole kaleidoscope of inexplicable errors, slack reporting, half-innuendos, suggestions and downright disbelief of the past fifty years hardened into a coherent suspicion that a fraud of almost unbelievable pretensions and magnitude had been perpetrated on science. Dawson's error over the height of the Piltdown gravel corrected by Edmonds. Oakley's remarks on the whiteness of the dentine beneath the ferruginous stain of the teeth. C. W. Lyne's statement in 1916 that the canine was worn to a degree out of keeping with its youth. Woodward's misgivings about the staining solution which Dawson had used on the first skull fragments, and his statement in 1912 that it would have been difficult to attribute the ape's mandible to a human being but for the teeth. In fact the description 'ape' pulsed through the history of Piltdown man's jaw with the insistence of the counterpoint of a Bach fugue.

Weiner mentioned his suspicion to Le Gros Clark. This led to the examination of the Piltdown casts in Oxford University's department of anatomy. The claims for the human features of the jaw rested entirely on the flat wear of the molars. Inspection of the casts revealed features consistent with artificial abrasion of the crowns. Weiner's next step was to reproduce the Piltdown molars. He used specimens from a chimpanzee jaw, filing down the crowns to form flat biting surfaces. He stained them with potassium permanganate. According to Le Gros Clark[1] when Weiner showed him the result he 'looked at the teeth with amazement, for they reproduced so exactly the appearance of the unusual type of wear in the Piltdown molars'.

Weiner, Le Gros Clark and Oakley met at the Natural History Museum at South Kensington. Le Gros Clark said later that a study of human and ape teeth had shown the anatomists that there were a certain number of reliable features by which natural wear of teeth could be distinguished. Because the first molar erupts earlier than the second molar it is usually more worn; the

[1] *The Exposure of the Piltdown Forgery.* Paper delivered to the Royal Institution 20 May, 1955. Reprint.

outside edges of upper molars overlap and grind down the opposing edges of the lower teeth; when enamel is worn from the molar caps this produces shallow cavities in the unprotected and soft underlying dentine; the biting surfaces of adjacent teeth function as a unit in the backward and forward and side to side motion of chewing so they present a uniform surface.

The original Piltdown teeth were produced and examined by the three scientists. The evidence of fake could be seen immediately. The first and second molars were worn to the same degree; the inner margins of the lower teeth were more worn than the outer—the 'wear' was the wrong way round; the edges of the teeth were sharp and unbevelled; the exposed areas of dentine were free of shallow cavities and flush with the surrounding enamel; the biting surfaces of the two molars did not form a uniform surface, the planes were out of alignment. That the teeth might have been misplaced after the death of Piltdown man was considered but an X-ray showed the lower contact surfaces of the roots were correctly positioned. This X-ray also revealed that contrary to the 1916 radiograph the roots were unnaturally similar in length and disposition.

The molar surfaces were examined under a miscroscope. They were scarred by criss-cross scratches suggesting the use of an abrasive. 'The evidences of artificial abrasion immediately sprang to the eye,' wrote Le Gros Clark. 'Indeed so obvious did they [the scratches] seem it may well be asked—how was it that they had escaped notice before?' He answered his question with a beautiful simplicity. 'They had never been looked for . . . nobody previously had examined the Piltdown jaw with the idea of a possible forgery in mind, a deliberate fabrication.'

The wear of the canine was confined to the crown, in fact a considerable portion of the enamel was worn away. This conflicted with evidence that the tooth was a young one which had not yet, or only just, completed eruption. This fact was established by a later X-ray which showed that the pulp cavity possessed the youthful feature of being wide open at the apex of the root. Closer examination of this tooth revealed that the perpetrator of the hoax had made a mistake. A small patch stated by A. S. Underwood in 1916 to be secondary dentine, a normal development as a reaction to excessive wear, was nothing of the kind. It was an over-abrading which had been remedied by a plug of some plastic material, remarkably like chewing-gum.

The canine surfaces showed the same fine scratches. The pulp cavity was full of sand. This had always been taken to be the result of the tooth's being rolled about on the bed of the River Ouse in antiquity, the cavity being gradually infiltrated with fine grains through the root's open apex. But the X-rays revealed that the sand grains were loose and not cemented together with the ferruginous matrix of the Piltdown gravel. They were also the wrong size for Piltdown, being one to two millimetres in diameter; the local sand grains were much finer.

Le Gros Clark agreed that this alarming turn of events was enough to warrant a full-scale examination. A series of chemical and mechanical tests were conducted on the entire Piltdown illusion. These tests were quite rightly claimed to be the most complete and exhaustive of any carried out on a fossil and could not have taken place without strong representations to the British Museum. The British Museum's report of the investigation (issued 1953) said that since the discovery of Piltdown man some forty years ago he had been the source of continuous controversy but that it was probably true to say that most anthropologists had remained sceptical and frankly puzzled by the contradictions. There was, said the report, another explanation—the mandible and canine were actually those of a modern ape (chimpanzee or orang-utan) 'deliberately faked to resemble fossil specimens'. But it was not until J. S. Weiner had put forward this proposition 'fairly and squarely' as the only possible solution to the Piltdown puzzle that a critical restudy of all the Piltdown material was decided on.

The report, quite short considering its implications, calmly gave the evidence yielded by the Piltdown teeth, then gave the results of a new series of fluorine tests. It explained also that Oakley's previous test had served well enough to place the Piltdown cranium and mandible in the Upper Pleistocene but it had not distinguished, nor was it intended to, between this and a later date. Oakley's original tests, it was explained, were not accurate enough when applied to samples of less than ten milligrammes of sample with the consequence that no difference in the fluorine content of the skull and mandible had been observed. But improvements in technique had resulted in greater accuracy. The result was that the cranium might well belong to the Upper Pleistocene but the mandible, canine and isolated molar (from Piltdown II) were quite modern. These results were[1]:

[1] *The Solution of the Piltdown Problem.* Bull. Brit. Mus. (Nat. Hist.) Geol., vol. 2, no. 3.

	% Fluorine
Local Upper Pleistocene bones	0.1
Local Upper Pleistocene teeth	0.1
Piltdown I cranium	0.1
Piltdown II frontal	0.1
Piltdown II occipital	0.03
Piltdown mandible (bone)	0.03
Piltdown molar	0.04
Piltdown canine	0.03
Isolated molar (Piltdown II)	0.01
Molar of recent chimpanzee	0.06

The report continued that dating by organic content of fossil teeth and bones had long been regarded as fallacious and that no serious attempt had been made to date the Piltdown remains by these means. But work on bones from early occupation sites in North America conducted by G. S. F. Cook and R. F. Herzer had shown that nitrogen present in living bones was lost at a relatively slow and uniform rate and this could be used as an important supplement to the fluorine analysis. The results of these tests were[1]:

	% Nitrogen
Fresh bone	4.1
Piltdown mandible	3.9
Neolithic bone (Kent)	1.9
Piltdown cranium	1.4
Piltdown II frontal	1.1
Piltdown II occipital	0.6
Upper Pleistocene bone (London)	0.7

Nitrogen content of dentine samples

Chimpanzee molar	3.2
Piltdown canine	5.1
Piltdown I molar	4.3
Piltdown II molar	4.2
Piltdown Upper Pleistocene horse molar	1.2
Upper Pleistocene human molar (Surrey)	0.3

The report said that the black coating on the bones described by Dawson as 'ferruginous', or iron-stain, was in fact a tough flexible paint-like substance (the National Gallery suspected

[1] *Ibid.*

Vandyke Brown paint). The cranium was deeply stained but the coating on the mandible was superficial. This discrepancy indicated that stain had been used to make one resemble the other and to make both appear aged.

The report now pointed a small finger at Dawson, so subtly it is not immediately apparent. It quoted Woodward on the potassium chromate dip and said that the analysis at the Clarendon Laboratory, Oxford, had confirmed that all the cranial fragments seen by Woodward in the spring of 1912 (before the commencement of systematic searches) did contain chromate; on the other hand there was no chromate in the fragments collected that summer—either in the right parietal or the small occipital fragment found *in situ* by Woodward himself. As Woodward was now himself conducting the excavations, said the report, it was not suspected that the mandible would be stained for he would have advised Dawson of his mistake. But in fact it was stained: unavoidable evidence that the faking of the mandible and canine is so extraordinarily skilful, and the perpetration of the hoax so entirely unscrupulous and inexplicable, as to find no parallel in the history of palaeontological discovery.

The report concluded:

Lastly, it may be pointed out that the elimination of the Piltdown jaw and teeth from any further consideration clarifies very considerably the problem of human evolution. For it has to be realized that 'Piltdown man' (*Eoanthropus*) was actually a most awkward and perplexing element in the fossil record of the Hominidae, being entirely out of conformity both in its strange mixture of morphological characters and its time sequence with all the palaeological evidence of human evolution available from other parts of the world.[1]

The report was signed by Dr J. S. Weiner, Department of Anatomy, University of Oxford, K. P. Oakley, Department of Geology, British Museum (Natural History), and W. E. Le Gros Clark, Department of Anatomy, University of Oxford.

When told of the deceit Sir Arthur Keith said: 'I think you are probably right, but it will take me some time to adjust myself to the new view.' Though not as deeply involved as Woodward the effect of this news on an eighty-six-year-old man who for

[1] *Ibid.*

over forty years had believed implicitly in the Sussex fossil can be imagined. He died eighteen months later on 7 January, 1955, at his home at Downe. He had been pruning fruit trees the previous day.

The only other survivor was Père Teilhard de Chardin. According to his biographer Robert Speaight, the priest, who now belonged to the Wenner-Gren Foundation in New York, was invited to give his views on the forgery in an article. But he preferred not to make a public statement. In a reply to a letter from Oakley which told him of the exposure he said[1]:

No one would think of suspecting Woodward. I knew pretty well Dawson—a methodical and enthusiastic character. When we were in the field I never noticed any suspicion in his behaviour. The only thing which puzzled me, one day, was when I saw him picking up two large fragments of skull out of a sort of rubble in a corner of the pit (these fragments had probably been rejected by the workmen the year before). I was not in Piltdown when the jaw was found. But a year later when I found the canine, it was so inconspicuous among the gravels which had been spread on the ground for sifting that it seems to me quite unlikely that the tooth would have been planted. I can remember Sir Arthur [Smith Woodward] congratulating me on the sharpness of my eyesight. Don't forget; the pit at Piltdown was a perfect dumping place for the farm and cottages. It was flooded in winter, and water in the Wealden clay can stain at a remarkable speed. In 1912, in a stream near Hastings, I was unpleasantly surprised to see a fresh-sawed bone (from the butcher's) stained almost as deep brown as the human remains from Piltdown. Had a collector possessing some ape bones thrown his discarded specimens into the pit? The idea sounds fantastic; but, in my opinion, no more fantastic than to make Dawson the perpetrator of a hoax.

The idea of an ape-bone-bearing collector in such a little inhabited part of Piltdown is fantastic. The other alternative was not so. On 23 November, 1953, *The Times* broke the news. A two-column picture of the jaw and canine arrested attention and a full report of the revelations was carried under the headlines 'Piltdown Man Forgery: Jaw and Tooth of Modern Ape'. The story continued:

[1] Robert Speaight: *Teilhard de Chardin: A Biography*.

The authors of the [Bulletin] article do not identify the perpetrator of this fraud—but 'Who did it?' is a question many will ask. The discovery of the 'Piltdown Skull' was due to Charles Dawson, a solicitor who lived at Hastings and who was an amateur of fossils. He died, highly regarded by scientists, in 1916, aged sixty-two... These finds he took to Sir Arthur Smith Woodward, of the British Museum (Natural History), an authority of international reputation and unassailable integrity.

The story mentions Teilhard de Chardin and describes him as then a young priest studying for Holy Orders. Having placed these participants beyond suspicion the correspondent concluded with the following accusation:

Thus two witnesses of the highest character either found, or helped to find, the bones now known to be spurious, and it is hard to resist the conclusion that the jaw and tooth had been put there by some third person in order that they might be unimpeachably discovered. If that third person were to prove to be Charles Dawson it would be but one more instance of fame (since money was certainly not the object here) leading a scholar into dishonesty. That the deception—whoever carried it out—has, though cunning and long successful, at last been revealed is a tribute to the skill of modern palaeontological research.

The *Manchester Guardian* gave the story similar prominence. In its fifth leader it said that the Piltdown skull had lost some of its importance but the revelations still caused a considerable flutter among scientists and laymen. The newspaper told how the discoverer of the Swanscombe skull, A. T. Marston, had steadfastly maintained that the skull and jaw could not possibly belong to the same individual, that he had been much criticized but was now vindicated. The leader continued:

... the report reads like a story of shrewd detection but what science cannot say—and what, after forty years, is probably left uninvestigated, is who the extraordinarily skilful and entirely unscrupulous hoaxer was. Piltdown Hoaxer is certainly a most successful specimen of Forging Man.

The newspaper chose as its precedents Thomas Wise, the 'discoverer' of first editions of poets and Van Meegeren and his 'Vermeers', but pointedly said that these forgers had been found out in their lifetimes. It concluded:

... but this one, we are probably justified in assuming, died in the knowledge that whoever had the last laugh he would not be there to hear it.

A reader objected to the view that the identity of the hoaxer was best left unrevealed. M. J. Lighthull of the University of Manchester said that such information would help reduce wasted effort by accelerating detection in future instances.[1]

The *Daily Telegraph* accompanied its story with the opinion of Dr A. E. Wilson of Brighton Technical College who knew the Piltdown site well. He said:

In Sussex we have always been a little doubtful about the jaw. We thought it was possibly of an ape of 50,000 years ago, contemporary with the cranium, but never suspected until now that it was that of a modern ape and had been faked. It was introduced into the pit after it was known that the cranium had been found and further researches would take place. This was done by someone who knew a good deal about fossilising bones. These were very heavily faked and seem to have been done by someone indulging in faking for its own sake. He could derive no financial satisfaction from it. I do not think that Mr Dawson had anything to do with this hoax. He was genuine, keen and anxious over such matters.

Marston told the newspaper that he was convinced that the mandible and the canine tooth were not faked but that he had never been convinced that they belonged to a human being. He mentioned Dawson's use of the hardening solution which had dyed the bones a chocolate brown. This, said Marston, was the extent of the supposed faking.

The *Daily Express* came to the defence of Dawson. Under the headline of 'That Man—The Great Whodunit. Did Charles Dawson give Mr Piltdown his fake jaw?', the newspaper said that no answer had been given in the British Museum bulletin.

[1] 26 November, 1953.

George Eade, a solicitor's clerk who had worked with Dawson in 1910-14, said that the lawyer would never have stooped to such a thing. Sixty-year-old Margaret Morse Boycott knew Dawson when she was a member of the Piltdown Golf Club and said:

> He was an insignificant little fellow who wore spectacles and a bowler hat. Certainly not the sort who would put over a fast one.

Professor H. J. Fleure told the newspaper that it was most unlikely that Mr Dawson had anything to do with this. The TV personality and archaeologist Sir Mortimer Wheeler thought the 'new Piltdown discovery removes an awkward customer from the line of human evolution, and at the same time redounds greatly to the credit of the three scientists concerned . . .'

The *Daily Sketch* did not think so.

> Anthropologists refer to the hoax as 'another instance of desire for fame leading a scholar into dishonesty' and boast that the unmasking of the deception is 'a tribute to the persistence and skill of modern research'. Persistence and skill indeed! When they have taken over forty years to discover the difference between an ancient fossil and a modern chimpanzee! A chimpanzee could have done it quicker.

The *Sydney Morning Herald* entirely missed the local-interest point that an Australian, the late Sir Grafton Elliot Smith, had been connected with the Piltdown discovery but thought that maybe it was the century's biggest scientific hoax. The following day the newspaper's third leader cited the precedent of Thomas Chatterton and added that an unnamed German archaeologist had detected Mithraic worship in the Roman army with the help of a bronze bull's head, which later revealed itself as part of a British army can-opener. The editorial concluded:

> Such errors, no doubt, are very regrettable and very humiliating for the learner but they are a useful reminder of the need for caution. And they are very funny.

The *New York Times* said that Sir Arthur Keith and the late Franz Weidenreich had negative views about the jaw; the latter had stated bluntly that the jaw was that of an orang-utan. The story concluded that the writers of the bulletin were not prepared to say categorically that it was Mr Charles Dawson who had planted the jaw. The newspaper quoted the president of the Royal Society, Professor Edgar Adrian, as saying that 'the hoax . . . was rather sad but exceedingly interesting', and reported that Fleure thought the hoax 'a very clever deception by someone with some scientific knowledge—perhaps a student who wanted to play a practical joke'.

The newspaper's editorial on 24 November said that some eminent comparative anatomists were the subject of 'considerable unearned ridicule' and that :

> Apparently nothing pleases the mind of the multitude more than the spectacle of a learned professor fooled by some able forger. Who planted the bones? Someone who knew his bones and chemistry . . . Perhaps an overpowering sense of humour, perhaps to prove that he knew as much as comparative anatomists and anthropologists.

In his column Meyer Berger told his readers that the Piltdown hoax hadn't caused as much astonishment at the American Museum of Natural History as might have been expected. Berger continued :

> Almost unanimously the men and women who work on the Oldest Races of Men series at the museum agreed twenty years or so ago that Old Piltdown was not one creature but two. They made no public issue of it for ethical reasons. There is, and always has been, a sly reference to the Piltdown exhibit in the museum as to the dual nature of the Old Boy from Sussex Downs. 'The brain case', says the card in the case, 'represents a very early and human type . . . The lower jaw much resembles that of a chimpanzee'. The museum may have to change this label. It will say, in effect, 'This restoration, once thought to be a genuine reproduction, has since proved to be spurious'. Nothing sharper than that.

Two days after its first report[1] *The Times* revealed that the

[1] 23 November, 1953.

forger's depravity had not ended with the supposed human remains. Not only was it now discovered that the Piltdown flints had also been artificially stained, but Kenneth Oakley told the newspaper that the Piltdown II fragments were as phoney as Piltdown I. The report commented that it was hard to resist the inference that the forger 'whoever he was had the coolness and scholarly skill to try to outmanoeuvre expert doubts about the 1912 remains by making possible in 1915 the discovery of a corroborative kind'.

This facilitated the accusation :

Mr Charles Dawson makes his appearance in the second discovery as in the first. Sir Arthur Smith Woodward . . . is said never to have been shown the second site, and Dawson died before he fixed it on the map.

The story continued that Oakley had told the newspaper that the flint implements 'were not all they should be', that they had been artifically stained to look more than their age. The famous elephant thigh bone implement had also been worked in a way that would be impossible with a crude flint implement. In fact, said the newspaper, the implement was too perfect.

The reader was further informed that :

The Piltdown ape-man is not the first forgery to deceive scholars. In archaeology there has been a number of deceptions. One was the eighteenth-century case of Beringer, whose students carved objects and left them for their unsuspecting master to find. Another case, in zoology, involved the Austrian Kammerer, who sought to prove the so-called inheritance of acquired characteristics. In lay terms, it turned out that somebody had made the swellings in newts on which proof of the theory depended by injecting Indian ink.

The writer was obviously having a hard time finding precedents. It would have suited his purpose better if he had cited the almost parallel case of the Moulin Quignon jaw. But from the substance of the two examples quoted it will be noticed they were of the 'student japing the master' kind. They may even have been chosen with care.

On 24 November the Piltdown forgery was rated a *Times* first leader which gave a lengthy and informative exposition of the story of evolution and how Piltdown man had been the cuckoo in the palaeontological nest for too long. From this it was but a short step to the House of Commons.

In the House on 25 November a motion was tabled by W. R. D. Perkins and five other members 'That this House has no confidence in the Trustees of the British Museum (other than the Speaker of the House of Commons) because of the tardiness of their discovery that the skull of the Piltdown man is a fake'. The three principal trustees of the British Museum were the Archbishop of Canterbury, the Lord Chancellor and the Speaker. Two days later Brigadier Terrance Clark asked if time could be afforded for the motion on the Piltdown hoax (Cheers). Mr Bowells said he understood the caution of its sympathizers for it offended against the rules of the House that members should not attack the Lord Chancellor and the Archbishop of Canterbury who were both members of the House of Lords (laughter). The speaker said : 'My attention has been drawn to the matter and I am not sure how serious the motion is (laughter). I shall have to consider it, but speaking for my co-statutory trustees . . . I am sure that they, like myself, have many other things to do besides examining the authenticity of a lot of old bones (loud laughter). Mr Cruickshank, Lord Privy Seal, said that Brigadier Clark's question was awkward because his predecessor was also a Trustee and he was himself *ex-officio* (laughter). But as he had told the House two years ago, the (Conservative) Government had found so many skeletons to examine when they came into office that he had not found time to extend his researches into skulls (laughter). Mr. Beswick cried : 'What has happened to the Dentists' Bill ?' (laughter). Cruickshank said he had no announcement to make on that, beyond that it was not a fake (laughter). Brigadier Clark asked to be allowed to withdraw his name from the motion in view of the excellent answer he had received (laughter). The Prime Minister, Sir Winston Churchill, said nothing. The parliamentary levity brought a furious letter to the *Manchester Guardian*. The correspondent said : 'By all means let the people laugh—and the Commons—but these matters are not fundamentally funny.'[1]

[1] 3 December, 1953. C. D. Orey. St. John's College, Cambridge.

But another debate at the heartland of palaeontology, at the Geological Society on 25 November, did not pass off so gaily. Oakley had explained with the help of lantern slides why the team of experts had concluded that the ape mandible had been faked to match the Upper Pleistocene brain-case. The next scheduled speaker was the finder of Swanscombe man, Dr Alvan Marston. The meeting was clearly expecting his usual scientific views on the jaw but it did not get them. Instead Marston said he was there to protest against the attacks that had been made on Charles Dawson in *The Times* and in the BBC broadcast the previous Saturday. He said:

> It has been very strongly hinted, if not definitely stated, that Mr Dawson took the canine tooth and lower jaw of an ape . . .

The chairman, Professor W. B. R. King, interrupted Marston. The meeting, he said, was not attempting to justify or condemn anything that had appeared in the newspapers or on the BBC, but it was hoped to get Marston's views on the jaw itself. But Marston persisted. He had received a letter from Barkham Manor confirming the integrity of Dawson. The chair again intervened but the speaker continued: 'They should not attack this man—it is so simple to prove that the canine tooth was not modern'. He then showed a number of lantern slides which in his opinion proved that the Piltdown canine and jaw were not modern but in fact those of a fossil which had not been artificially stained or abraded. He then returned to his theme. He asked how the British Museum could accuse a dead man's memory and besmirch his name? How could they account for the fact that a lawyer had such deep insight into anatomy and physiology that he could puzzle the greatest anatomists for years? The charge, he said, had been made to hide their own ineptitude and that the 'sycophantic humility' of the museum tradition had itself been playing a hoax on public opinion. Now they had made a scapegoat of the dead Dawson who could not answer back. He shouted: 'Let them try to tackle me'. He again asked the chairman to read the Barkham Manor letter which was 'from a person who knew that Dawson didn't fake anything'. But the chairman declined, saying that the revelations did not accuse Dawson in any way, and merely said that the skull was faked. Marston made further attempts to read the letter but was restrained by the chair. K. P. Oakley then rose and said he had taken part in the broadcast in question. He said that he had stated that they did not know who was responsible for the hoax. J. S. Weiner, another of the broad-casters, said that they had accused nobody. They did not know who had perpetrated the hoax. The hubbub at this meeting was wrongly reported in the United States to have developed into a series of fist-fights.

But someone must have been putting in some hatchet work. *The Times* surely had not exonerated Woodward and Teilhard de Chardin and left Dawson out on a limb on its own account. Dawson's step-son, F. J. M. Postlethwaite, wrote to the news-paper[1] that he had read with considerable indignation its Museum correspondent's insinuation and that he could not overlook 'this unnecessary sentence in an otherwise excellent statement of fact'. Postlethwaite said he had spent short periods at Dawson's home while on leave from the Sudan 'during 1911 and 1912 when the search for the fragments was in progress', and so had Sir Arthur Smith Woodward and Teilhard de Chardin. He then incorrectly said that as the pieces were found they were handed to Woodward for safe custody. He appears to have hoped that this statement would cause his step-father to be removed from suspicion on the grounds that he could not have stained the fragments, but of course this did not follow. Dawson could have stained them before they were planted at Piltdown. On his step-father's character Postlethwaite com-mented :

Charles Dawson was an unassuming, thoroughly honest man and very painstaking when he wrote *The History of Hastings Castle* entailing years of research. From an early age he was interested in flint implements and fossils, uncovering the bones of some saurians near Hastings and natural gas in Heathfield. His interests extended in many directions, but it is doubtful if he could be described as a great expert in any single subject. Until the discovery at Piltdown he did not display any par-ticular interest in skulls, human or otherwise, and so far as I know had none in his possession. To suggest that he had the knowledge and skill to break an ape's jaw bone in exactly the right place, to pare his teeth to ensure a perfect fit to the upper skull and disguise the whole in such a manner to

[1] 25 November, 1953.

deceive his partner, a scientist of international repute, would surely be absurd and personally I am doubtful whether he had the opportunity of doing so. No—Charles Dawson was at all times far too honest and faithful to his research to have been accessory to any faking whatsoever. He was himself duped, and from statements appearing in the Press this is the opinion of those who knew him well, some of whom are scientific people.

Teilhard de Chardin in fact told *The Times*[1] that 'from his acquaintanceship with Dawson and Smith Woodward it was virtually impossible to believe that Dawson, still less Smith Woodward, could have been guilty of the hoax'. His qualification is unfortunate, though probably unintentional.

The British Museum, duped for forty years, was in a highly vulnerable position. The advertising tenet that there is no such thing as bad publicity certainly did not apply in this case. To its credit the museum decided to tell the whole story, albeit a qualified one, in the form of a 'special' exhibition at South Kensington, containing four sections. First, *The Problem of Piltdown man* with a display of the original finds with photographs of the excavations in progress and palaeontologists discussing the Piltdown skull in the Geological Society rooms in London (in fact the John Cooke portrait). The second section showed the fraud being detected, the revelation of the fluorine analysis and the evidence of the staining and artificial abrasion. The third dealt similarly with the Piltdown II skull. The fourth pointed out Piltdown man's positon hitherto in the story of evolution. To this was added the following notice :

The removal of the 'ape-jawed Piltdown Man' from the fossil record considerably clarifies the problem of our ancestry. The Piltdown braincase is still regarded as a genuine fossil of Upper Pleistocene age. It is interesting on account of its unusual thickness, the absence of brow-ridges, and the primitive characters of its endocranial cast. While not so old as the Swanscombe skull, it is nevertheless important as representing an early member of our own species.

It might have been more tactful if the British Museum had avoided the use of Woodward's original description of the skull

[1] 26 November, 1953.

and the exhibition did tend to give the impression that its purpose was to announce a triumph for British palaeontology rather than its deception for so many years.

Martin A. C. Hinton, former Keeper of Zoology at the British Museum, wrote to *The Times*[1] that in 1912 he was working as a volunteer in the Geology and Zoology departments and he had not seen the Piltdown material until the reading of the Dawson-Woodward paper. Hinton said that as soon as he saw the jaw and the tooth he knew that, had they come into his hands for description, 'they would have been referred without hesitation to the chimpanzee which was already known to occur in some of the Pleistocene deposits of Europe'. His future chief, Oldfield Thomas, had been of the same opinion. But Gerrit Miller had published the results of his interpretation of the Barlow casts, and Thomas and Hinton had been delighted for it relieved them of the necessity of expressing an opinion that would have aroused hostility at the museum at the time. Hinton said that 'Pycraft's feeble criticism of Miller was replied to with great skill and dignity and there the matter ended as far as Thomas and I were concerned'. That they were faked specimens had not entered either mind for they had been accepted by the Geological Department, and neither Thomas nor Hinton had access to the originals.

Later another letter to the newspaper also mentioned that lack of access to the real specimens had made the deception undetectable. This gives the impression that science had been deceived by plaster casts but, as shown earlier, this was not the case. Keith had remarked long ago (1913) on the ease of access to the specimens by anatomists.

Next July came further evidence of the pains taken by the perpetrator of the Piltdown fraud to achieve his end. A new method of dating bones had been applied to the Piltdown bones. Mineral phosphates contain uranium and this is infiltrated into fossil bones by soil water. The longer the bone remains in a deposit the more uranium it absorbs. There is a progressive build-up of the isotope with advancing geological age which can be measured by radiometric assays. The impregnation of the bone, like fluorine, is proportional to the uranium content of the deposit, so the test could give a fair idea as to where the specimens had originated geographically.

By this means it was ascertained that the elephant molar

[1] 22 December, 1953.

(*elephas planifrons*) could certainly not have been supplied by Britain. In fact the geological deposits in France, Italy and India where this type of fossil had been found in fair quantity must also be absolved from blame. The most likely place was Tunisia. In striking contrast, the low radioactivity of the hippopotamus tooth could indicate a site in Malta or Sicily. *The Times* said in its third leader that the Geological Society meeting at which the latest advent was announced had accomplished Piltdown man's complete destruction.

> ... not a single thing is thought to be genuine in the sense that it was actually found there [at Piltdown]. Never was a bogus goldmine so successfully 'salted' as were those Sussex gravels. It would be easy to say that the moral lies in the gullibility of scientists but that would be to miss the point, no injury could be risked from experimental methods of investigation. But once suspicion of fraud was aroused retribution came with sure steps. The striking thing is not that the scientists were gulled, even for a long time, but the extraordinary patience, thoroughness, scientific ingenuity and teamwork by which the exposure was finally brought about.

The leader listed the authorities to be commended as the Department of Geology and Minerals, British Museum; Department of Human Anatomy, Oxford University; Atomic Energy Department, Geological Survey; Physics Department, King's College, London; Government Chemist's Department; Microchemical Department, Oxford University; National Gallery; Soil Survey.

The leader commented finally:

> What chance has a single malefactor against such an armoury? And yet perhaps he has the last laugh. His crime, indeed, is discovered, but he himself has eluded detection—at least, so far.

These winsome, yet sinister words were prophetic. Charles Dawson had slipped up. His conduct of the Piltdown hoax or fraud as it came to be called was impeccable but he had reckoned without J. Mainwaring Baines, curator of Hastings Museum, where Dawson's private collection of archaeological curios had rested since his death in 1916.

At Hastings was proof that Dawson was not only a forger but that he had plagiarized his *History of Hastings Castle*. Baines announced in his annual report to the museum trustees in November 1954 that enquiries had been proceeding since Piltdown man had been announced as a fake some twelve months before. The prickspur from Lewes that Dawson claimed to be Norman had not been recognized by the British Museum. Grave doubts had also been cast on a small axehead which he claimed he had found in a slag-heap at Beauport, near Hastings, a Roman iron-working site. From this site Dawson had also acquired a small statuette, a replica of a colossal statuary group at Rome. Said Baines: 'This statuette had been accepted by the Society of Antiquaries at the time (1893) but some doubt was cast on it and the story of its discovery seemed to be as enveloped in mystery as the Piltdown skull'. It had been submitted to a number of authorities and although it was undoubtedly of cast-iron it was almost certainly of recent date 'and might have been brought home from the Continent by Dawson'. Another suspicious item was the anvil marked 1515.

If this was not enough, said Baines, some months ago a local bookseller had brought to his notice a manuscript volume relating to Hastings Castle. He had immediately recognized the hand-writing as that of William Herbert, who carried out excavations at Hastings in 1824, for he had examined that author's notes in the London Guildhall library. The words of the manuscript and Dawson's *Hastings Castle* were almost identical, although rearranged and with a lot of extraneous matter added. Baines wrote:

It appears that this bound volume of manuscript was the actual one used by Dawson, for in a preface he makes reference to it in five lines saying that he had made full use of it. There can be little doubt in my mind that Dawson used Herbert's material and, saving his conscience in a few lines, had passed it off as his own work.

Baines himself qualifies his accusation by admitting that Dawson's preface refers to 'free use' of Herbert's manuscript but even so he fails to do justice to the dead lawyer. Dawson not only made full acknowledgement to William Herbert in his *History*. He explained how he had used the manuscript, considerably augmenting it with Herbert's further drafts in the

Guildhall library. He said that on hearing that he was writing a history of the castle Lord Chichester (the fourth earl) had presented him with the Herbert record. The record, wrote Dawson enthusiastically, was 'noted and planned in almost every detail'. Dawson goes so far as to state that Herbert had made good use of an earlier historian's work, Moss's *History of Hastings*, without acknowledging his debt to that writer. Dawson said he was also indebted to nine other authorities whom he names. In fact the attribution amounts to eighty-four lines: thirty-two in the case of Herbert and fifty-two devoted to the other authors. Moreover the attribution is couched in fulsome terms and is a far cry from the niggardliness alleged by Baines.

Baines' attack did in fact bring about some sort of defence of Dawson. John Thorne of the Battle and District Historical Society wrote to *The Times*[1] to point out Baines' error over the attribution.

There was also objection to the reference to the cast-iron statuette from R. L. Downes of the Faculty of Commerce, University of Birmingham. He said that as he had originated the investigations referred to by Baines he wanted to make it clear that all that could be said with certainty about the statuette was that it was cast-iron and a miniature replica of a Roman statue. Downes said his suggestion of a recent and Continental origin was only one possible explanation—the possibility of its being genuine could not be ruled out. The other three objects were doubtful but if they were fraudulent there was no evidence to prove that any particular person was responsible and it would be unwise to draw any conclusions from such debatable evidence. He concluded :

> We must wait for a complete review of the evidence of Mr Dawson's activities, ranging from his honest and talented work to his undoubted deceptions, before passing any judgement on him or on such debatable specimens.

The following year Dr J. S. Weiner's work *The Piltdown Forgery*[2] was published. His excellent account of the events that led to the discovery that a hoax had been perpetrated on science is marred by a strong bias against Dawson. This reveals itself in Weiner's choice of witnesses; in the main bandwagoners who had

[1] 19 November, 1954.
[2] Oxford, 1955.

apparently known of Dawson's deception and had kept mum for forty years. I have no wish to doubt the motives of these witnesses but their revelations must be flavoured by a desire to get out from under, to remove themselves from the ranks of the gulled. In the book Woodward and Teilhard de Chardin are summarily dismissed as suspects and appear as lay figures manipulated by the puppeteer and arch-villain Dawson.

But singular would be the author capable of completely objective appraisal. Weiner obviously believed in Dawson's guilt from the outset, just as I was biased in favour of Dawson's innocence. But even Weiner, after skilfully implicating the deceased lawyer and completing his destruction, had to remark at the end of the narrative that the evidence of Dawson's guilt which he had assembled was insufficient to prove anything beyond all reasonable doubt and 'that our verdict must rest on suspicion and not proof'.

Chapter 18

IT WOULD BE difficult to envisage a more ideal situation for the passing off of a bogus fossil man than that which existed at the British Museum's Natural History Department in 1912. The department's keeper, Sir Arthur Smith Woodward, although pre-eminent as a palaeoicthyologist, was certainly no human anatomist. This shortcoming was amply demonstrated by the misreading and malconstruction of the Piltdown cranium. Sir Wilfrid Le Gros Clark drew my attention to another surprising example of what he describes as 'the odd custom of the Natural History Museum at that time'[1]. Woodward's subordinate in charge of the anthropology section—the section which dealt with fossil humanity—was W. P. Pycraft, an ornithologist. It is due to Pycraft's poor knowledge of human anatomy that *Cyphanthropus*, the 'Stooping man' of Rhodesia, was credited with a stoop and peculiar gait that he did not possess. He mistook one part of the pelvis for another and reconstructed 'an impossible kind of acetabulum' (the cavity which receives the thighbone). In fact the pelvis is quite like that of modern man. Rhodesian man had no stoop and walked normally. Le Gros Clark pointed out 'this remarkable error' to Pycraft in 1928.

It is not, then, unjust to claim that Woodward's Natural History department was incompetent to handle Piltdown man or for that matter any kind of human skeleton—antique or modern. Charles Dawson may have decided to take advantage of this astonishing state of affairs but surely it would take a skilful anatomist to recognize an incompetent one.

One of my main objections to the assumption that Dawson is inevitably the culprit is that as the discoverer he was wide open to suspicion. He is too obvious a culprit. Even a cursory study of the events which surrounded the discovery of fossil men would have warned Dawson clearly that such finds are highly controversial. If the bogus fossil escaped detection by his friends at the museum he surely could not have expected that it would withstand scientific enquiry for ever.

[1] Letter to the author. 18 September, 1970.

I find it impossible to believe that Dawson would pit his meagre knowledge of anatomy (if it is accepted that he had any at all) against that of any skilled human anatomist. The strain on the nerves would be too great. The threat of exposure would be perpetual. If the forgery had been detected any time in the next ten or twenty years (for Dawson had at least this expectancy of life) then he would have had to face the odium and full wrath of Science. Surely the destruction of the high esteem earned by his many other discoveries would be too high a price to pay? Even if he knew he was about to die, would he be prepared to sacrifice his posthumous esteem? It was most unlikely.

As it was Piltdown man had a charmed life. Because of the poor quality of the original X-ray photographs the bogus jaw remained undetected at the outset. Le Gros Clark has emphasized that the forger's crude workmanship on the teeth was there for all to see if only someone had looked for it. The same critical examinations in 1912 would have revealed as much. Although advanced microchemical techniques were used in 1953 to prove that Piltdown man was bogus, no more than Dr J. S. Weiner's suspicions and a visual examination started his decline. One point that seems to have passed unnoticed hitherto is that owing to the British Museum's incompetence the skull of Piltdown man was reassembled to a smaller size than it actually was. Surely the forger could not have foreseen this circumstance?

Another matter quickly dismissed was the high degree of specialist skill that went into the conception of Piltdown man. The forger supplied the correct clues in the form of 'remains' from which certain (and erroneous) deductions would be arrived at. Any evidence that the skull had possessed features found in modern man other than the noble brow were missing. The brow was needed to supply the paradox. The connecting mechanism on the jaw by which it is hinged into the skull (condylar process) was missing. If present this feature would have clearly shown that the jaw could not have belonged to the skull. The Piltdown teeth are masterpieces of ape plus human features.

I argue that a forgery of such subtlety is beyond the conception of a layman such as Dawson. Most anatomists, including Dr J. S. Weiner, think otherwise : that the anatomy of Piltdown man is well within the scope of a knowledgeable layman. One might wonder to what degree this knowledge might extend before it was classed as 'professional' or 'expert'. After all, what is an anatomist other than a knowledgeable layman?

I have, however, an unexpected ally in one of the detectors of the Piltdown forgery. Sir Wilfrid Le Gros Clark remarked to me in a letter that: 'The forgery is extremely skilful and the forger (possibly in collaboration with someone else) certainly knew the relevant details of palaeontology, archaeology and anatomy'[1]. As this reservation was made by a former professor of human anatomy in the University of Oxford one may be forgiven for wondering whether it might not be something of an understatement.

The cleverness of the forgery is also far underestimated. A high degree of knowledge was required to ensure that Science, although eager, would find such a fossil man plausible. One present view on the evolution of mankind, briefly, runs from the early primates (prosimians) of the Eocene, roughly fifty million years ago, such as the tarsoids, small tree-dwelling animals, through early apes such as *Dryopithecus* and *Proconsul,* then in order *Australopithecus, Pithecanthropus* (Peking and Java man), Neanderthal man, then Modern man through his earlier forms such as the Cro-Magnons. Piltdown man neatly played the part now filled by *Australopithecus.* In fact there is a striking resemblance. The American authority E. A. Hooton stated after the revelations of 1953 that if *Australopithecus* had not been brought to light by Raymond Dart then Science would still be looking for something very much like Piltdown man. He was a highly plausible 'missing link'.

But, as was revealed in 1953, if the conception of Piltdown man was knowledgeable and skilful, the workmanship was not. It is now known that some of the fragments missing from Piltdown man I can be supplied by Piltdown man II. It is impossible to accept that Dawson could have believed that such an obvious device would for long have remained undetected. It is far more likely that this was the forger's next step. He was presenting the British Museum with another chance to detect that the whole affair was an absurdity. Another manifestation of a desire to reveal all must have been the mysterious elephant thighbone tool. The knife marks on this bone are only too clear. That this feature escaped notice is almost beyond belief.

It has been claimed[2] that Dawson was once accidentally interrupted while actually engaged in dark experiments with potassium bichromate stain and human bones. This was damning

[1] Letter to the author. 22 July, 1970.
[2] See The *Piltdown Forgery.* J. S. Weiner.

evidence. But in those times the 'hardening' of fossil bones by such methods was quite usual. The Galley Hill fragments were hardened in this way. Woodward himself innocently commented that the elephant thighbone was given similar treatment by the British Museum (see page 139). Dr Kenneth Oakley has informed me that 'staining' is a hopelessly inadequate way of describing what must have happened to the Piltdown fragments before they were planted. The skull, he said, must have been boiled in some acidulous solution. He suspects iron sulphate. So drastic was this treatment that the calcium phosphate normally present in bone was entirely changed to calcium sulphate. Potassium bichromate is not detectable at all.

Quite a lot was also made of suggestions that a number of people in Sussex, particularly members of the Sussex Archaeological Society, suspected, knew even, that Dawson had forged Piltdown man; that he was known as the 'Wizard of Sussex', a faintly bantering title which suggested that he discovered rare fossil bones or antiquities with suspicious ease. It is surprising, therefore, that his accusers were able to contain themselves for forty years. This has been explained as the result of the closely-knit comradeship of amateur archaeology : the exposure of Dawson would in some way have reflected on the honour of Sussex archaeology. I do not believe it for a moment. We have a strange parallel case in the bogus trimaran circumnavigation of Donald Crowhurst. The mere suspicion that something was not quite right was enough to launch a private letter to the *Sunday Times* adjudicators from Sir Francis Chichester. It is noticeable that single-handed circumnavigation has not gone into a decline as a consequence. Another sure indication that these 'suspicions' owe a lot to hindsight is that the headquarters of these doubters of Dawson, the Sussex Archaeological Society, offered to take over the upkeep costs of the Piltdown excavation site. A strange act indeed if the Society was suspicious.

Since the revelations of 1953 in which he played a prominent part, Kenneth Oakley has continued to examine the Piltdown specimens with a view to discovering the source. He stresses that his work is heavily supplemented by the work of others. Oakley has now proved that the Piltdown cranium is nowhere near as old as had been previously thought. It is not Pleistocene, and no more than a mere 620 ± 100 years B.P. This result was obtained by supplementing the fluorine, nitrogen and uranium estimates with the C-14 (carbon dating) technique.

This highly accurate dating method has also ascertained that Piltdown man's orang-utan jaw is not 'modern' in the true sense, nor could it have been easily come by. It is in fact attributable to 500 ± 10 years B.P. Like the skull the ape jaw is 'mediaeval'.

This result pushes the forgery even farther beyond the range of Dawson. It has been stated that Dawson could have obtained the jaw 'off the peg' from any dealer of zoological specimens. But mediaeval orang-utan jawbones are a rarity; even if available such a purchase would have attracted much attention. Oakley at last saw a breakthrough. A number of such specimens were brought to England in 1875 by the zoologist A. H. Everett. While on the island of Sarawak Everett discovered that the natives suspended the truncated heads of orang-utans from the rafters of their huts. Many of these 'fetishes' or 'trophy-heads' had hung there for centuries. In 1879, Oakley discovered, Everett's collection was presented to the British Museum. Oakley checked the collection against the fossil catalogue: they were all present. Oakley thinks it possible that Everett may have withheld a specimen or two, even selling them to a dealer. But the trail had ended. He had proved, however, that the Piltdown jaw was a rarity and by no means easily obtainable. If Dawson had come by one then the fact would have been well known.

It is a similar story with the 'Pre-Chellean' flint implements from Piltdown. I was at first inclined to suspect that these flints, like those of Moulin Quignon, were produced by the iron-struck method. Oakley assures me that this is not the case. He says that the Sussex specimens were manufactured by the true primitive method—by striking flint against flint; that they are genuine Neolithic 'wasters'—partially completed tools that were rejected by primitive man on discovery of some incipient flaw in the material.

Oakley's researches, and those of his collaborators, suggest that the Piltdown animal remains came from different sources of supply. The rhinoceros and mastodon teeth most likely are from the Tertiary Red Crag deposit in Suffolk. The elephant thigh-bone 'implement' may have come from the gravel in the region of Swanscombe, Kent. The strangest fragment, however, is the molar tooth found by Teilhard de Chardin. It is undoubtedly that of an *Elephas planifrons*. This highly radioactive molar could not have come from England. The only site where such highly radioactive remains have been discovered is at Ishkul,

Tunisia. This tooth has another claim to attention. It was the first *planifrons* tooth ever discovered. Such a discovery was not repeated until well into the 1920's. Now that this information is to hand some idea of the true importance of the Piltdown assemblage can be appreciated.

The most convincing evidence against Charles Dawson is that Piltdown was his special province. Even now it is an isolated place. By his own admission Dawson had regularly visited the site 'since just before the end of the last century'. This adds up, for it was in 1898 that Dawson was appointed to the stewardship of Barkham Manor in the grounds of which the Piltdown pit was discovered. Indeed, the manor house overlooks it. At any time Dawson could have 'planted' the bones without attracting notice, that is if he did not introduce them as the search progressed.

But was Dawson the only person to know about Piltdown and the expectations of the gravel? Dawson said that such antique gravel had not been 'experienced' in Sussex by geologists. Where did he get this information? Having discovered what he suspected was antique gravel at Piltdown Dawson must have spoken or written of it to many. Woodward stated that Dawson frequently sought advice about his finds from experts. So it is not impossible that the lawyer's surveillance of Piltdown was an open secret. Woodward counselled discretion in 1912. But Dawson had discovered the pit in 1898. Ten years had elapsed before the first piece of bone appeared at Piltdown in 1908.

Unfortunately there is no evidence of such an interchange. It is believed that the lawyer's private correspondence was destroyed when Castle Lodge was vacated in 1931. But reticence does not seem to have been Dawson's strong point. In fact, he was gregarious and garrulous. Therefore it is by no means unreasonable to suppose that such a lengthy search would have become known. That the pit was under regular scrutiny by an amateur enthusiast such as Dawson would have been sufficient for the forger's purpose. Who then was the forger?

Sir Arthur Smith Woodward has hitherto entirely escaped suspicion. He seems to have gained even more from Piltdown in the way of fame than Dawson. His long friendship with Dawson would have assured that the 'planted' bones would be returned to him almost automatically. We have only his word that Dawson discovered Piltdown man II. He had ready access to human and animal fossils. He could have sneaked the orang-utan jaw from the museum collection. But Woodward can, I think, be dismissed on the grounds that he was too dedicated, too studious, for such an undertaking. He was a queer fish—almost the archetypal boffin. His ascetic approach to his chosen subject was a by-word. He scurried about the museum work-rooms, head down, oblivious of the living world. This resulted directly in two nasty accidents.

On the first occasion he collided with a class exhibition case and fell to the floor snapping a leg. Woodward refused emphatically to go to hospital or to be attended by a surgeon. He set the limb himself with the result that henceforth he walked with a limp. Some human anatomist? A similar collision resulted in a broken arm. His younger assistants, with the expectation of being free of the Woodward thrall for a few weeks, were shocked from recumbent positions on benches by the conscientious professor's appearance for work the following day.

It is unlikely, therefore, that such a man would even dream of perpetrating such a fraud. Especially if one takes into account his nigh on a lifetime's search at Piltdown.

The other successful searcher at Piltdown was Père Teilhard de Chardin. The evidence against the priest is as black, if not blacker, than that against Dawson. One has merely to recall the incredulity of Dawson and Woodward when Teilhard de Chardin discovered the missing canine tooth in a stretch of gravel which had just been thoroughly searched. Oakley's discovery in connection with the *Elephas planifrons* molar is highly significant in this case. Before his arrival at Ore Place, Hastings, the student-priest had actually stayed near Ishkul, Tunisia.

Teilhard de Chardin is a hard man to place. His lifelong struggle with his religion made him deeply introspective. He was a prolific author but one can gather little of the quality of the man from the output. The books are for the most part quasi-scientific explanations of his conception of the place of evolution within religion. In this last task he sees no contradiction imposed by one on the other.

The priest has by no means escaped suspicion in some quarters. Sir Wilfred Le Gros Clark told me that because of the Tunisian association he at one time strongly suspected Teilhard de Chardin. Oakley agreed, but like Le Gros Clark, he feels that not only lack of the requisite anatomical knowledge but the whole nature of the man must exonerate him.

The discovery that Piltdown man was a deception deeply hurt Teilhard de Chardin. According to Oakley he took the news far harder than Sir Arthur Keith. He miserably told Oakley that throughout the vicissitudes of his life the main consolation was that he had helped to discover the Piltdown man. Teilhard de Chardin might have been putting on an act but he did in fact arrive in England too late to have 'planted' the original find in 1908. It is just possible however, that he might have added the *Elephas planifrons* molar to gain some kudos. That he likewise planted the controversial canine is highly doubtful.

Sir Arthur Keith, as one of the world's paramount comparative anatomists, is possibly the only person who can escape suspicion purely on prestige. He is further exonerated by his misinterpretation of the skull, by treating it as that of a primitive hominid which had existed too early in time to have developed the more prominent left side. If anything, the joke was on him as much as on Woodward. But contrary to expectations he took the terrible news quite calmly. Oakley recalled the visit he paid with Dr J. S. Weiner to the old man's home at Downe. He had, Keith said, in any case heard the news on the radio. He said at the outset of the interview: 'I know why you have come to me . . .' The visitors gave Keith the full story. He said that they were probably right 'but it will take me a little time to adjust to the new view'. Poor Keith. How bitter that moment must have been for him. Someone had made a fool of him for forty years.

But now let us return to Woodward's ill-fated construction of the first Piltdown skull. Owing to an imperfect knowledge of human anatomy, shared by the bird man Pycraft, he made a grave error over the reconstruction. Another mistake was his failure to recognize that the cranial bones of Piltdown man II rightly belonged to Piltdown man I. By contrast the American Ales Hrdlička found himself able to suggest that the Piltdown II molar must have come from Piltdown I after an examination which cannot have been more than brief. The incompetence at South Kensington is understandable for clearly the department did not know what it was about. But the most surprising feature of the whole mess was the non-intervention of Grafton Elliot Smith.

Not only was Smith an accomplished human anatomist but he was also an expert on prehistoric and ancient human skulls. He had certainly examined enough of them not many years before during his archaeological survey of Nubia. Smith was called in to the affair well before the unveiling of Piltdown man in December 1912. That he stood by and watched the baffled Woodward and Pycraft wrestle with the reconstruction is therefore certain. By no stretch of the imagination can it be accepted that he too was incompetent. A word from him would have put Woodward on the right track; certainly so in the case of the side ridge of the skull which Woodward took for the median ridge. His complete failure to assist Woodward is in my opinion, highly incriminatory.

What then was Smith's motive? Two immediately come to mind. First, if a sufficiently primitive man were to be discovered in England, this would lend support to Smith's almost obsessive views on migration. He argued that as the new waves of culture spread from 'somewhere in the Middle East' the exponents of the new learning, so to speak, drove the more primitive occupants further out. A near-animal Piltdown man as far west as Britain would lend admirable support to this view.

Alternatively, at the time of the 'planting' of the fossils, Smith was in what might be considered a backwater appointment in Cairo. It is therefore possible that he coveted the job at South Kensington. He must have known that neither Woodward nor Pycraft were human anatomists. His cataloguing of the Hunterian Collection had brought him into close contact with both.

I was at first inclined towards the second motive. I thought that as Smith grew in professional stature and the forgery refused to let itself be discovered, he allowed the matter to stagnate. He could not do otherwise, for a sudden revelation at this late stage would be highly suspicious. But as my research advanced, and I realized that Smith was a highly likely suspect, my view of the actual motive changed. In its place came the conviction that Smith would have loved a chuckle at the expense of what he thought, possibly correctly, was stick-in-the-mud palaeontology and anatomy. Somehow the whole affair reeks of Smith.

At the time of the Piltdown discoveries Smith was mostly in Egypt. But his tumultuous appearances in England coincide remarkably with the turn of events in Sussex. Smith had all the qualifications, both esoteric and professional, for what I believe is more accurately called the Piltdown hoax. Access to the remains of extinct fauna would have presented little difficulty to a professor of palaeontology. If Dawson had attempted such a remarkable aggregation then suspicion would have been drawn to him at once. Moreover, Smith's work in Nubia had made available a vast collection of human skulls. In his catalogue there are many thousands that are 'mediaeval'. Many have peculiarities caused by disease and whim of nature. Not a few are as thick in section as the Piltdown skull.

But what would have been Smith's excuse when the Piltdown forgery was detected, as he must have thought it inevitably would be? Would his pontifications about the value of the Pilt-down skull bring him a share of the opprobrium heaped on Woodward? At first this seems an insurmountable objection to my hypothesis, but it is in fact not so. I have examined all Smith's writings on the subject with care and in not one instance does he fail to state carefully that his findings were based on the examination of a *plaster cast* of the skull. He even used his argument with Keith to imply that these plaster casts were in-accurate. If Keith had access to the actual skull, he said, like Woodward, then Keith would have to revise his opinion as to the morphology of the skull. He did not think plaster casts were inaccurate in 1903 when he wrote from Egypt to Symming-ton advising him to have a good look at them (see page 102). Another clue to his method is that even as late as November 1915 he wrote that he had actually seen the skull fragments for the first time. It seems highly unlikely that three years had passed without sight of the actual fragments, that his Geological Society paper was based on the examination of a mere plaster cast. In fact, would any anatomist wage war with an authority such as Keith on the basis of a plaster cast when Woodward would have been only too pleased to show him the original?

I asked Oakley if it were not possible that the Piltdown skull might have come from Egypt, from Nubia. He replied that there was as much for the proposition as against it. All that was known of the skull, he said, was that it was Caucasian in type and over a half-century old. Egyptians certainly have Caucasian skulls, he said. Oakley must have guessed the drift of the question for he asked me whether in the course of my research I had not come to some conclusion as to the identity of the Piltdown forger. At the time I did not know that Oakley had studied under Sir Grafton Elliot Smith. The naming of Smith did not bring an objection from him. He raised his eyebrows. Indeed, Oakley thought that I could be right. He recalled Smith's arrogant delivery of a lecture. Oakley was not impressed with this superiority or by the air of conceit that Smith exuded. It is only fair to mention, however, that Sir Wilfrid Le Gros Clark was most favourably impressed by the Australian, by Smith's kindness and assistance in the way of laboratory space at University College when Le Gros Clark returned from a tour of fossil men sites overseas. Le Gros Clark also considers that the evidence against Dawson is considerable but he does suspect a professional accomplice.

One might speculate endlessly on the permutations of layman and scientist. Could Dawson have been in league with Smith against Woodward? This is not at all likely. It will be recalled that Dawson and Arthur Smith Woodward had been friends for many years. Dawson was a regular house guest. Lady Woodward had a special tablecloth on which eminent scientific visitors were invited to scrawl their signatures. It was an honour that had been extended to Dawson. Any such treachery would have been entirely foreign to Dawson.

So Piltdown man can be summed up as a hoax that went sour. It was certainly not intended as a forgery that would stand the test of time. It was skilfully contrived but clumsily put together. Although the realization that Sir Grafton Elliot Smith might be the hoaxer dawned on me about halfway through the preliminary research for this book, try as I may I have not been able to come up with concrete evidence of the Australian's participation. In fact it is hard to visualize anything that would come into this category other than a straightforward confession. I do hope, however, that I have shown that Dawson does not fit the bill. And that Smith does.

One thing that certainly emerges is the extraordinary waste of time, the absorption of brilliant minds, that was the result of the Piltdown hoax. The blind Woodward dictating the results of a search which lasted over a quarter of a century creates a poignant picture. Or is it too unkind to suggest that all concerned would have wasted their time anyway?

Sir Wilfrid Le Gros Clark is inclined to take a brighter view. He anticipates with relish the discovery of yet another Piltdown man. 'What would Science think then?' he asked me. In a more serious vein, he said that the major outcome of the Piltdown episode was that Science was now on its guard; that it would be impossible for a similar fraud to be perpetrated. Maybe all budding palaeontologists should be taken down to Sussex to

see the now derelict stone tribute to Charles Dawson at Piltdown just to make sure.

Many a hero has lost his glory posthumously because a
historian has credited him with the peculiar gift of talking in
italics. Others have been brought down by being quoted out of
context. Grafton Elliot Smith was ill-advised enough to tell the
1912 Geological Society meeting that the association of the
simian (ape) jaw with a human brain was not surprising to anyone familiar with recent research on the evolution of man. Now
that the whole Piltdown edifice has crashed down, how strange
this remark sounds. Could he have been laughing at his colleagues?

Grafton Elliot Smith also told poor Dawson that Piltdown
man's brother or cousin from Talgai was found at a place
called Pilton in Queensland. In fact, there is no such place in
the whole of Australia. Could Smith's eyes have watered just
a little as he watched the innocent dupe Dawson swallow this
gobbet of false information?

Let us be even unkinder with a little test of absolutely no
consequence. Turn to the picture of the Piltdown men facing
page 161. One of this distinguished group almost definitely was
the Piltdown forger—or hoaxer. *Nature* assures us that all are
excellent likenesses. Pick the hoaxer out for yourself. I will not
state the obvious.

Appendices

APPENDIX I

Brief Glossary

Acromegaly A disturbance of the pituitary gland causing accelerated growth, particularly of the nose, cheekbones and jaw. There are authenticated instances of the afflicted strongly resembling Neanderthal man. This disease was used to great effect to deny that this or that fossil man was indeed a fossil at all. Sir Arthur Smith Woodward similarly despaired of Rhodesian man and suspected the disease in this case.

Aurochs An extinct species of wild ox; now erroneously applied to the modern European bison, *Bos bison*, still extant in Lithuania.

Autochthones An early description of primitive man, implying that he had sprung from the soil. The ancient Athenians claimed to have done just this. The philosopher and writer Sir Thomas Browne (1605–82) observed in *Religio Medici* (*c.* 1635) that 'there was never any *autochthone* but Adam'.

B.P. Before the Present. An estimate of the age of a fossil human being is now given in a number of years B.P.

Brachycephalic If the width of a skull is 80 per cent or more of its length it is said to be *brachycephalic*, implying roundness. If the width is less than 75 per cent of the length it is *dolichocephalic*, implying length. Between 75 and 80 per cent the skull is said to be *mesocephalic*.

Coprolite A round fossil resembling a stone supposed to be the petrified excrement of an animal. There are many early reports of *coprolites* being found in British caves and attributed to the hyena.

Cranial capacity An estimate of the brain volume. Millet seed, even rice, was once commonly used to arrive at this measure.

Dentrites The presence of these 'brilliants' on fossil bones or flint implements was said to indicate vast antiquity. Also *limnites de fer*. The theory is now discredited.

Devonian A geological age. See Fig. I.

Drypopithecus A fossil ape.

Endocranial cast A plaster cast on the interior of a skull. Great anatomical sport was had with these casts, some authorities drawing mighty conclusions from what they considered were impressions of the brain on the bone. Modern thought tends to belittle the importance of such deductions but there are instances of some of the earlier findings being valid. Sir Wilfrid Le Gros Clark told the present author that because of the crudity of the earlier plaster casts they were open to all sorts of false interpretations and conjecture. Modern endocranial casts are plastic, which has resulted in a greater degree of accuracy and reliability.

Flint implements   Primitive stone tools worked by the hand of man. For culture types see Appendix B.

Fossil   As a rule fossils are formed by the least destructible part of the body, such as bones in the case of faunal fossils. Under favourable conditions these parts become impregnated with mineral salt derived from the deposit in which they are buried. Most resistant to decay in faunal skeletons are, strangely, the teeth.

Gisement   The conference of French and British geologists and archaeologists used *gisement*—the finding of flint implements *in situ* at Moulin Quignon in 1863—as valid evidence that the implements were authentic works of primitive man.

Glaciation or Glacial   A major icing-up of the earth's surface during the Pleistocene. There were four European glaciations named *Wurm*, *Riss*, *Mindel* and *Gunz*. The intervening 'warm' period is known by its preceding and following glaciations, e.g. Riss-Wurm *Interglacial*. A temporary rise in temperature during a glaciation is termed an *Interstadial*.

Holocene   The geological age in which we live. In fact Pleistocene conditions still apply, the condition of polar ice being unknown in 200,000,000 years. That another ice age with its glaciation will again be experienced by this planet is highly likely. The present author calculates that on previous form this should happen in about 15,000 years time. See *Table I*.

Hominid   A creature with strong affinities with man. Earlier workers used abilities such as firelighting and tool manufacturing as qualification for the title *hominid*. Modern thought, however, relies more on anatomical features of similarity but as has been observed more than once the qualification is not entirely anatomical. It seems much easier to define what isn't a hominid than what is.

Interglacial   See Glaciation.

Interstadial   See Glaciation.

Loess   Wind-born dust of immense use to stratigraphers, for such deposits mark 'warm' periods of the Pleistocene.

Marsupial   An animal, such as the kangaroo and the opossum, which has an abdominal pouch for carrying its young.

Matrix   A mineral or rocky mass surrounding a fossil bone.

Mesocephalic   See Brachycephalic.

Moraine   A stratigraphical term for an accumulation of debris marking the extent of an ice sheet.

Neolithic   New Stone Age. See Palaeolithic.

Pachyderm   Order of mammals invented by Cuvier which included ungulates or hoofed animals such as the elephant, rhinoceros, hippopotamus and horse. More recently, the term implies the thick-skinned quadruped the elephant.

Palaeolithic   The Old Stone Age. An expression of antiquity of indefinable pretensions. At first used to contrast with Neolithic or New Stone Age but later used generally for fossil men for which vast claims of antiquity were being made. Palaeolith was another and earlier term for 'eolith'.

Palaeontology   The study of fossils.

Phylum   A tribe or race of organisms related by descent from a common ancestor.

Pithecoid   Resembling or pertaining to the apes, especially the anthropoids. It is more common now to use *simian*.

Pleistocene   The age previous to the present (Holocene), first age of the Quaternary. Duration generally accepted to be in excess of 1,000,000 years but according to some authorities as much as 3,000,000. See *Table II*.

Pliocene   The age immediately preceding the Pleistocene and the final age of the Tertiary, duration about 9,000,000 years

Quadrumana   Order of mammals which includes monkeys, apes, baboons, and lemurs, whose hind as well as forefeet have an opposable digit or thumb so giving the animal, as it were, four hands. The expression Bimana is used for the two-handed variety such as man.

Quaternary   Successor to the Tertiary, including the Pleistocene and Holocene.

Rock-shelter   An overhang of rock forming a shelter thought to be a usual habitat for human beings during the mild weather of an Interglacial.

Secondary   Now usually called the Mesozoic. See *Table I*.

Simian   See Pithecoid.

Sulci   A fissure or depression between two convolutions of the brain.

Tertiary   The age preceding the Quaternary, from the Palaeocene to the Pliocene, duration about 60,000,000 years.

Travertine   Limestone deposited by water in which it was held in suspension.

Tuffa   Or *tuff*. A consolidation of volcanic ash.

Villefranchian   In recent terminology Villefranchian refers to the preglacial part of the Pleistocene.

APPENDIX II

Possible correlation of archaeological and geological terminology for sub-divisions of the Pleistocene.

Upper Pleistocene	Wurm Glaciation Riss-Wurm Interglacial
Middle Pleistocene	Riss Glaciation Mindel-Riss Interglacial Mindel Glaciation Gunz-Mindel Glaciation
Lower Pleistocene	Gunz Glaciation Pre-Gunz (pre-glaciation)

Possible correlation between flint cultures and geological terminology in the Pleistocene.

Magdalenian	Wurm III Glacial
Solutrian Gravettian	Wurm II/III Interstadial
Aurignacean	Wurm II Glacial
Chatelperronian replacing Mousterian	Wurm I/II Interstadial
Main Mousterian and Upper Levalloisian	Wurm I Glacial
Early Mousterian, also Middle Levalloisian	
	Riss-Wurm Interglacial
Tayacian and Micoquian (Acheulian VI, VII)	
Acheulian V, Tayacian High Lodge, Clactonian and Lower Levalloisian	Riss II Glacial Riss I/II Interstadial Riss I Glacial
Acheulian III/IV and Proto-Levalloisian	Pre-Riss 'Cold Phase'
Acheulian III also Clactonian	
	Mindel-Riss Interglacial
Aucheulian I-II facies	
'Abbevillian' i.e. facies of Early Clactonian	Mindel II Glacial Mindel I/II Interstadial

Table I

Geological Time Table (from *The History of the Primates,* British Museum, Sir Wilfrid Le Gros Clark).

GEOLOGICAL TIME-SCALE†

AGE IN MILLIONS OF YEARS	GEOLOGICAL SYSTEMS (Maximum thickness in feet)	ERA	TIME RANGES OF LIFE GROUPS
3 * —	QUATERNARY *		MAN
12 —	PLIOCENE 15,000 ft.	CAENOZOIC ‡	
25 —	MIOCENE 21,000 ft.		
40 —	OLIGOCENE 26,000 ft.		
60 —	EOCENE 30,000 ft		BIRDS
70 —	PALAEOCENE 12,000 ft		
	CRETACEOUS 51,000 ft.	MESOZOIC	MAMMALS
135 —	JURASSIC 44,000 ft.		REPTILES
180 —	TRIASSIC 30,000 ft.		
225 —	PERMIAN 19,000 ft.	PALAEOZOIC	AMPHIBIANS
270 —	CARBONIFEROUS 46,000 ft.		AGNATHANS AND FISHES
350 —	DEVONIAN 38,000 ft.		LAND PLANTS
400 —	SILURIAN 34,000 ft.		SEAWEEDS AND INVERTEBRATE ANIMALS
440 —	ORDOVICIAN 40,000 ft.		
500 —	CAMBRIAN 40,000 ft.		
600 —	Unknown thickness	PRO-TEROZOIC	
	PRE-CAMBRIAN		
	Unknown thickness	AZOIC	
Origin of Earth's Crust — 4500 —			

Table II

Approximate datings for the four great glaciations and inter-glacials of the Pleistocene.

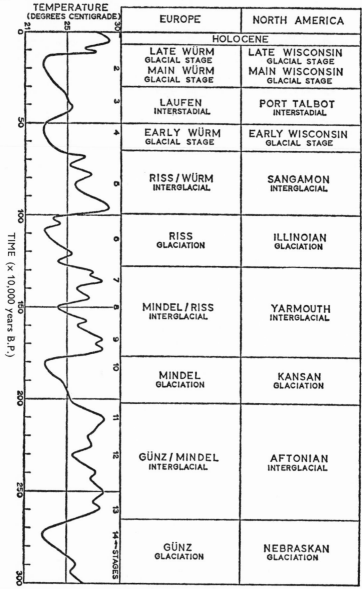

TEMPERATURE (DEGREES CENTIGRADE)	EUROPE	NORTH AMERICA
	HOLOCENE	
	LATE WÜRM GLACIAL STAGE / MAIN WÜRM GLACIAL STAGE	LATE WISCONSIN GLACIAL STAGE / MAIN WISCONSIN GLACIAL STAGE
	LAUFEN INTERSTADIAL	PORT TALBOT INTERSTADIAL
	EARLY WÜRM GLACIAL STAGE	EARLY WISCONSIN GLACIAL STAGE
	RISS / WÜRM INTERGLACIAL	SANGAMON INTERGLACIAL
	RISS GLACIATION	ILLINOIAN GLACIATION
	MINDEL / RISS INTERGLACIAL	YARMOUTH INTERGLACIAL
	MINDEL GLACIATION	KANSAN GLACIATION
	GÜNZ / MINDEL INTERGLACIAL	AFTONIAN INTERGLACIAL
	GÜNZ GLACIATION	NEBRASKAN GLACIATION

The temperatures in the left-hand column, obtained from cores drilled from the bed of the Caribbean Ocean, reflect changes in surface water.

SELECT BIBLIOGRAPHY

Anters, E. 1947. 'Dating the Past' (review), *J. Geol.*, vol. 55.

Barbour, G. 1965. *In the Field with Teilhard de Chardin*, Herder and Herder, New York.

Black, D. 1925. 'The Human Skeletal Remains from Shakuot'un', *Palaeontologia Sinica*, 1925, vol. i, fascide 3.

——. 1927. 'Lower Molar Tooth from Choukoutien Deposit', *Palaentologia Sinica*, 1927, vol. ii.

——, Teilhard de Chardin, P., Young, C. C., and Pei, C.C. 1933. 'The Choukoutien Cave Deposits with a synopsis of our present knowledge of the Late Cenozoic of China', *Mem. Geol. Surv. China*, Ser. A., no. 11.

Blake, C. C. 1864. 'On the Alleged Peculiar Character and Assumed Antiquity of the Human Cranium from Neanderthal', *Proc. Anthrop. Soc.*, 16 February, 1864.

Bordes, F. 1957. 'Some Observations on the Pleistocene Succession in the Somme Valley', *Proc. Prehist. Soc. Lond.*, vol. 22 (1956).

Boule, M. 1911–13. 'L'Homme fossile de la Chapelle-aux-Saints', *Annls. de Paléont.*, 6, 7, and 8.

——. 1921. *Les Hommes Fossiles*, 2nd edn., Masson et cie, Paris.

——, Vallois, H. V. 1946. *Les Hommes Fossiles*, 3rd edn., Masson et cie, Paris.

——, Breuil, H., Licent, E., Teilhard de Chardin, P. 1928. 'Le Paléolithique de la Chine', *Arch. de l'Institut de Paléontologie humaine*, memoir iv, 1928.

——. 1929. 'Le Sinanthropus', *Anthropologie* 39, pp. 455–60.

Bovyesonie, A. and Bardon, L. 1908. 'Découverte d'un squelette humain moustérien à La Chapelle-aux-Saints, Corrèze', *C. R. Acad. Sci. Paris*, 147: 1414, 1415.

Breuil, H. 1912. 'Les Subdivisions du Paléolithique supérieur et leur signification', *C.R. Congr. Internat. d'Anthrop. et d'Arch. Préhist.*, 14th sess.

——, Koslowski, L. 1931–2. 'Etudes de Stratigraphie paléolithique dans le nord de la France, la Belgique et l'Angleterre', *L'Anthropologie*, vol. 41.

Broca, P. 1865–75. 'On the Human Bones found in the cave of Cro-Magnon, nr. Les Eyzies', In *Reliquae aquitanicae*. Lartet, E., and Christy, H., Williams and Norgate, London.

Broom, R. 1938. 'The Pleistocene Anthropoid Apes of South Africa', *Nature* 142: 377–9.

——, Schepers, G. W. 1946. 'The South African fossil ape-men, the Australopithecinae', *Trans. Mus. Mem.*, 2: 1–272.

Buxton, L. H. Dudley. 1928. 'Excavations in Beluchistan', *Arch. Surv. India Report*, 1929.

Cambell, B. 1964. *Classification and Human Evolution,* Methuen & Co. Ltd., London.

Capitan, L. and Peyrony, D. 1909. 'Deux squelettes humaines au milieu de foyers de l'époque moustérienne', *Rev. anthrop.* 21: 148–50.

du Chaillu, Paul. 1861. *Explorations and Adventures in Equatorial Africa,* London.

Chang, K. C. 1960. 'New Light on Early Man in China', *Asian Perspec.* vol. 2 (1958), no. 2.

Clark, W. Le Gros. 1950. 'Evolution of the Hominidae', *Quart. J. Geol. Soc. Lond.,* 150, part 2.

——. 1955. *The Fossil Evidence for Human Evolution,* Chicago University Press, Chicago.

——. 1955. 'The Exposure of the Piltdown Forgery', *Royal Institution paper,* 10 May, 1955.

——. 1955. 'Further Contributions to the Solution of the Piltdown Problem', *Bull. Brit. Mus. (Natural History),* vol. 2, no. 6, 1958.

——. 1965. *History of the Primates,* 9th edn., British Museum.

Coon, C. S. 1963. *The Origin of Races,* London.

Cuénot, C. 1958. *Pierre Teilhard de Chardin, les Grands Etapes de son Evolution,* Plon, Paris.

Dart, A. 1925. 'Australopithecus africanus: The Man-Ape of South Africa', *Nature,* 115: 195–9.

——. 1926. 'Taungs and its significance', *Nat. Hist.,* 3: 315–27.

——. 1948. 'The Makapansgat Proto-Human, Australopithecus prometheus', *Am. J. Phys. Anthrop,* 6: 259–284.

Darwin, C. 1859. *The Origin of Species by means of Natural Selection,* John Murray, London. Also 1902 edn., Grant Richards, London.

——. 1871. *The Descent of Man,* John Murray, London.

Darwin, F. 1887. *The Life and Letters of Charles Darwin,* London.

Dawson, C. 1909. *The History of Hastings Castle,* 2 vols., London.

——. 1913. 'On the Discovery of a Human Skull and Mandible at Piltdown, Sussex', *The Hastings and E. Sussex Naturalist,* vol. 2, no. 2, 25 March, 1913.

—— and Woodward, A. S. 1913. 'On the Discovery of a Paleolithic Human Skull and Mandible in a Flint-bearing Gravel . . . at Piltdown (Fletching) Sussex', *Quart. J. Geol. Soc. Lond.* 69: 117–151.

—— and Woodward, A. S. 1914. 'Supplementary Note on the Discovery of a Paleolithic Human Skull and Mandible in a Flint-bearing Gravel . . . at Piltdown (Fletching) Sussex', *Quart. J. Geol, Soc. Lond.,* 70: 82–90.

Day, M. H. 1965. *Guide to Fossil Man,* Cassell, London.

Dubois, E. 1894. 'Pithecanthropus erectus, eine menschenaehnliche ubergangsform aus Java', *Landesdruckerie,* Batavia.

——. 1922. 'The Proto-Australian Fossil Man of Wadjak, Java', *Proc. Acad. Sci. Amst.,* 23: 1013–1051.

Emiliani, C. 1955. 'Pleistocene Temperatures', *J. Geol.,* vol. 63.

Flint, R. F. and Brandtrer, F. 1961. 'Climatic Changes since the Last Interglacial', *Amer. J. Sci.,* vol. 159.

von Fuhlrott, C. 1859. 'Menschlicke Uebereste aus einer Felsengrotte des Dusselthals', *Verh. naturh. Ver. der preuss. Rheinl.,* 16: 131–133

Garrod, D. A. E. and Bate, D. M. A. 1937. *The Stone Age of Mount Carmel*, vol. I, *Excavations at the Wady el-Mughara*, The Clarendon Press, Oxford.

Geikie, A. 1885. *Text-book of Geology*, 2nd edn., London.

Geikie, J. 1877. *The Great Ice Age*, 2nd edn., London.

Gorjanoric-Kramberger, K. 1906. *Der diluviale Mensch von Krapina im Kroatia*, C. W. Kradels Verlag, Weisbaden.

Grabau, A. W. 1927. 'Summary of the Cenozoic and Psychozoic deposits with special reference to Asia', *Bull. Geol. Surv. China*, 1927, vol. vi.

Gregory, W. K. 1922. *The Origin and Evolution of the Human Dentition*, Williams and Wilkins, Baltimore.

Grenet, P. 1965. *Teilhard de Chardin*, trans. Rudorff, R. A., Souvenir Press Ltd., London.

Hawkes, J. 1963. *Prehistory and the Beginnings of Civilization*, vol. I, George Allen and Unwin, London.

Henri-Martin, G. 1947. 'L'Homme fossile tayacian de la grotte de Fontéchevade', *C.R. Acad. Sci. Paris*, 288: 598–600.

Holmes, A. 1944. *Principles of Physical Geography*, London.

Howells, W. 1960. *Mankind in the Making*, London.

Hoyle, F. 1950. *The Nature of the Universe*, Oxford University Press, London.

Hrdlicka, A. 1922. 'The Piltdown Jaw', *Amer. J. Phys. Anthrop*, Ser. 5.

Huxley, T. H. 1863. *Evidence as to Man's Place in Nature*, Williams and Norgate, London.

Jones, F. D. 1929. *Man's Place among the Mammals*, Edward Arnold, London.

——. 1948. *Hallmarks of Mankind*, Baillière, Tindall and Cox, London.

Jones, N. 1926. *The Stone Age in Rhodesia*, Oxford University Press, London.

Keith, A. 1915. *The Antiquity of Man*, Williams and Norgate, London. Also 2nd edn., 2 vols., 1925.

——. 1928. 'The Evolution of the Human Races', *J. Roy. Anthrop. Inst.*, vol. 58.

——. 1931. *New Discoveries: The Antiquity of Man*, Williams and Norgate, London.

——. 1948. *A New Theory of Human Evolution*, Watts and Co., London.

——. 1950. *An Autobiography*, Watts and Co., London.

King, W. 1864. 'The Reputed Fossil Man of the Neanderthal', *Quart. J. Sci.*, 1: 88–97.

King, W. B. R. 1955. 'The Pleistocene Period in England', *Quart. J. Geol. Soc.*, vol. iii.

Lawrence, J. W. P. 1935. *Stone Age Races of Kenya*, Oxford University Press, London.

Leakey, L. S. B. et al. 1933. 'The Olduvai Human Skeleton', *Nature*, vol. 131.

——. 1959. 'A New Fossil Skull from Olduvai', *Nature*, 184: 491–493.

——, Leakey, M. D. 1964. 'Recent Discoveries of Fossil Hominids in Tanganyika; at Olduvai and near Lake Natron', *Nature*, 202: 5–7.

——. 1965. *Olduvai Gorge, 1951–1961*, Cambridge University Press, Cambridge.

Lubac, M. 1967. *L'Obéisance du Père Teilhard de Chardin*, Paris.

Lyell, C. 1830–33. *The Principles of Geology*, London.

Lyne, C. W. 1916. 'The Significance of the Radiographs of the Piltdown Teeth', *Proc. Roy. Soc. Med.*, 9 (3 Odont Sect.): 33–62.

Marston, A. T. 1936. 'Preliminary Note on a New Fossil Human Skull from Swanscombe, Kent', *Nature* 138: 200–01.

——. 1950. 'The Relative Ages of the Swanscombe and Piltdown skulls with special reference to the results of the fluorine estimation test', *Brit. Dent. J. London*, 88: 292–9.

Miller, G. S. 1915. 'The Jaw of Piltdown Man', *Smiths. Miscell. Coll.*, Washington, 65: 1–31.

——. 1918. 'The Piltdown Jaw', *Amer. J. Phys. Anthrop.*, Washington (N.S.) 1: 25–52.

——. 1920. 'The Piltdown Problem', *Amer. J. Phys. Anthrop.*, Washington 3: 585–6.

——. 1928. *Smiths. Rep. for 1928*, Washington, 1929.

Moir, J. R. 1911. 'The Flint Implements of Sub-Crag Man', *Proc. Prehist. Soc. E. Anglia*, 1: 17–24.

——. 1927. 'On Deposits at Hoxne, Suffolk', *Proc. Prehist. Soc. E. Angia*, vol. 5.

——. 1935. *Prehistoric Archaeology and Sir Ray Lankester*, Adlard & Co., Ipswich.

Morant, G. M. 1925. 'Study of Egyptian Craniology from Prehistoric to Roman Times', *Biometrika*, vol. xvi.

de Mortillet, G. and A. 1900. *Le Préhistorique: Origine et Antiquité de l'Homme*, 3rd edn., Paris.

Oakley, K. P. 1948. 'Fluorine and the Relative Dating of Bones', *Advanc. Sci.*, London, 16: 336–337.

——. 1949. *A Reconsideration of the Galley Hill Skeleton*, Bull. Brit. Mus. (Natural History) Geol., vol. 1, no. 2.

——. 1950. 'New Evidence on the Dating of Piltdown Man', *Nature*, 165.

——. 1951. 'A Definition of Man', *Science News*, Harmondsworth, London.

——. 1953. 'Dating Fossil Human Remains', in *Anthropology Today* (edit. Kroeber, A. L.), Chicago University Press, Chicago.

——. 1957. 'Stratigraphical Age of the Swanscombe Skull', *Am. J. Phys. Anthrop.*, Washington, 15: 253–60.

——. 1958. 'The Dating of Broken Hill (Rhodesian) Man', in *Hundert Jahre Neanderthaler* (ed. von Koenigswald, G. H. R.) Kemunk en Zoon, Utrecht.

——. 1961. *Man the Toolmaker*, 5th edn., British Museum (Natural History) Geol., London.

——. 1964. *The Problem of Man's Antiquity: an Historical Survey*, Bull. Brit. Mus. (Nat. Hist.) Geol., vol. 9, no. 5.

——. 1969. *Framework for Dating Fossil Man*, 3rd edn., Weidenfeld and Nicolson, London.

Owen, R. 1840–45. *Odontography,* Hippotyte, Baillière, London.

Pei, W. C. 1929. 'The Discovery of an Adult Sinanthropus Skull', *Bull. Geolog. Soc. China.*, vol. 8.

de Perthes, C. B. 1846. *Antiquités celtiques et antédiluviennes: de l'industrie primitive ou des arts à leur origine*, Abbeville.

——. 1863. 'Moulin Quignon', *L'Abbevillois*, 9 April 1863, Abbeville.

Pycraft, W. P. et al. 1928. *Rhodesian Man and Associated Remains*, ed. Bather, F. A., Brit. Mus. (Nat. Hist.) Geol.

Ramstrom, M. 1919. 'Der Piltdown-fund', *Bull. Geol. Inst. Uppsala.*

Raven, C. E. 1962. *Teilhard de Chardin*, Collins, London.

Selenka, M. L. and Blankenhorn, M. 1911. *Die Pithecanthropus-Schichten auf Java*, Verlag von Wilhelm Engelmann, Leipzig.

Schaafhausen, H. 1858. 'Zur Kenntnis de Eillensten Rasseuschädel', *Archiv. Anat. Phys. Wiss. Medicin*: 453–478.

Schoelensach, O. 1908. *Der Unlerkeifer des Homo heidelbergensis aus den Sanden von Mauer bei Heidelberg*, Verlag von Wilhelm Engelmann, Leipzig.

Smith, A. 1917. 'A Pleistocene Skull from Talgai, Queensland', *Proc. Roy. Soc. Queensland*, 4 October, 1917.

Smith, G. E. 1918. *The Evolution of Man*, Oxford University Press, London.

——. 1931. *The Search for Man's Ancestors*, Oxford University Press, London.

Speaight, R. 1967. *Teilhard de Chardin*, Collins, London.

Teilhard de Chardin, P., and Licent, E. 1924. 'On the Discovery of a Palaeolithic Industry in Northern China', *Bull. Geol. Soc. China*, vol. 3.

Teilhard de Chardin, P. 1956. *Lettres du Voyage*, Grasset, Paris.

——. 1957. *Nouvelles Lettres du Voyage*, Grasset, Paris.

—— 1959. *The Phenomenon of Man*, Collins, London.

——. 1960. *Le Milieu Divin*, Collins, London.

True, H. L. 1902. *The Cause of the Ice Age*, Cincinnati.

Underwood, A. S. 1913. 'The Piltdown Skull', *Brit. Dent. J.*, London, 56: 650–652.

Vallois, H. V. 1954. 'Neanderthals and Praesapiens', *J. R. Anthrop. Inst., London*, 84: 113–130.

von Virchow, R. 1872. 'Untasuchung des Neanderthal-Schädele', 2 *Ethn.* 4: 157–165.

de Vries, H. and Oakley, K. P. 1959. 'Radiocarbon Dating of the Piltdown Skull and Jaw', *Nature*, vol. 184: 224–226.

Wallace, A. R. 1866. *The Malay Archipelago*, London.

——. 1903. 'My Relations with Charles Darwin', *Black and White*, 17 January, 1903.

Warren, S. H. 1948. 'The Crag Platform, its Geology and Archaeological Problem', *S. E. Nat. and Antiq.*, vol. 53.

Waterston, D. 1913. 'The Piltdown Mandible', *Nature*, 92: 319.

——. 1913. 'Discussion on Piltdown', *Quart. J. Geol. Soc. Lond.*, 69: 150.

Weidenreich, F. 1945. 'Giant Early Man from Java and South China. Anthrop'. *Pap. Amer. Mus.*, 40: 1–135.

Weiner, J. S., Oakley, K. P. and Clark, W. Le Gros. *The Solution of the Piltdown Problem*, Bull. Brit. Mus. (Nat. Hist.) Geol., vol. 2, no. 3.

Weiner, J. S. 1955. *The Piltdown Forgery*, Oxford University Press, London.

Woo, J. K. and Chao, T. K. 1959. 'New Discovery of a Sinanthropus mandible form Choukoutien', *Vertebrata Palasiatica,* 3: 169–72.

Woodward, A. S. 1917. 'Fourth Note on the Piltdown Gravel with evidence of a second skull of Eoanthropus Dawsoni', *Quart. J. Geol. Soc. Lond.*, 73, part I: 1–10.

——. 1921. 'A new cave-man from Rhodesia, South Africa', *Nature*, 108: 371–2.

——. 1948. *The Earliest Englishman,* Watts and Co., London.

Wymer, J. 1955. 'A further fragment of the Swanscombe skull', *Nature*, 176: 426–7.

Zdansky, O. 1923. 'Ueber ein Saugerknochenlager in Choukoutien', *Bull. Geol. Surv. China.*, vol. I, No. 5.

——. 1927. 'Preliminary Notice on two teeth of a hominid from a cave in Chehli (China)', *Bull. Geol. Soc. China,* 5: 281–4.

Zeuner, F. E. 1946. *Dating the Past,* 1st edn., London. Also 4th edn., 1959.

——. 1959. *The Pleistocene Period*, 2nd edn., London.

Index

Index